Enterprise Development:
The Challenges of Starting,
Growing and Selling a Business

Colin Barrow, Gerard Burke, David Molian and
Robert Brown

CENGAGE
Learning™

Australia • Brazil • Japan • Korea • Mexico • Singapore • Spain • United Kingdom • United States

CENGAGE
Learning™

Enterprise Development, 1st Edition
Authors: Colin Barrow, Gerard Burke

For product information and technology assistance,
contact **emea.info@cengage.com**.

For permission to use material from this text or product,
and for permission queries,
email **emea.permissions@cengage.com**.

British Library Cataloguing-in-Publication Data
A catalogue record for this book is available from the British Library.

ISBN: 9781861529893

Cengage Learning EMEA
Cheriton House, North Way, Andover, Hampshire, SP10 5BE
United Kingdom

Cengage Learning products are represented in Canada by Nelson Education Ltd.

For your lifelong learning solutions, visit
www.cengage.co.uk

Purchase your next print book, e-book or e-chapter at
www.cengagebrain.com

Printed by Lightning Source, UK

Contents

1 The challenges of getting into business 9

List of figures

List of tables

Introduction

Ever since Professor David Birch's seminal work at MIT in 1979 (*The Job Generation Process*), demonstrated that two-thirds of the increase in employment in the United States between 1969 and 1976 had been in firms with fewer than 20 workers, there has been an almost worldwide interest in stimulating new enterprises. Many governments have been attempting to develop programmes to stimulate entrepreneurship (e.g. among indigenous Malays in Malaysia) or to provide support to the growing small business sector (e.g. the work of the Small Business Administration in the USA).

The governments of most developed economies see new enterprises as the wellspring of economic growth and job and wealth creation. Nevertheless, encouraging more and more entrepreneurial individuals to take the first brave steps towards starting a new venture will not, by itself, achieve these highly desirable economic aspirations – as demonstrated by the large numbers of businesses which fail in the first few years. In order to create sustainable jobs and wealth, these businesses not only need to be started, they also need to grow. And ultimately the entrepreneur needs to harvest the wealth that their enterprise and endeavours have created.

This book covers all three of the major stages of enterprise development: starting a business, growing a business and selling a business. It is intended as a guidebook for those about to set out on one of these key entrepreneurial journeys and for those who are part way through them.

Structure of the book

Robert Wright, a qualified commercial pilot and graduate of the MBA programme at Cranfield School of Management, founded Connectair as a feeder airline bringing passengers in to the main UK airport hubs, such as Heathrow and Gatwick, where they would connect with the major carriers flights. Getting the business off the ground was a long haul during which Robert and his very small team turned their hands to just about every possible activity within the business. Robert himself, as well as being MD, was also at times the person who checked passengers onto the flight, the pilot, the steward and the baggage handler!

Over the next few years of frantic activity, Robert successfully grew the business to a point where it employed 60 people and made a comfortable profit. He had achieved his original vision, was enjoying his work, earning a good living and declared himself 'happier than ever before.'

At this point, he found himself contesting extra take-off and landing slots at Gatwick with one of the major charter airlines. Connectair's 20-seater planes needed the same slots that the charter airline wanted for its 747s and Robert realized that these slots were worth a lot more to the charter airline than they were to him. After protracted negotiations, the charter airline offered £6.25 million for Connectair in order to obtain the slots.

While flying to the US to negotiate the sale Robert's business-class companion, on discovering the purpose of his visit, congratulated him on having covered in five short years the 'three basic challenges of enterprise development'. These are:

1. the challenges of getting into business
2. the challenges of growing the business
3. the challenges in deciding whether to re-invest or exit.

These three sets of challenges form an appropriate structure for this book. As a result, the book is split into three sections – one named after each of the sets of challenges.

Each section is then broken down in to a number of chapters which cover the key individual challenges within that stage of enterprise development. Each chapter begins with an introduction and objectives, and concludes with a summary. The introduction sets the scene for the issues to be addressed in the chapter and puts them in the context of the other chapters in that section. The objectives set out the key issues to be addressed in the chapter. The summary consolidates what has been covered in the chapter.

Our approach to the challenges of enterprise development

Our overall approach is predicated on the belief that good preparation and planning will be a significant aid in dealing with each of these sets of challenges. In other words, you're more likely to start successfully, grow successfully and exit successfully if you've researched carefully, analysed rigorously and planned thoroughly. On the other hand, we are not saying that having a great plan is all you need to start and grow a new business. On the contrary, as you will see as you progress through the book, you also need a good business proposition, an appropriate personality, an effective team around you and, perhaps, a little bit of luck. But as the great golfer Gary Player said, 'The more I practise, the luckier I get!'

From this planning perspective, it is also clear that each of the three sets of challenges corresponds to a distinct business planning requirement, each designed to cope with quite different problems, namely:

1. A business plan, to minimize start-up risks
2. A strategic growth plan
3. An exit plan.

How to use this book

This is not an academic book. It is a practical book aimed at people who are seriously interested in actually starting, growing and/or selling their business. We hope to inspire potential entrepreneurs to start more sustainable businesses, and existing entrepreneurs to grow their businesses more successfully and quickly, by sharing insights from other successful growth businesses and by providing a toolkit to rummage through when facing a challenge.

Case studies

We find that, in the case of entrepreneurs, the entrepreneur's own story is often as valuable and full of insights as the theory. For this reason, we are featuring 11 case studies, with which we are particularly familiar, in detail. We will return to these case studies repeatedly throughout the book to illustrate different points. Each excerpt has been carefully chosen to illustrate key issues in the life cycle of an enterprise at that particular stage. In this way, the story of these businesses should build up through the book. Each of these recurring examples is briefly introduced below.

Assignments

Perhaps the most practical part of the book is the assignments which can be found at the end of each chapter. These assignments suggest work to be done in applying the ideas introduced in that chapter. In all cases, we have written these assignments on the assumption that the reader is a potential or existing entrepreneur.

If you are a potential entrepreneur considering starting a business, then your primary interest will probably be in Section 1: *The Challenges of Getting into Business*. By working through the assignments at the end of each chapter in Section 1 applied to your business idea, you will build up most of the information you need for a start-up business plan.

If you are an existing entrepreneur who is seeking to grow your business, then you should learn most from Section 2: *The Challenges of Growing the Business*. If you complete the assignments at the end of all the chapters in this section related to your business, then you will have most of what you need in order to put together a growth strategy.

If you are an entrepreneur who is considering selling your business, then your focus should be on Section 3: *The Challenges of Deciding Whether to Re-invest or Exit*. Working through the assignments in this section should help you make this key decision and the work that results will form part of your exit plan.

In addition, we anticipate that the book will also be useful as part of teaching and education programmes at undergraduate, postgraduate and executive levels. In these circumstances, it is possible that readers may not have a business idea or existing business on which to base the work done on the assignments. Nevertheless, there is much to be learned from completing the assignments. Therefore, in the introduction to each section we suggest ways in which readers without a business or business idea can undertake the assignments.

Acknowledgements

Throughout the book, the thinking we set out, and the suggestions we make, have been heavily influenced by the work we have done at Cranfield School of Management and with individual entrepreneurs. In particular:

1. In working with several hundred MBA students and alumni who have launched new businesses and whom we have had the pleasure to support and help.
2. In working with the owner-managers of over 600 growing businesses, with turnover between £1 million and £20 million, participating in the Business Growth and Development Programme which we have run since 1988. The vast majority of these businesses have outperformed their sector in terms of growth and many of the owner-managers have subsequently sold their businesses at significantly higher values.

Through these activities, we are privileged and humbled to spend most of our working lives with truly remarkable individual entrepreneurs and their businesses. It is true to say that we have learned from them at least as much as they have learned from us! We are truly grateful. They are our inspiration. We hope that, through this book, we can share some of that inspiration.

Businesses used as case studies throughout the book

Any business book, even one about entrepreneurial ventures, can easily become dry and heavy going unless it is illustrated with real life examples. That is why you will find case studies liberally sprinkled throughout this book. All of these case studies are real – real entrepreneurs and their real businesses.

Some of these examples recur repeatedly in different chapters through the book. By using this approach, we hope to give you a small sense of the journey that these entrepreneurs have taken from foundation through growth and ultimately to maturity.

These recurring examples have all been developed as a direct result of our working with these entrepreneurs and their businesses. Some of the founders are alumni of the Cranfield MBA while others are past participants of the Business Growth and Development Programme (BGP) which we have run for the past 17 years.

They have been chosen in order to represent a broad range of businesses and entrepreneurs, and because between them they illustrate many of the crucial issues in developing an enterprise. All those involved in the recurring case studies have given their permission for us to tell their story, for which we are very grateful.

We briefly introduce each of these recurring case studies here. In most cases, more information along with teaching notes can be found on the companion website or via the European Case Clearing House.

We are deeply honoured to have worked with these entrepreneurs and their businesses, in some cases, right from the pre-start-up days. We are delighted that they are being successful and are pleased to be able to tell their stories here. We hope that they provide as much inspiration for you as they do for us.

ChocExpress (Hotel Chocolat)

ChocExpress – renamed Hotel Chocolat in 2003 – is a highly successful direct sales business set up by Angus Thirlwell and Peter Harries. The two founders met when they were working in IT and saw an opportunity to sell promotional mints and chocolates to corporate buyers. Out of this, they created a business selling chocolates as delivered gifts.

The full case study describes how the business was first established, and how the partners diversified into supplying supermarkets before returning to their original business model. Subsequently, they created a highly successful website to complement their direct mail and direct marketing activities.

Today, Hotel Chocolat is the dominant supplier of delivered chocolate gifts in the UK and, increasingly, in mainland Europe. You are welcome to browse at www.hotelchocolat.com.

This case study was winner of the Entrepreneurship category in the European Foundation for Management Development (EFMD) Case Awards in 2002.

Cobalt Telephone Technologies

Cobalt was started in 1997 by Harry Clarke from a Portakabin in someone else's car park. An engineer by profession, Harry had seen as an employee how other companies were integrating computing and telephone systems. He was convinced that he could do it better, and started a business to prove it.

The case study describes how Harry bootstrapped the business and survived the first few years precariously. Since there was no one else to do it, Harry taught himself how to sell and developed some highly effective approaches in the process.

When the big opportunity came, Harry seized it – and the business has gone from strength to strength ever since. See www.ctt.co.uk.

Cobra Beer

Cobra Beer was founded in 1990 by Karan Bilimoria, an Indian national who stayed on in the UK after qualifying as an accountant and lawyer. Dissatisfied with the beers available at that time (in the most crowded beer market in the world), he determined to brew the perfect beer to accompany Indian food.

The case study describes how he struggled to set up the business, initially importing from India, found distributors and made his early sales to Indian restaurateurs. Through bootstrapping his finances, Karan built a successful firm until disaster struck and his business was boycotted for reasons unconnected with Cobra.

The case study then relates how Cobra recovered and continued on its brand-building path, winning numerous awards for its innovative advertising and high-growth strategy. A detailed history of the brand and examples of the company's advertising are available at www.cobrabeer.com. This case study was a winner of the Entrepreneurship category in the EFMD Case Awards, 1999.

Fitness Express

Fitness Express was created by David Courteen and Steve Taylor to provide a service for hotel and corporate leisure centres. Having qualified in physical education studies, David and Steve spotted an opportunity to manage health and fitness centres under contract to hotel owners. They extended the concept to the corporate sector and for approximately ten years developed the company solely through organic growth and retained earnings. In 2000, they took the opportunity to sell the business to a major public company.

The case study describes how the two partners developed a service culture unique to the leisure industry and pursued a strategy of controlled, low-risk expansion. The selling process and the final sales agreement are also documented in detail. The partners have continued to be involved with the business following the acquisition. See www.fitnessexpress.co.uk.

InternetCamerasDirect (InternetDirect)

InternetCamerasDirect (now InternetDirect) was founded by Nigel Apperley while he was still at business school. He was influenced by the Dell computer direct sales model and believed that it could be applied to the digital camera market. Accordingly, he started a business from home, initially as a hobby and then as a full-time career. The company successfully made it through the boom and bust of the dot com frenzy, focusing on a narrow product range and carefully refining the business model of selling exclusively through internet channels.

The case study describes the ups and downs experienced by Nigel and his team as the company has expanded. See www.internetdirect.co.uk.

Light Emotions

Light Emotions is the brainchild of two electronics engineers, Christophe Mermaz and Dominique Pecquet. They met while working as employees in their native France and decided to set up a company to exploit patented technology developed by Dominique. Their first product was a glass which illuminated when water was poured into it and switched off when the glass was emptied. They believed this to be ideal for parties and launch events. From this, Light Emotions went on to develop a unique light stick product for the safety industry, again based on the company's unique technology.

The case study describes how the duo first got into business and the choices facing them when their original sales and distribution plan failed to deliver the necessary results. To view Light Emotions' technology for yourself, visit www.lightemotions.com.

Iviewcameras

Iviewcameras was created by Pete Rankin in 2002 and began trading while Pete was studying full-time for an MBA. The idea came about when Pete spotted that the price of wireless CCTV (closed circuit TV) cameras had fallen dramatically, making them affordable for private individuals to purchase via the internet.

Having quickly researched the market, and sold some equipment to friends and family, Pete and some colleagues from business school established a company. To get into the market he agreed a partnership deal with Nigel Apperley of InternetDirect (see above), whereby Iviewcameras would use the infrastructure already established by InternetDirect.

The case study describes this low-cost entry strategy and how Pete and his team built sales in a market which was still in its infancy. The marketing of Iviewcameras was greatly helped by Pete's appearing on a popular daytime TV show to demonstrate how CCTV could be used in the home. A clip from this programme and the current product range can be viewed at www.iviewcameras.co.uk.

The Impact Programme

The Impact Programme is a small consultancy and training organization which was acquired via a management buy-in (MBI). The lead MBI manager, Christopher Young, was approached while still at business school by an old business contact. The opportunity was to buy into an IT-related business which had lost it way. Existing management was divided and the company was losing money.

The case study describes how the business was turned around by Christopher and the team, and covers the key aspects of rejuvenating a failing organization through sales-led leadership. Visit www.impact-sharing.com.

Moonpig

Moonpig is a greetings card business which sells and distributes solely over the internet. Founder Nick Jenkins set up the business in 1999 immediately on leaving business school. Moonpig's unique offer is that buyers can select from a wide range of humorous greetings cards which they can then customize on line. Moonpig then prints the card and sends it anywhere in the world.

The business very nearly collapsed as a result of the dot com débâcle, but recovered and grew strongly from 2001 onwards.

The case study describes how Nick raised successive rounds of finance to support Moonpig's rapid growth. Visit www.moonpig.com – but beware: the cards are intended for the adult market.

Real Burger World

Real Burger World (RBW) was established by Naz Choudhury in 2003, with the aim of reinventing the fast food hamburger. With a family background in the catering industry, Naz had a long-held ambition to establish his own restaurant. RBW's main point of difference is to provide a high-quality, freshly prepared alternative to the mainstream fast food offerings.

The case study describes the early days of finding the right site for the first outlet and creating a credible business plan that outside investors would find attractive. RBW was the subject of a television programme made by Channel 4 and shown in the UK in April 2004. Excerpts from the programme are available to view at the company's website, www.realburger.co.uk.

Top Golf and World Golf Systems

Steve Jolliffe developed his first successful business undertaking market research. Having sold it, he was in search of a fresh challenge. He found it in the form of the golf driving range. A keen golfer, he was struck by how uninspiring it is to go to a driving range and practise hitting golf balls into a muddy field. His solution was to implant an electronic chip inside a golf ball, and to transform a tired driving range into an entertainment centre for golfer and non-golfer alike.

The case study describes the technical challenges of the early days and then the growth of the business into an international franchising operation as Steve and his partners have sought to take their idea global. To take a virtual tour of the Top Golf centre, visit www.topgolf.co.uk.

The challenges of getting into business

As we have already noted, there is a very wide interest, across many countries, in stimulating new enterprise. For example, in the UK, the period since the government-sponsored Bolton Committee inquiry into small firms in 1971 has seen a resurgence of small firms in the UK. While for the most part this has been fuelled by the growth in self-employment (rising from 6.5 per cent of the UK labour force in 1965 to nearly 15 per cent by 2003), by 2004 there were approximately 3.8 million businesses registered for VAT in the UK. The annual births and deaths of firms, indeed, occur on a large scale, e.g. in the second quarter of 2003 new firms registering for VAT numbered 108 000, while some 113 000 were de-registering, giving a net reduction to stock of 5000 in the quarter, the first significant reduction for several years.

And the UK is by no means alone. Survey after survey shows that, in just about every developed economy, more people than ever before are starting businesses or are interested in doing so. If you are one of these people, then this section is specifically aimed at you.

Of course, the first thing that you will need is a business idea. Sources of successful business ideas and approaches to generating ideas are considered in Chapter 1. Thereafter, the chapters in this section will lead you through a process of investigating your business idea. The work that you do on the assignments at the end of each chapter will form the basis of what is required for a start-up business plan.

To plan or not to plan?

As we have already mentioned, our overall approach to all stages of business is predicated on the belief that thorough planning and preparation will be of significant value in overcoming the challenges to be faced. On the other hand, some people would argue that there is no advantage in writing a business plan for a start-up business since it immediately becomes out of date. So why not just get on with starting the business? The US entrepreneurial magazine *Inc* has shown that nearly two-thirds of new businesses started without a formally produced business plan. Of *Inc's* top 100 fastest-growing companies in one particular year, 41 per cent had started with no business plan at all, and 26 per cent had only a 'back of envelope'-type plan.

However, while writing a business plan is no guarantee of future business success, there are nevertheless several compelling arguments for undertaking such an exercise. These include the following:

1. It is usually less costly to make your first mistakes on paper rather than in the marketplace (i.e. to fail in the market research phase of plan preparation to locate sufficient 'real' customers to justify the venture rather than, without research, to take premises and lease obligations and then come to the same negative conclusion.)

2. The business 'idea' and concept will undergo modifications, and perhaps improvement, in the rigorous process of researching markets and presenting findings to potential investors.

Case Study

Mark Sanders, a participant on the Graduate Enterprise Programme at Cranfield University, originally planned to design and manufacture his innovative Strida bicycle. But, research in to market size and product costings quickly convinced him of the need to sub-contract manufacture, thereby reducing risk to himself and ensuring quicker access to the market.

3. Those entrepreneurs needing financial assistance, either from the outset or at a later stage, whether from banks, venture capitalists or business angels, will all find the preparation and presentation of a business plan to be an essential and educational part of the financial negotiation.

Case Study

It was Robert Wright's fourth business plan, written and re-presented over a period of 18 months, which finally secured venture capital support from 3i for Connectair. The fourth plan had identified a viable customer, British Caledonian, and a totally different airport connection from his original idea, in part suggested by the venture capitalist organization. Wright went on to build a successful business which he sold for over £6 million. He then bought it back again (for significantly less) and, having renamed it City Flyer Express, grew it once more and ultimately sold it again for £75 million to British Airways.

Avoiding the mistakes of others

One other key reason to produce a business plan is to try to avoid, as much as possible, the mistakes others have already made. When starting a business, these mistakes can be very costly and often result in the failure of the business. So, let's briefly consider the main reasons why start-up ventures fail.

Whilst there are millions of businesses starting up, many of these survive only a relatively short time. Typically, over half of all independently owned ventures will have ceased trading within five years of starting up. One comprehensive study of all 814 000 firms started up in the US in a particular year followed their destinies for eight years. That research indicated that only 28 per cent of all the start-ups in the study (see Figure 1.0.1) survived as independent entities, which after all is the primary goal of most people starting a business.

The Office of the Official Receiver in the UK lists the following causes of business failures:

- insufficient turnover
- poor management and supervision
- lack of proper accounting

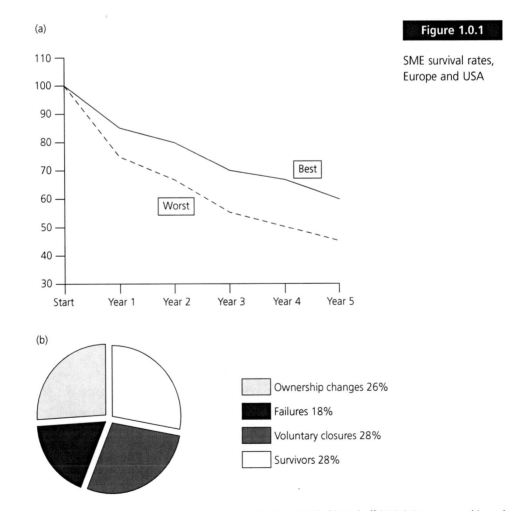

(a)

Figure 1.0.1

SME survival rates, Europe and USA

(b)

Ownership changes 26%

Failures 18%

Voluntary closures 28%

Survivors 28%

Sources: (a) European Observatory for SME research (October 1997); (b) Kirchoff (1994) *Entrepreneurship and Dynamic Capitalism*

- competition
- not enough capital
- bad debts
- excessive remuneration to the owners.

In our view, these are for the most part symptoms rather than causes. The causes of failure come under the following general headings.

- *Nothing new to say*: Many people starting a business have no clear idea as to why people should buy from them rather than from their existing supplier of competitive products and services. Indeed, many would-be entrepreneurs have little or no idea what governs their potential customers' purchase decisions. Trying to sell sausages to consumers who are largely preoccupied with buying sizzle can be an unproductive exercise. If there is nothing distinctive about your product or service, or the way you plan to do business, you must surely question why anyone would want to buy from you. It may only be that your opening hours are different and that customers feel that matters; or that you keep your promises while operating in a sector, such as building or the motor trade, which is renowned for low integrity. You must have an edge that matters in the market.

- *Lack of expertise*: Starting a business from scratch calls for remarkable versatility. The typical entrepreneur types the invoices with one finger in the evenings, does the books at the weekend, sells on Monday, makes the goods from Tuesday and delivers whenever he or she can. People whose only experience has been in a large firm may find it difficult to become a jack-of-all-trades. But, while being able to turn your hand to many tasks is important, you still need some experience of the industry you plan to start up in. Going into an entirely new area forces the entrepreneur onto a near impossibly steep learning curve. Not only do you have to learn how to start a business, and all the new tasks that involves, but you also have to learn about a new market with customers, suppliers and workers about whom you know practically nothing. All learning has to be bought at some price. For those lacking expertise in the sector they are going into, this learning is often gained by making mistakes, which in turn consume scarce cash resources. This goes some way to explaining why business failure rates are so much higher in the early years.

  At no time does this lack of expertise show up faster, and with more disastrous consequences, than during a recession. It's during such periods that lots of people are propelled into entrepreneurship through redundancy, or forsake their own industries believing that the best opportunities lie elsewhere. However, it is clear that the further you move away from what you know and understand, in terms of products/services, customers or markets, the lower are your chances of success. The lowest-risk route to market is to build on either your product/service expertise or on your knowledge of the market, and ideally on both.

- *Cash flow crises*: Too few new businesses prepare cash flow forecasts at the outset and maintain a permanent one-year projection when they begin to trade. Received wisdom is that all forecasts are wrong, which can lead the unwise to believe they are a waste of time. Paradoxically, it's exactly because events are so unpredictable that cash flow projections are essential. Expenses occur that you did not anticipate; customers take longer than expected to find and then take longer still to pay up. These, and a dozen other unforeseen, and to some extent unforeseeable, factors make it vital to make a realistic estimate of the likely timing of cash movements in and out of the business, whist building in a margin of safety.

One other factor to remember is that cash that flows into a business hasn't had any of the automatic deductions knocked off it as, for example, has a pay cheque from an employer. Too often entrepreneurs yield to the temptation to use this cash to maintain their standard of living and when the bills come in – from suppliers or for tax – they can't pay them.

- *No management accounts*: Cash management is only one aspect of the financial information an owner needs to remain in control of the business. Profit and loss accounts, balance sheets and key performance ratios such as gross margin, debtor days and stock turn all have a part to play in a prudent and well run business. It is not merely useful to understand the basics of accounting, for company directors it is a legal requirement. It is an offence for the directors of a limited company to continue trading once they know – or should have known – that their business is in trouble.

  Poor financial control is a major reason why many businesses fail. Owner-managers often leave financial questions to their accountants to sort out at the year end. They often have the erroneous belief that keeping the books is an activity somehow divorced from the 'real' task of getting customers or making products. By the time the first set of figures is produced, perhaps up to 18 months after trading has commenced, most start-up businesses are already too far down the road to financial failure to be saved. The final accounts then become all too final and a good business proposition has been ruined by financial illiteracy, something that could easily have been prevented with a modicum of outside help and advice.

- *Falling out*: Hidden in these reasons why early stage businesses fail is the failure in relationship between business partners. If the business is going to have any chance of success, it is essential that the partners can work together harmoniously and trust each other. Business partners need to be temperamentally suited, have complementary skills and be prepared to compromise without falling out.

  There are no hard and fast rules about selecting a business partner, but most successful partnerships seem to occur where people have known each other for some time, ideally as business associates rather than just as friends.

Many of these reasons, or 'mistakes', can be avoided by thorough planning, careful thought and detailed research.

For all of the above reasons, and whatever the nature of the business idea, would-be entrepreneurs would be well advised to complete the essential steps of the business planning process. In essence, the business plan is designed to reduce risk for the entrepreneur (and for any investors).

Contents of this section

Accordingly, this first section deals with *The Challenges of Getting into Business*, the main ones of which are:

1. How do you find a good business idea?
2. Do you have the right personal qualities for success?

3. Is there a market opportunity in your business sector?
4. What is your business model and market entry strategy?
5. Can you make a profit?
6. What is the most appropriate legal form for your business?

Each of these elements is examined in turn in the six chapters which make up this first section.

While we discuss alternative options for getting into business in Chapter 1, most people who want to work for themselves think in terms of starting their own business from scratch. Accordingly, this section of the book is written largely from the point of view of starting a new business. However, much of what we have to say is relevant to entrepreneurial businesses in general and, even if you are considering buying a business or taking one of the other options discussed in Chapter 1, we recommend that you work through all the chapters in this section.

Assignments

As with the remainder of the book, each chapter concludes with a series of assignments which suggest work to be done in applying the ideas introduced in that chapter. If you are a potential entrepreneur, then by working through these assignments applied to your business idea, you will build up most of the information you need for inclusion in a start-up business plan.

If you are using this book to learn about starting businesses, but do not have a business idea of your own, then we suggest that you work through the assignments in Chapter 1 in order to generate an idea which you can use as the basis of the assignments for the remaining chapters.

1　How do you find a good business idea?

Introduction and objectives

Let's assume that you want to join the ranks of entrepreneurs and face the challenges of getting in to your own business. The first challenge is, of course, *'What* business?'

In this first chapter we will explore various ideas, which successful entrepreneurs have come up with to create their businesses. By the end of this chapter, you should have a good understanding of each of the following three broad options:

- Identifying your own idea and starting the business from scratch.

- Buying an existing business.

- Running an autonomous part of someone else's business (e.g. taking a franchise or an agency, or participating in a multi-level marketing programme).

You should also be in a position to do some creative thinking in order to come up with your own business idea.

Finding your own idea and starting from scratch

There is a widely held misconception that the secret of being a successful entrepreneur is to come up with a truly original idea. The reality is somewhat different.

Firstly, there are very few truly original ideas. Most successful business ideas are either slightly different versions of existing ideas, or are based on the entrepreneur's previous experience, know-how and/or contacts. Indeed, there is much to be said for copying an existing idea since at least you know that it can be made to work.

Secondly, as we have learned to our own cost (and sometimes embarrassment) it is almost impossible to be sure which ideas will work, and which will not, at the very outset. In other words, only the market can decide whether something is a 'great idea' or not.

And, thirdly, all sorts of people have ideas for new businesses all of the time. Some of these ideas, no doubt, have the potential to be the basis of great businesses. But, it is only the true entrepreneur who will take an idea and actually build a business around it. In other words, the secret of success is far more about having the nerve, energy, passion, commitment and skill to build a business than it is about having a great idea.

It's a good start to have an idea which appears from the outset to have some compelling features, an addressable market and which you are likely to be interested in. But, let's not worry too much about whether the idea is wholly original.

Sources of business ideas

Looking at where successful entrepreneurs get their business ideas, we can see that the following are the most likely sources.

- *Your previous experiences in business*: What have you done in your career to date? What special skills and/or knowledge have you acquired which could be the basis of a business? If you are currently employed by a business, could you do what you do now except working for yourself? Can you see a better way of doing what you do?

- *Your hobbies and interests*: Arguably, the most important factor in indicating success in a start-up is the passion the entrepreneur has for the business. So, hobbies, interests and other things that you already enjoy doing are a potential source of business ideas. This is often the case with 'craft-based' businesses but can also be the basis of much larger businesses.

- *Your own skills*: Do you have any particular skills which other businesses and/or individuals would be prepared to pay for? This is the basis for nearly all consultancy and professional advisory businesses.

- *Your experiences as a customer*: Most of us have had bad experiences as a customer or have been frustrated at not being able to buy what we want in the way we want. Many entrepreneurs use such experiences as a spur to creating a business, assuming that there must be other people who have had the same experiences and are just waiting for someone to come along and do it better.

    For example, as an expatriate Indian, one of the things that Karan Bilimoria liked about living in England was the ready availability of Indian food, with a Tandoori restaurant on every high street. One of the few things he disliked, however, was the lack of the right kind of beer to drink with the curry of his choice. It was bizarre, but in a market of hundreds of different beers everything he tried was too 'gassy'. What he wanted, he decided, was a beer with the smoothness of a real ale, but the refreshing qualities of a lager. He felt sure that there were many other consumers who felt the same way and decided to start Cobra Beer.

- *Your existing business relationships and network*: Do you have good relationships with customers for a given product or service? Can you ask them how satisfied they are with existing suppliers? Do you have other contacts who may be aware of opportunities and unmet needs?

Case Study

Angus Thirlwell and Peter Harries were working for an IT company when they decided that they wanted to go into business together and for themselves. Angus's father, a successful entrepreneur himself, had commissioned peppermints, packaged in his company's logo, as a promotional 'giveaway' for customers. Customers loved them and the stock soon ran out. When he tried to re-order, Angus's father found that the supplier had stopped trading. Angus and Peter concluded that there must be other commercial customers out there for such products and set up the Mint Marketing Company which later became Geneiva Chocolates, ChocExpress and ultimately, Hotel Chocolat.

- *A new invention or technology*: Have you invented something, or do you know someone who has, which could be the basis of a business?

    For example, Christophe Mermaz was enthralled by Dominique Pecquet's invention of a champagne glass which lights up when there is liquid in it and switches off again when it is emptied. Christophe and Dominique set up Light Emotions to exploit the invention. Although it is tempting with an invention, to aspire to setting up a business to manufacture and sell the items, this can be a very long and hard road to commercial success. James Dyson and his washing machines are a classic example here. Sometimes, it may be preferable to license the invention to an existing business for them to exploit.

    Are there new technologies which create opportunities for new businesses or ways of doing business? The most obvious recent example of this is the internet as a direct sales channel. Despite the bursting of the so-called 'internet bubble', there are many internet-based businesses which are making healthy profits and the internet remains a relatively easy way of getting in to business compared to more traditional routes, particularly for retailing.

    For example, in searching for his business idea, Nick Jenkins identified the potential of the internet to reach large numbers of consumers. He also realized that in order to build a truly distinctive online business, he needed an idea where the internet allowed him to add distinctive value. After some months of researching, he came up with the idea for Moonpig, a service which allows users to modify the text on greetings cards so that they are personalized for the recipient.

    A key lesson here is that those internet businesses which are making money have focused on the same core business concepts that have helped more traditional businesses to be successful – and it is these concepts on which this book will focus. For this reason, it is clear that you don't necessarily need to be a technology specialist in order to build a successful business around the technology. For example, Nigel Apperley, founder of

InternetCamerasDirect, an online retailer of cameras, was previously an insurance salesman!

- *Copy something that already exists*: As already mentioned, there are very few completely original ideas. So, why not look at business ideas which have been successful in other circumstances (e.g. in another country or with a different type of product) and copy them? Ideally you can make it even better than it was before.

Case Study

Nigel Apperley was at business school in 1999 when he developed the idea that was to change his life. A successful insurance salesman, Apperley was fascinated by the internet boom. In class, he was inspired by a case study of the Dell business model of selling computers to customers direct, and how that transferred to the emerging online sales channel.

To succeed as an internet retailer, he concluded, you needed a product in an identifiable niche with a high enough sales transaction value per customer to fund marketing and re-investment. Apperley rapidly focused on digital cameras and camcorders as the best candidates. After carefully looking at the market, he chose to specialize in digital cameras and related accessories.

Three years later, when the business was set to achieve turnover of £20 million (€28 million) Apperley freely admitted that much of his success was the result of deliberate imitation!

Techniques for generating ideas

We believe that anyone is capable of generating good ideas for businesses – but, of course, not everyone is capable of building a business on those ideas. Nevertheless, in addition to being aware of all the potential sources of ideas, it may also be helpful to use some more creative approaches to generate new ideas or enhance existing ones.

One simple technique that an entrepreneur we know uses very successfully is to carry a small notebook with you. Whenever you come across something that might lead to an idea for a business (e.g. you hear about a new invention, see an interesting existing business or have a bad experience as a customer) make a note of it. Then, set aside a short amount of time each week or month to review your notes to see whether any of the ideas are appealing.

The other main technique for idea generation is brainstorming. This is a well-known technique for encouraging creativity and is best done in groups. There follows a step-by-step guideline for using brainstorming to come up with new business ideas.

1. Start by defining the question as closely as you can. The more specific you can be about the question, the more effective the brainstorming is likely to be. A question such as 'Has anyone got any business ideas?' is less likely to lead to specific business ideas than such questions as 'How

can we improve on the product/service currently delivered by xyz?' or 'How could we use the new abc technology as the basis of a business?'

2. Write out the question concisely and ensure that all the participants are in agreement.

3. Give yourselves a time limit. Often 25 minutes is enough, although the larger the group the more time is needed.

4. Appoint one person to record the ideas that are generated on a flipchart, whiteboard or electronic notepad.

5. Everyone else shouts out their ideas. No matter how daft or silly the idea, it must be written down. There must be no criticism of the ideas since this will restrict the generation of ideas. Moreover, ideas which appear silly at first may lead to other ideas that are good.

6. It is sometimes useful to give people other items or words from which to spark ideas. For instance, you might leave four or five objects on the floor of the room and ask participants to say how these affect the way they see the question.

7. Once the time has run out, select the five ideas you like best.

8. Write down five or six criteria for judging which ideas best address the question and judge each idea against them.

9. Don't ignore any of the ideas that come out of this process. They may be useful later.

Buying an existing business

At this stage, it is also worth asking yourself the fundamental question 'Do I start a new business or buy an existing business?' Inevitably, there are pros and cons to each approach.

The biggest advantage of buying a business is that the business is already established. Products/services are already developed, customers are already buying from the business and revenue is already coming in. The existing business may also have certain accreditations or licences which allow it to trade and which may be time-consuming or difficult for a start-up business to acquire.

On the other hand, the business will come with a history, some of which may not be advantageous to a new owner, and it will have existing owners whose needs will have to be met and who may be vitally important to the ongoing success of the business.

You may find that there are existing businesses that match your idea and which are for sale. On the other hand, if your idea is fundamentally new, there will be no other business like it and therefore no advantage in buying an existing business.

If the risky start-up stages have already been successfully negotiated, then it may be that there is less financial reward for you from an existing business compared to a pure start-up.

And, of course, you will have to pay for an existing business! If you cannot fund the purchase yourself, you will need to raise external finances. While investors and lenders are often more willing to back the purchase of an existing business, particularly if you have an experienced management team, it is likely that they will stipulate conditions, with the result that you may feel you are not in complete control – which may well have been the reason you wanted to run your own business in the first place.

Finding businesses to buy is fairly straightforward. In most countries, business for sale will be advertised in the main business newspapers and publications. There are also company brokers who specialize in buying and selling small companies. Some of these have websites on which you can search for businesses meeting certain criteria (e.g. by industry sector). Larger businesses for sale are often dealt with by corporate finance specialists.

There are a number of different ways to buy a business which are described below.

Buy the whole business

If the business you want is owned by a company, you can buy all the shares in that company to acquire the business. This is advantageous if you want to maintain the trading name of the company or do not want to bring the change of ownership to the attention of customers or suppliers. If the business is a partnership or sole trader, you can buy out the existing owners. This means you will get all of the business, both the bad bits and the good bits. If there are some particularly onerous obligations you are taking over from the previous owners, this should be reflected in the price you pay.

Buy some of the assets of the business

A business is made up of various assets and liabilities. Some of these will be valuable to you, and some may be of no use at all. For example, you may wish to buy the customer list and stocks of an existing business but may not wish to take on the property it trades from or its existing liabilities. This can be a good way of avoiding being landed with problems inherited from the old business.

Buy a part of the business

If the business you want to get into is going to be more than you can afford, it may make sense to buy a part of that business. Depending on the legal form of the business (see Chapter 6), you will then become either a shareholder or possibly a director or partner. In this case you need to be aware of the reputation of your prospective business partners. Going into business with them means you will take on their reputation by association. Ask around and get references if appropriate. Always formalize the relationship with your business partners by means of a comprehensive and professionally drafted legal agreement.

Management Buy-Out (MBO)

The term 'management buy-out' or MBO is applied to the sale of a business to the existing management team. Large companies are continuously reviewing their overall operating strategy. They often seek to dispose of, or close down, businesses they have acquired in the past that are not sufficiently profitable or that do not fit in with their future plans. If you work in such a business, this may be a way to get into your own business, though you will have to share that ownership with others. Big firms often favour buy-out teams since selling out to the management makes better headlines than closing a business down or making people redundant. Financial backers like them too, as both the management team and the business idea are to some extent proven, or at least the problems are more visible (and hence solvable, in theory).

Management Buy-In (MBI)

The term 'management buy-in' (MBI) is applied to the purchase of a stake in a business by an external manager or management team. As with MBOs, MBIs tend to be transactions backed by external investors such as venture capital (VC) firms. The opportunity for an MBI exists where current management are poor or lack expertise and, consequently, the business is under-performing. In this way, the business gets the injection of expertise it requires and the new managers share in the future profits they expect to generate. This could be an alternative to buying a part of the business from an existing owner.

Running an autonomous part of someone else's business

There also exists a range of options which lie somewhere between starting a new venture and buying an existing one. These usually consist of buying in and running an autonomous part of a larger business owned by someone else and include buying a franchise (e.g. a McDonald's restaurant), taking an agency (e.g. distributing home and personal care products door to door) and multi-level marketing. These options can combine some elements of running your own business with a pre-existing, and hopefully proven, business model.

When considering these options it is important to be absolutely sure of the background of the company from whom you are buying the franchise or for whom you are acting. It is also vital to be clear about the obligations you are taking on with regard to the company. For instance, there are many examples of unscrupulous scams concerning pyramid selling where naïve individuals have been obliged to buy large amounts of stock which they have been unable to sell.

Chapter summary

We are continuously approached by enthusiastic and talented people who tell us that they have a burning desire to start their own business – if only they had a good business idea! This chapter should have helped you gain an understanding of where business ideas come from and how you might generate your own.

We've considered where successful entrepreneurs get their business ideas from and concluded that most ideas are not entirely original. We've looked at a range of sources of business ideas and some techniques for generating them. We've also considered the various different options for buying an existing business and the 'middle ground' approaches, including buying a franchise or taking up an agency.

By reading this chapter and completing the assignments you should be in a position to generate at least one business idea which is worth further investigation through the remaining chapters of Section 1.

Assignments

1. Consider each of the following and make a list of any business ideas which emerge:
   - your previous experience in business
   - your hobbies and interests
   - your skills (particularly those which are unusual and for which people would be prepared to pay)
   - bad experiences as a customer of other businesses
   - your existing business relationships and network
   - any new inventions or technologies with which you are familiar or to which you might have access
   - businesses which are successful in other circumstances and which appeal to you (e.g. in another country or with a different product/service).

2. Do a brainstorming session, as described in this chapter, with friends and/or colleagues around one or more of the ideas which emerge from the above.

3. Consider whether it may be more appropriate to buy an existing business. Develop the habit of looking at the main business press to see what businesses are being advertised for sale. Have a look at some of the websites of company brokers in your country and see if any of the businesses advertised interest you.

4. Consider whether a franchise, agency or multi-channel marketing opportunity may be right for you.

Suggested further reading

De Bono, Edward (1990) *Lateral Thinking: A Textbook of Creativity*, Harmondsworth: Penguin.
Foster, Jack (1996) *How to Get Great Ideas*, San Francisco: Berrett-Koehler.

2 Do you have the right personal qualities for success?

Introduction and objectives

Before committing any significant amount of time, energy and money to getting into business, it is important to ask yourself: 'Can I do it?' In answering this question, you will need to address three issues which are considered in this chapter:

- *Am I really the entrepreneurial type?* The high failure rate for new businesses would suggest that some people are seduced by the glamour of starting up on their own when they might be more successful and more contented in some other line of endeavour.

- *Are my motivations and aims realistic?* Running a business is never easy and, on an hourly wage basis, is often less well-paid than working for someone else. So why do people set up their own business, and do your aims seem realistic in that context?

- *Is this business right for me?* Even if your answers to the first two questions are sound, this particular proposition might not be right for you.

Am I the entrepreneurial type?

To launch a new business successfully calls for a particular type of person. The business idea must also be right for the market and the timing must be spot on. The world of business failures is full of products that were ahead of their time.

The stereotypical entrepreneur is someone who is always bursting with new ideas, highly enthusiastic, hyperactive and insatiably curious. But, this is not always the case: people who start businesses have many different personality types. Peter Drucker, the international business guru, describes what his research has revealed:

Some are eccentrics, others painfully correct conformists; some are fat and some are lean; some are worriers, some relaxed; some drink quite heavily, others are total abstainers; some are people of great charm and warmth, some have no more personality than a frozen mackerel.

Drucker, P. (1999) *Innovation and Entrepreneurship*,
London: Butterworth Heinemann.

There is little point, therefore, in trying to match yourself up to this or that personality type. However, there are some fairly broad characteristics that are generally accepted as being essential if you are going to make a success of your own business.

Broad characteristics of entrepreneurs

A lot of commitment and hard work

Entrepreneurs have complete faith in their business idea. This self-belief is necessary if they are to convince the sceptics (such as the bank manager!) whose help they need. They are usually single minded and more than capable of putting in an 18-hour working day. This can put a strain on other relationships, so successful entrepreneurs usually involve their families and get them on their side too.

Business owners are likely to put in many more hours at work than their employees. A third of managing directors of small and medium sized enterprises (SMEs) admit to routinely working for longer than the EU Working Time Directive lays down. One in twelve MDs claims to work over 60 hours a week, week in and week out.

Working long hours is a curiously British disease, at least amongst European countries. Workers in Britain spend nearly 15 per cent more time at work than Europeans, and the gap is getting wider. Average working hours amongst UK workers have increased by 3 per cent over the past decade, whilst they have decreased in every other European country. In the Netherlands, for example, hours worked have declined by 5 per cent.

There is nothing illegal about the boss, or their immediate relatives if it is a family-run business, working as many hours as they like. The danger comes in two ways. If, by their behaviour, they influence or encourage other employees to work excessive hours, then they are breaking the law. Also, there is a considerable body of research that shows that people who consistently work excessive hours become progressively less and less productive and more prone to making mistakes. It could be argued that the occasional mistake by a junior employee is par for the course. But having the MD making mistakes every week is a recipe for disaster.

While most entrepreneurs remain unaware of the damage that prolonged stress can inflict, some large companies are now addressing the problem. High-technology companies such as Rank Xerox and IBM operate counselling schemes to help employees spot the danger signs, while some divisions of ICI give their entire workforce stress management training. This is not altruistic. The company wants to encourage balanced employees because they are more productive, so their reasoning is completely commercial.

But where does the balance lie? There is probably nothing wrong with working hard as long as you are having fun. The thing to remember is that running a business is more like running a marathon than running a sprint. Workaholics rarely seem to enjoy their work and behave more like addicts than enthusiasts. Jim Henson, creator of the Muppets, who died suddenly at 50, is held up as a warning to stoics and workaholics who persist in carrying on as usual during or after bouts of illness. A vigorous man in excellent health and with $120 million in the bank, Henson kept to his usual punishing work schedule while complaining of flu. One Saturday, he consulted a doctor who prescribed aspirin. On the following Tuesday, after continuing to work, he was admitted to hospital where he died of galloping pneumonia 16 hours later.

Acceptance of uncertainty

Managers in large businesses tend to seek to minimize risk by either calling up more information or delaying decisions until every possible fact is known. This response to uncertainty is one that challenges the need to operate in the unknown. In the world of large companies, there is a feeling that to work without all the facts is risky and, therefore, not prudent or desirable.

Entrepreneurs, on the other hand, know that by the time the fog of uncertainty has been completely lifted, too many people will be able to spot the opportunity clearly. In fact, an entrepreneur would usually only be interested in a decision that involved accepting a degree of uncertainty and would welcome, and on occasions even relish, that position. The uncertainty carries with it risk and it is through taking risks that many entrepreneurs reap their rewards, both financial and otherwise.

To be an entrepreneur, you need to be comfortable with uncertainty and you need to be happy to live with a certain amount of risk.

Good health

Apart from being able to put in long days in the early stages of the business, the successful entrepreneur needs to be on the spot to manage the firm every day. The entrepreneur is the essential lubricant that keeps the wheels of the business turning. They have to turn their hands to anything that needs to be done to make the venture work and they have to plug any gaps caused either by other people's sickness or because they just cannot afford to employ anyone for that particular job. They themselves cannot afford the luxury of sick leave. Even a week or two for a holiday is viewed as something of a luxury in the early years of a business's life.

Self-discipline

Entrepreneurs need strong personal discipline to keep themselves and their business on the schedule set out in the business plan. They must set the example for everything in their firm. Get that wrong and wrong signals are sent to every part of the business – both inside and out.

One of the most common pitfalls for the novice entrepreneur is failure to recognize the difference between cash and profit. Cash can make people feel wealthy, and if it results in a relaxed attitude to corporate status symbols, such as cars and luxury office fittings, then failure is just around the corner. This is explored further in Chapter 5.

Self-confident all-rounders

Entrepreneurs are rarely geniuses. There are nearly always other people in their business who have more competence, in one field, than they could ever aspire to. On the other hand, entrepreneurs have a wide range of ability and a willingness to turn their hand to anything that has to be done to make the venture succeed. They can usually make the product, market it and count the money, but above all they have self-confidence that lets them move comfortably through uncharted waters.

Case Study

Karan Bilimoria, founder of Cobra Beer, is certainly not a brewer by background. On the other hand, he has a broad and varied education, is a qualified accountant, has a degree in law and is extremely confident in himself and his vision for Cobra.

Karan grew up in India. His grandfather had been a general in the Ghurkhas and this meant that Karan's family was reasonably well off. He was well educated in India and came to the UK in 1982 to complete his accountancy training with one of the leading international firms, Ernst & Young. Even at this stage, he was thinking about the possibility of starting a business based on his knowledge of Indian and UK markets and cultures.

Not content with an accountancy qualification, he then won a place at Cambridge University to study law. On graduation, he began applying for jobs in banking but still hankered after starting his own business.

His first venture, formed in partnership with a family friend, Arjun Reddy, was selling polo sticks imported from India. Arjun's uncle then offered them the opportunity to act as distributors for a brand of Indian seafood. It was during this period that Karan became aware of the opportunity to create a beer that complemented Indian food.

At the beginning, Karan and Arjun did just about everything. They defined the brand, they found a master Indian brewer to make the beer, they sourced distinctive bottles, they negotiated with the Indian authorities to allow them to export, and they set up deals with UK distributors. And when these distributors subsequently pulled out of the deal, they loaded cases of Cobra into a Citroen 2CV, drove from one Indian restaurant to the next and sold the beer themselves! Neither Karan nor Arjun had much prior experience of any of these activities, but they had broad business knowledge, common sense, self-confidence, good connections with their market and total belief in Cobra.

Cobra has grown consistently every year since. The business now has sales of over £30 million and offices in four countries. In 2002, Karan won the prestigious Asian of the Year Award in the UK.

Innovative skills

Almost by definition, entrepreneurs are innovators who either tackle the unknown, or do old things in new ways. It is this inventive streak that allows them to carve out a new niche, often invisible to others.

Goal setting

Successful people in many walks of life set themselves goals and get pleasure out of trying to achieve them. Once a goal has been reached, they have to get the next target in view as quickly as possible. This restlessness is very characteristic of entrepreneurs. Sir James Goldsmith was a classic example, moving the base of his business empire from the UK to France, then the USA – and finally into pure cash, ahead of a stock market crash.

Self-evaluation for prospective entrepreneurs

Having established the broad characteristics of entrepreneurs, the big question is: Have you got what it takes? You may be able to get some feedback on how you match up against these characteristics by asking friends and colleagues. You may also have taken personality or psychometric tests in the past and the result of these may also be useful.

For our purposes here, we have put together the following simple self-evaluation questionnaire. The questions probe only those areas which are important to starting a business successfully and can be controlled or affected by the individual. If the statement is 'rarely true', score 1; if 'usually true', score 2; and if 'nearly always true', score 3.

1. I know my personal and business objectives.
2. I get tasks accomplished quickly.
3. I can change direction quickly if market conditions alter.
4. I enjoy being responsible for getting things done.
5. I like working alone and making my own decisions.
6. Risky situations don't alarm me.
7. I can face uncertainty easily.
8. I can sell myself and my business ideas.
9. I don't take time off sick.
10. I can set my own goals and targets and then get on with achieving them.
11. My family are right behind me in this venture – and they know it will mean long hours and hard work.
12. I welcome criticism – there is always something useful to learn from other people.
13. I can pick the right people to work with me.
14. I am energetic and enthusiastic.
15. I don't waste time.

A score of 30 plus is good; 20–30 is fair; below 20 is poor.

A high score will not guarantee success but a low one should make you think seriously about whether you really have the right personal qualities to be a successful entrepreneur.

On my own or with a team?

While most entrepreneurs start their businesses on their own, there are many instances where two or more people start the business together as a team. There are several advantages of the team approach including:

- You are likely to have complementary skills (e.g. one of you being the 'technical expert' while the other is good at sales).
- You have more resources from the outset.
- You may have complementary characteristics so that, although each of you individually may not possess all the characteristics of a successful entrepreneur, perhaps between you, you do.
- You can provide support and encouragement to one another when times get tough – as they inevitably will.
- You can cover for one another for sickness and other absence.

Indeed, if you are intending to start a business which requires external investment, then a team approach will usually be required. Not surprisingly, an investor's ideal proposal includes an experienced and balanced management team, who have all worked together for a number of years.

Of course, there are also disadvantages of the team approach such as:

- You are carrying a bigger overhead from day one.
- You will need to be clear from the outset about roles, responsibilities, ownership shares, etc.
- You may fall out with one another and thus put the business at risk.
- Decision-making may take longer since you will need to agree key decisions with the other members of the team.
- For some entrepreneurs, whose need for control is great and whose primary driver is to be their own boss, being part of a founding team may feel like the precise opposite of what they are looking for.

Ultimately, whether you choose to start on your own, or with a team, is a matter for you to decide. Nevertheless, unless you intend to remain a one-person business, then at some fairly early point in the life of the business you will need to start bringing on other key people.

Are my motivations and aims realistic?

Common motivations for starting a business

Set out below is a list of the most common reasons entrepreneurs give for starting a business. So you could start by seeing if you identify with these.

- being my own boss
- being able to make my own decisions and do things my own way

- having satisfaction in my own work and achievements
- making a lot of money (i.e. capital growth)
- being able to capitalize on specialist skills
- earning my money when I want
- having flexible working hours for existing or family commitments
- taking a calculated risk on my own abilities
- reducing existing stress and worry
- working without having to rely on others
- creating something which is mine
- changing the way things are done
- having a business to pass on to the next generation
- creating employment for the family.

There are two central themes connecting all these reasons. The first theme seems to revolve around personal satisfaction, which can be seen as making work as much fun as any other aspect of life. The second theme is wealth creation, which is essential if an enterprise is going to last any length of time.

Personal satisfaction (fun)

No one particularly enjoys being told what to do and where and when to do it. Working for someone else's organizations brings all those disadvantages and, in addition, most jobs have little real security. Even in countries where the culture of a job for life runs deep, such as Japan, in practical terms career spans are much shorter than in the past. Somewhere between six and nine years is the average time an employee stays with one firm.

But, if you work for yourself you can, in theory at least, construct your own work pattern and give yourself a job for life, albeit a changing one. The only person to blame if your job is boring, repetitive or takes up time that should perhaps be spent with family and friends is yourself.

Another source of personal satisfaction comes from the ability to 'do things my way'. Employees are constantly puzzled and often irritated by the decisions their bosses impose on them. All too often managers in big firms say that they would never spend their own money in the manner they are encouraged or instructed to by the 'powers that be'. They also feel constrained by company 'policy', which seems to set out arbitrary standards for dealing with customers and employees alike.

Big firms often fall into the trap of thinking that, just because they are big and have been around a long time, what they are doing must be right. IBM fell into that trap. After growing to dominate the computer world, in much the same way as Microsoft has, and facing similar accusing voices, the company stumbled and nearly fell. The outside view of the company was encapsulated in the phrase used at that time to describe their staff: 'button-down shirt, button-down mind'. IBM badly fumbled desktop computing, handing over the two most critical PC architectural control points – the systems software and the microprocessor – to Microsoft and Intel. Since any clone maker could acquire the operating system software from Microsoft and the microprocessor from Intel, making PCs became a brutal commodity business. In 1990 IBM was in serious trouble and newcomer Microsoft was in the ascendancy. By 2000 IBM had recovered and was a world-class business once again, itself a rare example of a stunning recovery. Britain's Marconi and Marks and Spencer will do well if they can manage similar recoveries. But stories abound about executives in these firms (and many others besides) who knew that their firm's arrogance and 'if it ain't broke, why fix it?' attitude was bound to lead them into trouble.

Running your own firm allows you to do things in a way that you think the market and your employees believe to be right for the time. Until, of course, you become big and successful yourself.

Wealth creation (making money)

Most Americans and Asians have no ambivalence about their desire to be successful in business and, hence, make lots of money. However, there is still a certain nervousness about admitting to wanting to make money in many European cultures – although that is changing fast. For example, two decades ago 70 per cent of the richest 500 people in the UK inherited their money, with many, such as the Duke of Westminster and the Queen, coming from the traditional 'landed gentry'. A minority of the very wealthy was what might be called 'self-made' first-generation entrepreneurs. Today the ratio is reversed. The vast majority of the current seriously rich are people who started up their own business. Bill Gates (Microsoft), Larry Ellison (Oracle), Richard Branson (Virgin), Jim Clarke (Netscape), Barrie Haigh (Innovex) and Anita Roddick (Body Shop) are just some examples of dollar billionaires who started businesses in the past few decades.

Apart from winning a lottery or inheriting a fortune, starting your own business is the only possible way to achieve full financial independence. That is not to say it is not without risks. In truth, most people who work for themselves do not become super-rich. But many do, and many more become far wealthier than they would probably have become had they remained working for someone else.

Entrepreneurs have something else going for them today when it comes to creating wealth. Most governments have recognized the value of entrepreneurship to their national economies. These governments vie with each other to make their business climate more 'friendly' to entrepreneurs and, in some cases, actually woo entrepreneurs to emigrate to a more favourable regime.

Disadvantages of running your own business

You are totally responsible for the success or failure of your business. This can be very exhilarating. On the other hand, it is risky and can be very stressful.

Running a business is much more risky than working for someone else. If the business fails you stand to lose far more than just your job. Not only will all your hard work have been to no avail, but you might also suffer severe financial hardship if your business owes money, since you may be personally liable to your creditors. This might mean selling your assets, including your home, and, at the worst, may result in bankruptcy. If you form a limited company (see Chapter 6), your personal liability to creditors is limited to the value of the shares you hold – in theory. But, in practice, banks usually require a personal guarantee from the director(s) to secure an overdraft or loan for the business, which to some extent negates the benefits of limited liability status.

Constant pressure and long hours are par for the course for most entrepreneurs. This can drastically affect your social and family life and also your health.

To give a flavour of what it is like being your own boss, here in their own words are selected comments from a range of entrepreneurs.

'It gives you a feeling of being totally in control of your own destiny which is very exciting.'

'You feel totally productive. You use your own time as you wish to spend it. Often this means working all hours of the day, six days a week – permanently. But it isn't a grind if you're doing it for yourself.'

'I have earned far more in personal reward than I have financial benefits. It has given me self-confidence which has made me calmer, less neurotic and more prepared to take risks than hitherto.'

'No longer being involved in office politics has given me an enormous feeling of freedom.'

'You get pleasure from the simplest things – just the fact that the office copier is working!'

'The ability to buy more and better material possessions is irrelevant compared to the sense of achievement you feel.'

'To begin with it's a very exciting feeling, you've stuck your flag in the sand. Then . . . there is a deadly pause while you sit and wait for the business to pour in. The bank manager, or your spouse, is going berserk and you wonder why you've done it. If you're sensible, you ride out this period by concentrating on planning the business properly and making sure you've got your costs right.'

'It's food for the soul.'

'It's good fun!'

But . . .

'It's very lonely knowing you are totally responsible for the success or failure of the business.'

'You have to be totally single-minded which can make you appear selfish to family and friends. It broke up my marriage.'

'You have to be prepared to turn your hand to anything that needs doing. A start-up business can't afford all the back-up services – secretarial help, tea lady, mail boy – you might have become accustomed to as an employee.'

'Some aspects of the work are unpleasant – e.g. cold canvassing for clients, chasing up slow payers, and doing VAT returns.'

'You must develop a strong sense of responsibility to your staff. You can't be cavalier with them. After all, their careers and jobs are in your hands.'

'You must be prepared to be ruthless however friendly you are with staff or suppliers. If staff are no good, you must fire them. If suppliers let you down, get rid of them.'

'It was a great relief going back to being an employee since I no longer had the burden of finding staff salaries each week.'

'These days everyone is trying to live on credit so the biggest problem is cash flow.'

'It's very terrifying at the beginning. You sit there waiting for the phone to ring and when it does you hope like hell it's a potential customer rather than someone you owe money to.'

'The paperwork and form filling is time-consuming and irritating. A government department returned a form to us because we omitted to indicate the type of business of a client even though the client was called the Bank of America!'

'I find the responsibility a constant worry – it brings me out in cold sweats every night.'

Despite the complaints, most entrepreneurs are pleased to have struck out on their own and would have no hesitation in starting up another business rather than work for someone else.

Is the business right for me?

So much for general self-analysis; now, to the particular. In the first chapter of this book, we considered a number of ways in which entrepreneurs typically identify business ideas. Of course, very few people have only one idea. Most people who are seriously interested in doing something entrepreneurial will have several ideas that catch their imagination – and some people are so creative that they have a constant stream of ideas. Whether you have many ideas or just one, you'll need to decide if the business is right for you.

Having identified possible ideas, you need to balance the possibilities against the criteria which are most important to you. These criteria might be things like: small amount of capital required; good anticipated profit; secure income; work satisfaction; no need to learn new skills; variety of work; the possibility of working hours that suit your lifestyle; opportunity to meet new people; minimal paperwork; opportunity to travel. You may have other criteria not on this list.

Firstly, make a list of the criteria which are important to you. Then, allocate each chosen criterion a weighting factor of between 1 and 5, where 5 is the most important to you and 1 the least. Now list the possible business opportunities you have identified and measure them against the graded criteria.

Here's a simple example to illustrate the approach. Jane Clark, an ex-secretary with school-aged children, needed work because her husband had been made redundant and was busy looking for another job. She was not in a position to raise much capital, and she wanted her hours to coincide with those of her children. She wanted to run her own show and she wanted to enjoy what she did. The criteria she selected are shown in Table 1.2.1.

Since minimal capital was a very important criterion for Jane she gave it a weighting factor of 5, whereas the opportunity to meet interesting people, being far less important to her, was only weighted one.

Jane then gave each of her three business ideas a rating, in points (out of five) against these criteria. A secretarial agency needed capital to start so was given

Criteria	Weighting factor (out of five)
Minimal capital required	5
Possibility to work hours that suit lifestyle	5
No need to learn new skills	4
Minimal paperwork	3
Work satisfaction	2
Opportunity to meet interesting people	1

Table 1.2.1

Criteria and weighting factors, Jane Clark

Criteria	Weighting factor	Secretarial agency		Back-up typing		Authors' manuscript	
		Points	Score	Points	Score	Points	Score
Minimal capital	5 ×	1	5	5	25	4	20
Flexible hours	5 ×	1	5	3	15	5	25
No new skills	4 ×	2	8	5	20	5	20
Work satisfaction	3 ×	4	12	1	3	3	9
Minimal paperwork	2 ×	0	0	4	8	5	10
Meeting people	1 ×	4	4	3	3	4	4
Total score			**34**		**74**		**88**

Table 1.2.2

Criteria and weighting results, Jane Clark

only one point. Back-up typing needed hardly any money and was allocated five points.

Her worked-out chart looked like Table 1.2.2.

The weighting factor and the rating point multiplied together give a score for each business idea. The highest score indicates the business that best meets Jane's criteria. In this case, typing authors' manuscripts scored over back-up typing since Jane could do it exactly when it suited her.

Chapter summary

Although many people harbour the dream of starting their own business and working for themselves, it is not necessarily right for everyone. So, before committing any significant amounts of time, energy and money to getting into business, it's important to ask yourself the fundamental questions which we have reviewed in this chapter.

Firstly, are you really the entrepreneurial type? Do you possess most of the broad characteristics of the successful entrepreneur? Would you be more suited to starting on your own or with a team?

Secondly, are your aims and motivations realistic and are they likely to be met by starting up on your own?

And, finally, is the idea that you've come up with the right idea for you?

These are challenging questions and it is easy to deceive oneself in answering them. However, we encourage all potential entrepreneurs to consider them very, very carefully. After all, starting a business is hard enough and risky enough without discovering part way down the track that you were never really cut out for it!

Ultimately, the most important single criteria is that you must be 100 per cent committed and passionate about your business. After all, if you're not, why should any customers or employees be?

Assignments

1. Carry out the self-evaluation check described in this chapter and see how closely you appear to fit the entrepreneurial style.
2. If you have already identified other people with whom you intend to start the business, get them to carry out the self-evaluation also. Are there any areas where you can foresee potential problems? What could you do to alleviate these problems?
3. Consider whether you are better suited to starting on your own or with a team? If the latter, do you already know the other people? Are you sure that they are the right people? If you don't already know the people, then which other people do you need? What characteristics and skills should they have?
4. Review your motivations for getting into business to see how well they compare with typical entrepreneurs.
5. Identify the criteria you are looking to satisfy in starting your business and weight them using the approach described in this chapter. How well does your proposed venture meet those yardsticks?

Suggested further reading

Drucker, P. (1999) *Innovation and Entrepreneurship*, London: Butterworth Heinemann.
Golzen, Godfrey (2003) *Working for Yourself*, London: Kogan Page.
Webb, Phillip and Sandra Webb (2002) *The Small Business Handbook*, Hemel Hempsted: Prentice Hall.

3 Is there a market opportunity in your business sector?

Introduction and objectives

You've got your business idea and you've thought carefully about your own drivers, motivations and characteristics. Now you need to demonstrate that your idea represents an opportunity to build a business – or, to put it more simply, that there are people who will buy what you are hoping to sell.

By the end of this chapter, you should have a good understanding of the market you are planning to enter and the following key topics:

- The role of vision statements in defining the business idea both for yourself and other people.

- How market research can help you sharpen your business idea and focus on your target customers and how to set about undertaking your own market research.

- Analysis of existing competitors, both direct and indirect.

Vision statements and business objectives

The first step is to be clear about the business sector within which the enterprise will function. One effective way to do this is to write a *vision statement* for the enterprise, to define the goal of the business and the opportunity that you are seeking to capture.

As we have seen, there is much debate over whether successful entrepreneurs share a common set of characteristics. There are, however, good reasons for thinking that many entrepreneurs have a clear vision of their goals, even if they are not sure how to achieve them!

Vision statements and objectives are important in two main ways:

- they concentrate your own and your (future) employees' efforts in a specific market
- and they concentrate attention on problems to be solved.

Large companies may spend long weekends at country mansions wrestling with the fine print of their vision statements. In principle, given the narrower scope of the new business, the task facing the new business owner should be less daunting.

Since vision statements and objectives are inevitably intertwined, let's take them first. Vision statements and objectives are statements of direction, intended to focus your attention on essentials, and to define your specific competence(s) in relation to the markets/customers you plan to serve.

Firstly, the vision should be narrow enough to give direction and guidance to everyone in the business. This concentration is the key to business success because it is only by focusing on specific needs that an early-stage business can differentiate itself from its larger competitors. Nothing kills off a new business faster than trying to do too many different things at the start.

Secondly, the vision should open up a large enough market to allow the business to grow and realize its potential.

In summary, the vision statement should explain:

- Which business you are in, and your purpose.

  Naz Choudhury, founder of Real Burger World, wanted: 'to turn the fast food industry on its head and give it the shake-up that has been long overdue. Our goal is to establish the first nationally recognized fast food chain serving fast food with real, natural and wholesome ingredients with prompt service and an inviting ambience.'

- What you want to achieve over the next one to three years.

  Within one year of opening his first outlet, Naz intended to open a second and possibly a third, once the Real Burger World concept was refined. Within three years, he intended to expand out of London into other parts of the UK and, quite possibly, continental Europe.

- How you will achieve your goals, your values and your standards.

  'We aim to provide "no-nonsense" tasty food at good value, which the eyes will delight in before the mouth devours. The Real Burger concept aims to revolutionize customer perceptions of the fast food burger experience, by

Figure 1.3.1

The pyramid of goals

redefining the product, service and ambience. Real Burger is differentiated by making our own burgers in open plan kitchens using only fresh "natural" ingredients.'

Case Study

Nigel Apperley, founder of InternetCameras-Direct, online retailer of digital cameras, was inspired by the Dell business model of selling computers to customers direct, and how that transferred to the emerging online sales channel. Right from the start, he was clear about his vision and objectives:

- The *vision* was to become Britain's leading web-based retailer of digital cameras.

- The *strategic goal* was to become a strong, financially independent company, highly branded and an attractive acquisition target for bigger industry players.

- The key to *achieving this* was: smart marketing; shrewd buying based on strong relationships with key suppliers; and superior customer service.

All of this was based on the Dell model!

Above all, vision statements must be realistic, achievable – and brief.

The vision statement can then be communicated widely, through meetings and company literature, to promote greater company cohesion and concentration.

Market research

Having narrowed your market focus by completion of your vision, you should now concentrate on researching the specific market segment, to determine the need for your own product or service.

You do not have to open a shop (or an e-commerce website) to prove there are no customers for your goods and services; frequently some modest do-it-yourself (DIY) market research beforehand can give clear guidance as to whether your venture will succeed or not.

The purpose of practical DIY market research for entrepreneurs seeking to prove, as far as possible, that there is a real market opportunity for their business idea is twofold:

1. To build *credibility* for the business idea the entrepreneur must prove first to his or her own satisfaction (and, typically, later to outside investors), a thorough understanding of the marketplace for the new product or service. This will be vital to attract the resources needed to build the new venture.

2. To develop a *realistic* market entry strategy for the new business, based on a clear understanding of genuine customer needs and ensuring that product quality, price, promotional methods and distribution channels are mutually supportive and clearly focused on target customers.

Otherwise, as the English proverb says, there is a danger of 'fools rushing in where angels fear to tread!'

In the army it is said that 'time spent in reconnaissance is rarely time wasted'. The same is certainly true in starting a business, where you will need to research in particular:

1. *Your customers*: Who will buy your goods and services? What particular customer needs will your business meet? How many potential buyers are out there?
2. *Your competitors*: Which established companies are already meeting the needs of your potential customers? What are their strengths and weaknesses?
3. *Your product or service*: How should it be tailored to meet customer needs?
4. *Price*: What should you charge to be perceived as giving value for money?
5. *Which promotional material is needed* to reach customers? What newspapers and journals do they read? Which websites do they log on to?
6. *Sales and distribution channels*: Which are most appropriate in reaching your customers?
7. *Location*: Where is most convenient for key customers, suppliers, staff skills and other resources?

Research is not just essential in starting a business. Once the business is launched, it should become an integral part of the ongoing life of the company. Customers and competitors change; products have life cycles. The good news is that once you have existing customers (and staff) to question, the research task becomes easier.

First steps

There are two main types of research in starting a business:

1. desk research, or the study of publicly available information
2. field research, involving fieldwork in collecting specific information for the market.

Both activities are vital for the starter business.

Desk research

Desk research is exactly what the name implies – research which you can carry out from your desk. This is typically high-level data regarding the environment and market.

Today, 'desk research' might be better named desktop or laptop research. Thanks to the internet, it has never been easier to access huge amounts of research on a bewildering range of product, service and geographic markets. And much of it is free.

In advanced economies, governments increasingly make available online statistics on the economy, the population, patterns of expenditure, trends in consumption and so on. If the data is published in hard copy form, it is normally available in public libraries or at government offices. Information collected by governments (or supra-national bodies, such as the European Union) which is typically of use to would-be entrepreneurs will include:

- *Macro-economic cycles*: Comparing the performance of the economy as a whole with different industrial sectors.
- *Trends in population growth or decline*: For instance, currently most western economies face a common problem in the form of an ageing population, a fall in the numbers of those of working age and a long-term decline in the birth-rate.
- *Regional economic performance*: Which regions are most and least affluent, which qualify for assisted status (and thus grants to aid new businesses)?
- *Patterns of household and personal consumption*: Where are consumers spending their money, and which sectors are declining or booming as a result of changes in lifestyle?

Government data can also provide lists of potential customers, whether companies or private individuals. For most purposes, however, it is usually more cost-effective to obtain 'qualified' lists of potential customers through agencies who specialize in compiling and selling such lists, or through trade and industry associations. (Of course, the most cost-effective way of all of finding potential customers is to use your own existing contacts, wherever possible. This is just one reason why relevant industry knowledge and experience is so valuable to the entrepreneur.)

Official statistics are usefully complemented by market research reports produced by specialists, such as the Economist Intelligence Unit, Datamonitor and Mintel (to cite three of the best-known European companies). Their reports are typically more focused on commercial issues, and will go into greater depth on a particular industry. They divide into those specializing in business-to-business, and those who deal with consumer markets. A little research on the web will soon highlight the experts in the area in which you are interested. As a rule of thumb, if the industry sector is significant – that is, involving turnover in the hundreds of millions or billions of euros – it will attract the attention of market research specialists. The downside, as you might expect, is that, since these are commercial organizations, they sell their information.

However, an important customer segment for market research is the commercially focused library. These can be found in business schools, for example, and sometimes also in government departments or agencies. Before you part with your hard-earned money, check which libraries you have access to already, or are eligible to use free or for an annual subscription. Then, find out which market research services the library subscribes to – you could save yourself a significant outlay.

The information you obtain through desk research is known as 'secondary' data, because it is collected by someone else. Primary data is information you collect yourself. Secondary data is extremely valuable in establishing the 'big picture' in terms of economic trends, potential market size, consumer lifestyle trends and so forth. On the other hand, it is most unlikely to answer the question 'is there a market for *my* product/service?' More to the point, it is dangerous to expect that it will do so. As business school faculty, we have lost count of the number of business plans we have seen which are based on gaining, for example, 1 per cent of a €5 billion euro market, but which cannot identify who will actually be the first customers for the business. From the viewpoint of the would-be entrepreneur, secondary data has some important limitations:

- The data provided is often at too general a level, and does not answer the specific questions that are vital to the new business.
- It may well be several years out of date, as a result of the time lag in collecting, processing and publishing the information.
- Data on the same market from different sources often conflict, because of different ways of defining the relevant population.
- The information may well indicate the type of potential customer for your business, but not who they are specifically.
- And it may well not answer the practical, detailed questions of how you reach your target, how you brand and position your business, your pricing policy, and so forth.

It is best therefore to view the conclusions from desk research as useful indicators which provide support (or not) for your business concept, but are in need of confirmation from your own fieldwork.

Case Study

Naz Choudhury had already established one restaurant when he decided to launch Real Burger World with a partner in 2003. His plan was based on certain key assumptions, substantiated by market research:

- UK consumers liked the convenience of fast food, but were increasingly concerned about the nutritional value of what they were eating.
- Consumers were open to new flavours and cuisines, and these could be incorporated into a hamburger-based food offering.

- People would pay a premium for freshly cooked food made from quality ingredients.

He summarized the conclusions from his desk research as shown in Table 1.3.1.

His thinking was also strongly affected by the bestselling book, *Fast Food Nation* by Eric Schlosser, which raised a number of questions about the activities of mainstream fast food operators. This reflected, he thought, growing public concern about what people were eating.

Table 1.3.1	*Drivers – What's been happening?*	*Expectations*
Naz Choudhury's drivers and expectations	*Pioneers* Pioneering by TV chefs such as Jamie Oliver and supermarkets opting to offer wider range of better, premium foods and ingredients have re-educated customers.	Desire for fresh, natural, wholesome food from all over the world. People want real food, not imitations!

▶

Table 1.3.1	Drivers – What's been happening?	Expectations
(continued)	**Competition** Owing to competition from the abundance of restaurants and eateries offering a plethora of foods from all over the world, customer expectations are far more developed than ever before.	Discerning customers. To eat good quality, wholesome food at value for money prices. Better than ever service.
	Lifestyle changes Work hard, play hard attitude to life. Longer working hours. Career focus. No more fixed lunch and dinner times.	To eat out more often, and to eat when they want: hence expecting better value, owing to increased eating-out spend.
	The world is a small place With multicultural societies, cheap airfares and holidays abroad, people are more culturally aware.	A diverse selection of foods from all over world to serve highly developed eating palates.
	Health People are searching for healthier lifestyles. Gymnasiums in abundance throughout UK.	To eat nutritious and wholesome food with fresh, natural ingredients which supports their health goals.
	Standard of living A better standard of living owing to a higher disposable income. People are getting married later and having fewer children later. Fast food staff poorly paid.	A modern experience in tune with their aspirations. Staff expect better pay.
	Environmentally aware People more aware about environment and society.	Environmentally friendly food and packaging is a customer-pleaser! More people eating vegetarian food as main meal than ever before.

Field research or primary data collection

If you want specific market data relating to your particular target customers, then the only way to obtain it is to get out and talk to them. This is called field research or primary data collection. If desk research addresses the question 'Is there a business opportunity?' at the macro level, field research addresses the same question at the micro level.

Some years ago, a team of entrepreneurs we know were considering opening a classical musical shop in a provincial French town, in the belief that there was a gap in the market. Their target market was younger consumers. Desk research revealed that, out of a total population of 250 000 people in the town, 25 per cent were under 30 years of age. But, this did not tell them what percentage were interested in classical music or how much they might spend on classical recordings. Field research (a questionnaire handed out to passers-by in the street) provided the answers of 1 per cent and €5 a week spent on average. This suggested a potential market of only €162 500 a year (250 000 × 25 per cent × 1 per cent × €5 × 52). Even allowing for the do-it-yourself nature of the exercise, this did not look like a realistic proposition. The entrepreneurs in question decided to investigate Paris and Lyon instead. But at least the cost had only been two damp afternoons spent on the streets, rather than the horrors of having to dispose of a lease of an unsuccessful shop.

Much fieldwork consists of interviews, with the interviewer putting questions to an individual respondent or possibly a group of respondents in what is known as a focus group. Many of us have been on the receiving end as interviewees, so we already have some knowledge of what is involved. Historically, most interviews have been conducted face to face, with telephone surveys the next most popular method. Then come postal surveys and discussion or focus groups.

More recently, email and the internet have become increasingly popular ways of soliciting opinion and attitudes. There are a number of online survey sites (e.g. www.zoomerang.com, www.snapsurveys.com, www.websurveyor.com) which will allow you to design and administer simple surveys either to your own network of contacts or to a sample that the site provides. In some cases, a restricted version of the service is available free of charge and this may be all that is required in the very early stages of planning your business. The main limitation of online surveys compared to face-to-face interviews is that you cannot offer clarification or enter in to any exploratory discussions.

Case Study

At the height of the dot com boom one of our MBA students, who was an experienced architect, intended to set up an online portal for the architecture profession. Unlike many other dot com entrepreneurs, he took the sensible step of doing some primary market research before beginning to spend time and money on designing, building and populating the site. He used an online survey tool to design a simple questionnaire which he then invited about 100 architects, who he already knew, to complete. Less than ten indicated that they would make use of the proposed portal. Our aspiring entrepreneur concluded that, if less than 10 per cent of the architects that already knew him would use the site, then those that did not know him would be even less likely to be users. And so he would struggle to generate enough traffic to be able to sell the advertising which was to be his main revenue stream. Sensibly, he decided not to proceed with the venture at that time.

There are numerous market research agencies that will undertake field research on your behalf. Like those companies who focus on providing secondary data, these tend to divide into specialists in business-to-business and experts on consumer markets. There is frequently a further subdivision between those who specialize in obtaining statistically significant data from larger samples (quantitative research) and those whose focus is on exploratory work, to understand the latent opinions or attitudes of a particular target group (qualitative research).

However, these also charge money which you may not be able to afford. So, if you intend to undertake some fieldwork on your own behalf, and you have no professional experience of market research techniques, bear the following guidelines in mind:

- Before you start, have you undertaken some basic desk research that enables you to frame your research in a sensible context? There is nothing worse than realizing at the end of such an exercise that you have failed to obtain some really crucial piece of information which could easily have been included.

- Before you embark on trying to do a piece of statistically representative work (see guidance later in this chapter), are you certain that you know what is on the 'agenda' of your target market? If you are unsure what is important to them, spend some time initially in informal discussions that are likely to generate insights which guide your questions to a wider sample.

Questionnaire design

However you conduct your research – in person, by telephone, on the internet – it will be driven by a questionnaire. At the outset, give careful thought to the following:

- Defining your research objectives. What is it exactly that you vitally need to know (for example, how often do people buy, how much do they spend on the average transaction)? Remember that few people have the time to spend more than a few minutes answering something which may be important for you but is trivial for them.

- Who are the customers to sample for this information and where might you reach them easily and cheaply? If you are investigating the market for household goods, for instance, most countries have big trade fairs which attract large numbers of people interested in products for the home.

- How are you going to undertake the research? Be realistic about the resources you have and the time that you can devote to the task.

When you are sure of the above, and only then, you are ready to design the questionnaire. There are five simple rules to guide this process:

1. Keep the number of questions to the minimum. 'Vital to know' is more important than 'nice to know'.

2. Start by asking for straightforward, easily answered, factual information. Capture data such as sex, age group, location, that you may need to refer to later. Progress to opinion once you have established the 'facts'.

3. Where possible, the answers should be either 'Yes/No/Don't Know' or consist of prompted alternatives, which can be ranked in order of importance (1–4).

4. Avoid ambiguity – make sure the respondent really understands the questions – and that interpreting the answers will be equally unambiguous.

5. Make sure that at the beginning you have a cut-out question to eliminate unsuitable respondents (such as those who never use the product/service in question).

Be prepared to pilot your questionnaire among a small sample of respondents first, and revise it if necessary.

You can increase your response rates by also following some simple rules:

- *Telephone interviewing*: This requires a very positive attitude, courtesy, an ability not to talk too quickly and to listen while sticking to a well-defined questionnaire.

- *Postal surveys*: Response rates can be dramatically improved by sending accompanying letters that explain the purpose of the questionnaire and why respondents should reply. Sometimes the offer of information is attractive (a summary of the survey findings, for example), or the offer of a small reward or the chance to take part in a prize draw. Enclosing a pre-paid envelope for the reply is guaranteed to increase the response rate.

- *Face-to-face interviewing*: How you introduce yourself is very important here. Make sure you are prepared, either by carrying an identifying card or with a rehearsed introduction. For example: 'Good morning, I'm from Organization X [show card]. We are conducting a survey and we would be grateful for your help.' You may also need visuals of the product you are investigating, such as samples or photographs, to ensure the respondent understands. Make sure these are neat and accessible. Once again, we urge you to try out the questionnaire and your technique on your friends, prior to using it in the street. You will be surprised at how questions which seem simple to you are incomprehensible at first to respondents.

- *Online surveys*: Response rates to these are highly dependent on the quality of the sample. If you use your own contacts and can provide their email addresses, then you are likely to get a better and more relevant response. The usual mechanism is to send an email which either includes the survey or a link to a website where the survey can be completed. The wording of this email is important in increasing response rates. It should be brief and should include who you are, what you are trying to find out, what the recipient might get if they respond, what they have to do to respond, an indication of how long it will take them to complete the survey and, most importantly, a big 'thank you'!

Sampling sizes

If you want to undertake fieldwork which is statistically significant, the size of the population surveyed is critical. The accuracy of your survey clearly increases with the size of sample, as Table 1.3.2 shows.

If, on a sample size of 600, your survey showed that 40 per cent of women in the town drove cars, the true proportion probably lies between 36 per cent and 44 per cent. For a typical entrepreneurial business, with a product that targets

With random sample of:	95 per cent of surveys are right within ... points	Table 1.3.2
250	6.2	Surveys: relation of
500	4.4	sample size to
750	3.6	accuracy
1 000	3.1	
2 000	2.2	
6 000	1.2	

thousands of buyers, we usually recommend a minimum sample of 250 completed replies.

Validation

The most convincing kind of market research is the type that can be confirmed from more than one source. Retailers such as Naz Choudhury of Real Burger World can confirm what interviewees say by reference to his own industry experience, by the data from secondary market research and by independent observation (this cross-referencing is known as triangulation). When all these more or less coincide, then you can have some degree of confidence that you have an accurate picture of what is going on.

Be warned, however. What people tell you is not always matched by what they do. This is not necessarily because interviewees deliberately mislead you. They may misunderstand the question, their memories may be at fault or they may give you the answer they think you want to hear. If the questions that are asked are about personal consumption or preferences, there is always a risk that they will give the answers that convey the image of themselves they wish to project. After all, which of us would rather be perceived as selfish, mean and ignorant as opposed to concerned for others, generous and enlightened?

Case Study

When Naz Choudhury was planning the opening of his first Real Burger World outlet in south London, he estimated the number of customers based on observing the number of people passing the location of the shop, the number of people using other fast food outlets in the vicinity, face-to-face interviews with potential consumers, research studies and his own experience in the industry. To help him get a hands-on 'feel' for his market, he also worked for three months in a mainstream fast food competitor. As a result, he knew that:

- The busiest times of day for his outlet would be between 11.00 am and 3.00 pm and between 6.00 pm and 8.00 pm.
- The busiest day of the week would be Saturday.
- December would be 20 per cent more busy than a usual month.

►

- February is the poorest trading month for food businesses, being 30 per cent less than a usual month, while January is also 20 per cent less than a usual month but not as bad as February because of people shopping at New Year sales.

Based on this detailed information, he was able to draw up a plan for staffing the outlet, calculating the total number of staff hours required, the number of members of staff and the associated staff costs.

Competitor analysis

Most people, when they contemplate starting a new venture, have a fair idea of who their competitors are, if only because most new ventures are launched into existing markets. By the time you have finished your market research, you should have a much clearer picture of the competition. The secondary research sources, such as Mintel or the Economist Intelligence Unit reports, typically provide market share data on the bigger players in each segment. Quantitative data, such as sales value, geographical markets, product segments and so forth combine to build a picture of each competitors' strengths and weaknesses. For instance, for every soft drinks company except Coca-Cola, reviewing international market data is typically a humbling experience. Around the world, with few exceptions, Coke dominates soft drinks, and companies like Pepsi and Schweppes battle for second place.

As a general rule, we recommend that new start-up businesses do not go head-to-head with giant multinationals. Having said that, the soft drinks market is enormous and highly fragmented – even Coke, with its full brand portfolio, has less than 20 per cent of worldwide consumption. It has taken less than 15 years for high-energy drink Red Bull to grow from nothing to a business that sells over a billion litres of product annually. There are opportunities for entrepreneurs in every marketplace.

How should you define your competition?

Some new ventures find this easier to answer than others. If you plan to serve a clearly defined group of customers in a specific location, the competition is easy to identify. For a fast food restaurant business, like Real Burger World, the direct competitors are the other fast food providers within close walking distance of each outlet who compete for the target customers' expenditure. If the average purchase value is £5 or less at lunchtime, then that eliminates the more expensive restaurant as a direct competitor because lunchtime expenditure there will be above £5. Time can also be an important criterion: the competitive set could be more tightly defined as:

- all fast food operators within 500 metres of the Real Burger World kiosk
- all fast food operators who can provide a 'meal solution' for less than £5
- and all fast food operators who can meet that demand in less than x minutes' queuing time (after which the customer drifts away).

There are also, of course, indirect competitors, or alternative 'meal solutions' outside the fast food competitive set. Examples might be a pub or a pizza restaurant, where the target customer chooses to spend 30 minutes sitting down to eat. Or it could be the sandwiches that the target customer prepares at home and eats in the office.

Other new ventures find this question of 'who are my competitors?' more difficult to answer. Moonpig is a specialist provider of greetings cards, which operates only on the internet. By logging onto their website, you can choose and customize a card which Moonpig then prints and sends to a recipient anywhere in the world. When Nick Jenkins created this business in 2000, he found that he had no real direct competitors, in the sense of other businesses that would customize greetings cards over the internet. On the other hand, he had indirect competitors selling greetings cards on every high street.

As a general rule, direct competitors are those businesses who compete for the same piece of the customer's expenditure that you plan to target. Your direct competitors are the ones who are most likely to respond to your entry into the market, since your target customers are also their core customers.

Often the easiest way to identify your direct competitors is to include this as part of your market research activity. Ask a sample of your target market which suppliers in your chosen segment are at the top of their mind. If the same handful of names keep emerging, these will form the competitive set in which you will be competing.

Indirect competitors are more typically alternative or substitute solutions to meet the same customer need: perhaps a different technology or a different service.

Remember that, in many markets, the customer can always choose not to buy at all, and so 'doing nothing' is often an indirect competitor. This is particularly true in markets for products or services which have not previously existed, for example, new technology products. Even if you have a unique product/service, do not underestimate the difficulty in overcoming the inertia of customers who don't necessarily see the desirability of your product/service in the way that you do.

Also, in many product markets, suppliers providing secondhand goods can be significant indirect competitors. Given the increasing popularity of 'car boot' sales and internet-based auctions such as e-bay, there may be many places where your customers can find a solution to their needs without necessarily buying from you or your direct competitors

Why should you study the competition?

We began this chapter by talking about the need to substantiate your business idea through research. An opportunity only exists if a customer is prepared to buy from you – as opposed to someone else. From the moment you start to work seriously on your new idea, therefore, you need to understand what else is out there in the market. If you do not know who the competitors are, and how well their offerings meet the customers' needs, how will you be able to:

- Verify that there is indeed a gap in the market?
- Identify where your competitors are weak and where they are strong?
- Satisfy yourself that your business concept is sufficiently better or different to withstand the inevitable market pressures?

All too often, we have seen business plans that have been prepared without taking sufficient account of existing competitors. At the point of launch or, worse still, after launching, the unlucky founders have discovered that there are suppliers already meeting the supposed gap in the market – and that the customer proposition needs to be radically redesigned.

What are the key things you need to know about the competition?

Generally speaking, the more you know about the competition the better. In particular, it is important to understand:

- What is the range of competitive offering – products and services, direct and indirect?
- For each one, what are their strengths and weaknesses, which parts of the market do they focus on and which do they neglect?

A more detailed set of questions regarding competitor research is included in the assignments at the end of this chapter.

How do you obtain information about the competition?

There is a wide range of ways in which you can obtain this information. The most obvious, but often overlooked, way is to buy your competitors' product/services yourself. This has the great advantages that you can examine the product/service itself and get first-hand knowledge of the way this company deals with customers. In some circumstances you can also deconstruct the competitor's product/service, identifying components and how they are put together. This is called 'reverse engineering' and can be very useful in identifying ways in which to improve on your competitors' offerings.

For example, the highly entrepreneurial British design guru and restaurateur, Sir Terence Conran, has claimed that he undertakes no market research at all. In reality, he confesses to spending nearly half of his time visiting competitors' restaurants and inspecting new and rival products.

You can also examine competitive advertising and promotion and, where appropriate, attend trade exhibitions where your competitors may be exhibiting. And, of course, as part of your field research you can ask potential customers about their experiences of your competitors.

Just like customer research, finding out what your competitors are up to is an ongoing task. In most markets competitors, like customers, change all the time. Never, ever, underestimate the opposition.

Chapter summary

It is an obvious and fundamental part of starting a new business to demonstrate that there are people who will buy what you are hoping to sell. In this chapter, we have considered:

- How to create a vision statement as a means of helping to define the business idea both for yourself and other people.
- How to use market research to help you sharpen your business idea and focus on your target customers.
- How to set about undertaking your own market research.
- The importance of carefully analysing your competitors, both direct and indirect.

In carefully considering these areas, you lay the foundations for matching your new business idea to the needs of the market. In our experience, this process often involves modifying the original concept, as you learn more about the market and the competition. Be prepared for this, and see it as something positive that will increase your chances of success. If, when this process is complete, you are still keen to proceed with your business idea, collate the results so that they can be incorporated into your business plan. Your conclusions will give you and potential investors confidence and lenders that your idea is both timely and appropriate for identified customers.

However, do not expect market research to provide all the answers. A major next step still lies ahead: determining your strategy for getting into the market, which will be addressed in the next chapter.

Assignments

Vision and objectives

1. Write a vision statement linking your product/service to the market segment and customer needs at which it is aimed.
2. What are your principal business objectives
   a) short term (say, one year)?
   b) long term (say, three years)?

Market research

3. What information do you currently have on the overall market, economic and demographic trends, etc.? What high-level secondary information do you still need to find and why do you need it? What desk research do you need to carry out to obtain this information?
4. What primary data do you need on customers and why will it be valuable? How will you go about obtaining this data and which field research approaches will you use?
5. Produce a plan of all the market research activities showing who will undertake each task, how much time and money will be needed to carry out each task and when all the data will be available.

Competitor analysis

6. Identify the range of competitor offerings – products and services, direct and indirect.

7. Answer the following for each direct competitor:
   a) What are they known for (for example, low price, high service levels, innovations)?
   b) Which part of the market do they focus on (for example, high net worth individuals)?
   c) Which part of the market do they neglect (and why)?
   d) What are their weaknesses (actual or perceived)?
   e) What are their strengths (for instance, big competitors generally buy more cheaply than smaller ones)?
8. For each indirect competitor (including 'doing nothing' and the secondhand market, if appropriate):
   a) Which part of the market is served (for example, cost conscious customers)?
   b) What are their strengths and weaknesses (actual or perceived)?

Suggested further reading

Barrow, Colin (2003) *The Complete Small Business Guide*, Oxford: Capstone Reference (for desk research guidance).

Crimp, Margaret and Len Tiu Wright (2000) *The Marketing Research Process*, Harlow: Pearson Higher Education.

4 What is your business model and market entry strategy?

Introduction and objectives

Let's assume that your research has convinced you that your business idea has a good chance of succeeding and that you have the right personal qualities to make it happen. Before you decide whether you can make money (addressed in a later chapter), there are three major questions relating to your market that you need to resolve:

- *Business model*: What are you going to do, for whom, and who is going to pay you for it? For example, are your customers individual consumers or are they other businesses?

- *Route to market*: How will you reach your end customer? For example, will you sell to them directly or through some form of intermediary?

- *Marketing strategy*: How will you sell to your target customers? For instance, who specifically are your target customers and what does your product/service offer them which is distinctively better than alternative ways of meeting their needs? What is the selling message and how will it be delivered?

By the end of this chapter, you should have a clear understanding of each of these three areas and how they relate to your business idea.

The answers to all three of these questions start with your (end) customer. Everything has to be defined in terms of customer needs and how you will satisfy them. Some customers who want good quality photographs may be less interested in the sophisticated technology needed to produce them. Others want to own the latest, leading-edge digital camera. People who enjoy a quality cappuccino in the coffee bar may want to reproduce that experience at home, not just to savour the taste but to re-live the moment of relaxation in the company of friends and family. For them, the look and feel of the coffee-maker may be as important as its performance. As well as meeting people's needs, solving a customer's problem can be just as effective a driver for starting a successful new venture. One highly successful serial entrepreneur we know well recommends that you always 'Identify the point of maximum pain'. What is it that is complicating a consumer's or a company's life, and which is a problem crying out for a solution? Take the pain away, and you have a proposition of value to your customer, for which he or she is willing to pay.

Business model

If you've done your market research as described in the previous chapter, you should have a good idea about whether there is demand for your product/ service. Nevertheless, it is worth pausing for thought about what precisely you are going to do, for whom and who will pay you.

One way to think about your business model is to use the simple model shown in Figure 1.4.1

Along the horizontal axis is the type of customer you are targeting. Business customers (we also include public sector and other types of organizations in this category) buy on behalf of their organization and they spend the organization's money. On the other hand, there are consumers who spend their own money. Along the vertical axis is the way that you reach your final purchaser, either directly or through an intermediary. If it is through an intermediary, you will have two kinds of customer to satisfy. By the end of this chapter, you should have a clear view on which of these four boxes is the one that best describes your business concept.

For some start-ups, the choice of business model is straightforward. InternetCamerasDirect, for example, the online retailer of digital cameras, sells direct to consumers. For others, the answer is not so simple. Consider the alternatives which were open to the start-up business Light Emotions.

Figure 1.4.1

Business model matrix

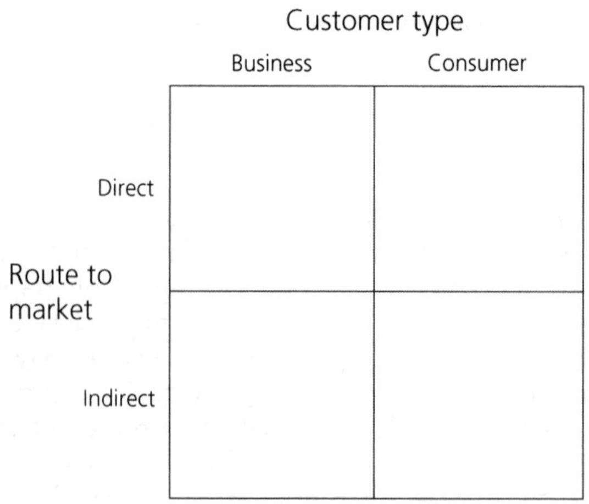

Case Study

Dominique Pecquet and Christophe Mermaz, two French engineers, set up Light Emotions in November 2000 to exploit Dominique's invention of a champagne glass which lights up when liquid is poured in and switches itself off when the glass is empty. The invention was intriguing and delighted everyone to whom they showed it. However, the first big question they had when setting up Light Emotions was 'What should be the business model?' For instance:

- Should they sell the glasses directly to end consumers? If so, should it be via a shop, a website, a mail order catalogue or some other means?
- Should they sell the glasses to party shops?
- Should they sell the glasses to party and event organizers and nightclubs?
- Should they do deals with event organizers where Light Emotions was allowed to have a presence at their events where the glasses were sold to consumers, with Light Emotions and the event organizers splitting the proceeds?
- Should they sell to champagne makers who could use the glasses as promotional gifts? If

so, should they go directly to the champagne makers or through marketing companies who already work with them?
- Could they sell the design to other companies who could then make the glasses?
- Were there other models?
- And, in each case, what would be the appropriate batch sizes and prices?

The answers to these questions vexed Christophe and Dominique for some time. Ultimately, they chose to focus on selling the glasses to drinks manufacturers for product launches. But the manufacturers would not deal directly with Light Emotions since it was such a young and small business. Instead, Light Emotions developed relationships with marketing agencies and event management companies who organized events on behalf of the drinks manufacturers. These agencies then recommended Light Emotions glasses as part of the launch events.

Even today, three years after starting the business, and now with a second product, they are still not sure that this is the most appropriate model with which to move the business forward.

Should you target businesses or consumers?

In most market sectors, the reality is that there are far more opportunities to sell to businesses, since there are so many more links in each and every supply chain. It is also generally easier and less costly to identify and target businesses of a particular type than consumers within a given segment. It also appears to be a more successful strategy for start-up businesses. Amar Bhidé, in his masterly study of successful start-ups in the US, *The Origin and Evolution of New Businesses*, concluded that the most consistently successful new ventures are

- those targeted at niche business to business markets
- where the average sales transaction is relatively high
- and the sale is made directly by the founder(s) of the firm.

Of course, the answer to this question is not necessarily either businesses or consumers. Some businesses have elements of both of these in them. For instance, most publishers of magazines and regional newspapers will in essence have two sets of customers – the readers, who may or may not pay a cover price for the publication, and the advertisers, who pay for advertising space so that they can promote their products/services to the readers. Equally, Moonpig, the online provider of personalized greetings cards, is primarily targeting consumers but also has business accounts with major companies to providing humorous Christmas cards. Businesses which have a genuinely hybrid business and consumer sales model are, nevertheless, the exception.

If you have any doubts about which should be your dominant target buying group, then consider the following questions:

- Will the target user group be buying your product/service for themselves or for the organization they work for?
- How tightly can you define your target user group, to be confident that your proposition meets their needs?

If, having answered these questions, you are still unsure whether you have a business-to-business (B2B, as it is sometimes called), or business-to-consumer (B2C) model, you probably need to rethink your business concept.

If you decide on a business-to-consumer model, then you also have choices over the mechanism by which your consumers will find you. Will it be a traditional shop, will it be a website, a mail order catalogue, door-to-door selling, 'party plan', or something else? Each of these options will have different sizes of market, different competitive and market dynamics, different types of customer who prefer to deal in this way, and different cost structures. It may be that you need to look at several of these options, making comparisons across these issues, before deciding which is the most appropriate for your venture.

At the start of a new venture, the key point is to focus on one model – you simply don't have the resources to be doing too many things at the same time. But, of course, be prepared to modify your model as you make progress.

Route to market

At the same time as considering who are your customers, and who will pay you, you should also consider how you will reach those customers. In some cases, it may make sense to sell to your customers directly. For example, business services such as legal or accountancy advice, banking or insurance are typically sold and marketed direct to the person – whether private individual or organizational buyer – who pays for them. Nigel Apperley's InternetCamerasDirect business focused from day one on selling direct to individual customers. On the other hand, many new ventures reach their customers through intermediaries as Christophe and Dominique of Light Emotions decided to do.

So, three questions suggest themselves:

1. Do I sell directly or through a third party?
2. Is the product or service bought by the end user or on their behalf?

3. If I sell indirectly can I meet the needs of both the intermediary and the final user?

Let's take each of these in turn.

Selling directly or using a third party

In his 1987 work, *Ogilvy on Advertising*, David Ogilvy, the advertising guru, cites a classic advertisement created by the McGraw-Hill Business & Professional magazines division. Facing the reader is a stony-faced senior executive. The text reads:

I don't know who you are.
I don't know your company.
I don't know your company's product.
I don't know what your company stands for.
I don't know your company's customers.
I don't know your company's record.
I don't know your company's reputation.
Now – what was it you wanted to sell me?

McGraw-Hill, of course, were promoting the cause of corporate advertising in their own publications. But, there is a clear and highly pertinent message here for the new or fledgling business. However good your business concept, building the trust, confidence and reputation that help to close sales in the early days is not easy. For that reason, many successful new ventures get started by selling to customers who already know the founder(s) of the business. For the same reasoning, finding the right trade partner or intermediary, especially a name well known to the target market, can be a powerful means of gaining credibility for your product or service.

Deciding whether to sell direct or to use an intermediary is largely based on two factors:

- Whether it makes sense to share the marketing and sales risk (and, inevitably, some of the reward) with someone who is already selling to your target customer base
- And the structure of the market into which you are selling.

Sharing the marketing and sales risk

For new ventures, it frequently makes better sense to exploit existing and well-established channels to market than to take the risk of selling directly. You should seriously consider selling through intermediaries if the following conditions apply:

- You and your business have little recognition or reputation among the target customers.
- There are efficient economies of scale which some form of partnership will enable you to exploit. These could be in terms of manufacturing, distribution, marketing, advertising, etc.

- There is a limited window of opportunity, accessible only through a trading partner who can help you get to market fast.
- Your business concept creates attractive new opportunities for the intermediary by, for example, increasing his product range or service offering.
- For your business to succeed, you need complementary assets, such as after-sales service, which you cannot offer on your own.

In this context, consider Light Emotions' decision to go to market through intermediaries. The company was young and unknown. They were anxious to get to market ahead of potential competitors, even though their technology was patented. And the glasses were an attractive 'menu' item for businesses already dealing with Light Emotions' end user market.

Structure of the market

Of course, none of this applies if, like Dell Computers or InternetCamerasDirect, the essence of the concept is exploiting a new, direct sales channel. Business concepts like these, however, are the exception rather than the rule. Most new ventures are, by their nature, evolutionary, rather than revolutionary, in their impact on the market. This means selling and marketing within the existing structure of your chosen industry. The defence, IT and automotive sectors, for example, all have complex supply chains in which small specialists sell to bigger specialists, who supply yet bigger specialists, and so forth. It may well be that the structure of your chosen market provides an obvious answer to the question of your route to market.

Is the product or service bought by the end user or on their behalf?

Business-to-business products and services are generally bought on behalf of an organization, not by each individual employee. Every office worker in a company may have a PC, but typically one person is responsible for the buying. Business buyers are notoriously conservative: before the mid-1990s, when IBM suffered a series of major setbacks, a common saying was 'no one ever got sacked for buying IBM'.

In these circumstances you will also, of course, need to ensure that your product/service meets the need both of the corporate buyer (who is typically cost-conscious) and the corporate user (who is typically much more interested in performance). This is one of the biggest challenges of business-to-business selling.

There is a related issue in some consumer markets, where the purchaser buys on someone else's behalf. For example, the heaviest consumers of soft drinks are young adults, teenagers and children. But, soft drinks consumed by younger children are usually bought by their parents. Most children have a natural liking for sweet tastes. Many parents are understandably concerned about their children's health and in particular their teeth. Consequently, soft drinks companies have a difficult balancing act to achieve, satisfying the child's taste for sweet beverages and at the same time convincing parents that the sweeteners, preservatives and other ingredients in their products are at an acceptable level. Ultimately, it is the parent who makes the buying decision. The Procter & Gamble brand Sunny Delight has done a remarkable job in marketing to the parent an 'acceptable' sweetened beverage, while retaining its credibility with the target consumer.

If I sell indirectly, can I meet the needs of both the intermediary and the end user?

This question can be more complex than at first sight appears. The glass distributor Autoglass has built a commanding position across Europe in the replacement of damaged car windscreens. Autoglass does not sell direct to the motorist, but if your windscreen is broken by a stone thrown up from the road, there's a good chance that an Autoglass employee will fix the problem while you wait by the roadside. The explanation is that Autoglass focuses on selling to the companies who insure your car – and the cost of their service is partly underwritten by the motoring insurance premium. Your need as a motorist is for the speedy replacement of your damaged windscreen to get you back on the road as quickly as possible. Autoglass achieves this through specializing in windscreens and through having an excellent network of depots. The insurance company, however, has a quite different set of needs. It wants a business partner which complies with its systems and processes (all insurance companies being very heavily dependent on their systems and processes), and which it can trust not to submit fraudulent claims. And it also needs to be confident that Autoglass will look after its customers to a high level of satisfaction – because dissatisfied customers do not automatically renew their insurance premiums!

The issue of meeting two sets of needs is not always just about systems and processes, however. It can also be a question of what the business is capable of delivering, and what fits with the values and aspirations of the founding management. The case study that follows provides an illustration.

Case Study

Angus Thirlwell and Peter Harris first met while working in the computer industry. Each had a strong drive to create his own business and eventually they decided to set up a new venture in partnership. The new business would have nothing to do with computers, however. Based on an idea that had come from Angus's father, himself a very successful entrepreneur, Angus and Peter created the Mint Marketing Company which produced peppermints for corporate customers packaged in the customer's corporate logo as promotional give-aways.

They began with £5000 start-up capital, two telephones and a list of potential customers. They manufactured some samples wrapped in the photocopied logos of their target companies, and mailed them to marketing directors at the companies concerned. The first mailing produced a response rate of 40 per cent, and they knew they were in business. The business grew rapidly and by 1990, two years after

▶

starting up, turnover was approaching £500 000.

By now customers were asking 'What else do you do?' and Angus and Peter took their next step. They extended the range to chocolates, and re-named the business Geneiva Chocolates Ltd. It was a risk, but a calculated one, since their analysis of the market suggested that there was a gap for a high-quality supplier, able to deliver exactly what the customer required within a tight deadline. The business employed a team of direct sales representatives, who called on major customers, supported by sales account managers in the office. Within two years, chocolate had taken over from mints as the major product line, and the business was employing around 25 in purpose-built offices near Cambridge, England.

In 1993 the two partners expanded the business yet again. They created two new subsidiaries:

- Geneiva Retail Chocolates was established to exploit a growing opportunity: to use the company's know-how and contacts to supply big supermarkets with own-label chocolates, at lower gross margins but also with significantly lower overheads.

- ChocExpress was created as a mail order gift company, selling direct to consumers, to compete in the delivered gift market (against, for example, Interflora)

Geneiva Retail Chocolates was an immediate success, winning contracts with major UK retailers such as Sainsbury and Waitrose. Within three years, turnover was close to £1 million. Unfortunately, dealing with the supermarkets proved much more problematic than Angus and Peter had expected. These big customers used own-label chocolates to compete in low-priced promotional campaigns, and expected their suppliers to take a hit on their margins as well. Seasonality was also a huge problem. There were massive sales peaks at certain times, such as Easter and Mother's Day, which put Geneiva's supply chain under extreme pressure. At the same time, supermarkets were unwilling to commit to long-term contracts, making planning very difficult.

The final straw came in Easter 1997. A big consignment of chocolate Easter bunnies melted on the shelves of one of their supermarket customers, for reasons outside Angus's and Peter's control. In spite of this, the customer withdrew the products and refused to pay. The two partners decided to wind up Geneiva Retail Chocolates and to focus on their mainstream business model, which was selling direct. 'It made us re-examine our values', said Angus. 'In fact it was a very positive experience for us, as it reaffirmed our values and culture and sharpened our appetite to do more of the sort of business that we found to be fun.' Their conclusions were encapsulated in a company culture table (shown here as Table 1.4.1), displayed prominently in the offices for employees and visitors alike to see:

Table 1.4.1	We are	We are not
ChocExpress (Hotel Chocolat) company culture table	Leaders	Followers
	Adders of value through our ideas	Wage slaves to other companies
	Always seeking to improve	Red tape merchants
	Exciting, excited and excitable	Dull and predictable
	Building something worthwhile	Short-termist
	Driven by our vision and teamwork	Driven by fear and politics

Marketing strategy

Your preliminary desk and field research ought to have given you some initial feel for customer needs and the segment of the market you wish to attack first. Your analysis of competitive offerings should have indicated weaknesses or opportunities which you may wish to exploit. You now need to be very clear about how you will market your product/service to your target customers. In particular:

- What is your specific target market segment?
- What will be your overall marketing strategy?
- What is the marketing and sales message and through what mix of marketing activities will it be delivered?

By addressing these questions in detail, you will create your marketing strategy. Let's look at each in turn.

Market segmentation

Market segmentation is the name given to the process whereby customers and potential customers are organized into clusters or groups of 'similar' types. For example, a shop or a restaurant has both regular customers and passing trade. The balance between the two is a fundamental issue that affects everything the business does.

In addition, each of these customer groups is motivated to buy for different reasons, and your selling message has to be modified accordingly.

Case Study

When Nigel Apperley started InternetCameras-Direct in 1999 he had a clear target customer segment in mind. They would be:

- IT-literate and comfortable with transactions over the internet
- early adopters (in the language of marketers) or people who were ready to trade up from conventional to digital cameras at a stage when the market was still relatively immature.

Given this tight definition, reaching this segment would not be too difficult. They would be readers of specialist photography magazines, and web-surfers. Apperley developed a two-pronged marketing communications strategy: high-impact advertisements in a limited number of publications, and clever deals with web search engines, to ensure that the InternetCamerasDirect website always appeared in the top ten search findings.

Business-to-business markets can be similarly segmented:

- by size and location of company (number of employees, turnover, geographic concentration)

- by category of trade (for example furniture, glass and ceramics)
- by level of technology and production process (such as types of buyer, or service requirements).

Here are some useful rules to help you decide on whether a market segment is worth trying to sell into:

- *Measurability*: can you estimate how many customers are in the segment?
- *Accessibility*: can you communicate with these customers? Just knowing they are out there somewhere is not much help.
- *Size*: a segment has to have a 'large' number of customers, although exactly what constitutes large will be relative to your business.
- *Open to practical development*: just being a large segment is not enough. The customer must have money to spend and be able to spend it.

Overall marketing strategy

Based on your market research, and armed with the results of your customer and competitive analysis, you are now in a position to consider the primary thrust of your marketing strategy.

Michael Porter, arguably the best-known of all business school gurus, famously concluded that there are three distinctive marketing strategies for a company to pursue, as outlined below.

1. Overall cost leadership   This is often characteristic of large companies, who are able to achieve economies of scale by major capital investment, operating on low margins by virtue of efficient control systems and to create barriers of entry through low pricing.

Case Study

Walmart dominates global retailing. On one day alone in November 2002, Walmart stores in the US sold $1.25 billion dollars' worth of goods. The company is three times the size of its nearest international rival, Carrefour, and has over 4000 stores across the world. Originally confined to groceries, today Walmart sells white goods, domestic electronics, home furnishings, computers, clothing, DIY equipment – the list is endless.

Walmart has built its leading position through a ruthless focus on its supply chain. By squeezing out inefficiencies and through constant innovation and re-investment, Walmart has the lowest unit costs of any company in its industry. Any competitor which has tried to challenge Walmart through a price war has always lived to regret it.

2. Differentiation   This is characterized by quality, good design and image, with high margins, based on achieving brand loyalty and unique products.

Case Study

While Real Burger World operates in the highly competitive fast food industry, the Real Burger offering is clearly differentiated through its healthy eating orientation, its use of imaginative flavours from around the world and the fact that it is freshly cooked.

3. Focus This is where a company serves one particular target market well, with low costs and high margins, creating barriers to entry by the very narrowness of the market and raising distribution barriers.

Case Study

InternetCamerasDirect is a highly focused business. At the start, the business supplied only digital cameras and only through one distribution channel, namely, the internet.

The temptation for new ventures to follow strategy 1 is often great. Many business founders quite rightly start their new businesses from a spare bedroom at home and pay themselves a minimum salary. This comparative cost advantage, combined with a simplified product or service, often leads the founders to believe that under-cutting competitors' prices will lead to rapid market penetration and growth. It may well lead to rapid sales growth in the short term. But this typically forces the business owner to add the extra overhead (in the form of offices, employees or promotions) which slim margins cannot support. The only real way to sustain the cost leadership strategy is through operating on a large scale and achieving this scale is likely to be beyond the capability of most start-ups in the early years. Of course there are examples of successful start-ups which have pursued this strategy successfully: the European airline industry has been transformed by the advent of low-cost operators such as Easy-Jet and Ryan Air. In both cases, however, these companies had very significant initial backing, sufficient to cover start-up losses.

Our collective experience of working with hundreds of new start-ups has emphasized the importance of strategies 2 and 3, differentiation and focus. For this reason, we urge start-up businesses to focus on a narrow target market and to maximize ways to differentiate themselves from competitors.

The marketing mix

In delivering your message to your target customer segment, in such a way as to differentiate yourself clearly, you have a choice of a wide range of marketing elements. Some are obvious such as pricing and promotional activities. Others are more subtle such as your business name and your distribution methods. The set of selected marketing activities for a given business is often referred to as the marketing mix.

The most appropriate marketing mix will be different for each individual business and will vary over time. In the following paragraphs, we have described the elements of the marketing mix which we consider to be the most likely to be appropriate at the start-up stage. These elements are:

- product/service definition
- business name
- intellectual property
- pricing
- promotional materials
- distribution and selling methods
- premises.

Product/service definition

It may sound blindingly obvious that you need to define your product/service. And yet many is the time that we have to ask would-be entrepreneurs who have been pitching their idea to us for 10 minutes or so, 'So, what exactly is it that you intend to sell?'

It is absolutely imperative that you can describe you product/service succinctly and compellingly, in a way that your intended customers will understand, in a maximum of about 30 seconds.

One very common mistake to which entrepreneurs are prone is to describe their product/service in terms of features. Features are what a product/service has or is, for example, its colour, its size or its functionality. This is often a particular problem when the product/service is highly technical or a piece of technology.

However, as all good sales people will tell you, customers buy *benefits*. Consider the experience of using Hotel Chocolat's (originally ChocExpress) delivered gifts service as shown in Table 1.4.2.

The customer pays for the benefit. The seller pays for the feature. So, having a close understanding of your customer needs and product/service benefits will enable you to focus your future marketing activities and to vary them as required. Hotel Chocolat mails catalogues to existing or potential customers several times a year, building its offer around different events in the calendar such as Valentine's Day, Mother's Day, Easter and so forth.

Table 1.4.2	Features	}	Benefits	Proof
Using Hotel Chocolat's gift service	A delivered box of high quality chocolates	which means to me ...	The pleasure of delighting someone I care for	A delighted phone call from the recipient.
	Sent direct to a loved one to mark a special occasion		A 'solution' to the perennial problem of finding a suitable gift	(And perhaps) a chance to sample this delicious gift!

Business name

Your company name can, in effect, be the starting and sustaining point in differentiating you from your competitors. Choose it carefully and protect it where possible by registering and trademarking it. Write it in a distinctive and memorable way. It is, after all, the visible tip of the iceberg in your future corporate communications effort, and will be used on all your promotional literature.

If you must use initials (and most companies in electronics, for example, do) try to make them into an acronym, to make recall easier: most of their customers know that IBM stands for International Business Machines. The European consumer electronics house AMSTRAD stands for Alan Michael Sugar Trading.

Given all the marketing investment you will make in your company name, you should check with a trademark agent whether you can protect your chosen name. The exact rules governing this differ from one country to another, but typically you cannot register descriptive words, surnames and place names except after long usage. ChocExpress was, as Angus Thirlwell puts it: 'A "no-brainer". We sell chocolates and we deliver them promptly and efficiently.' On the other hand, 'Geneiva Chocolates' was deliberately chosen to trade on the quality image of Swiss chocolate, and spelled with an 'i' inserted to absolve the company of any charges of misleading its customers (its suppliers are, in fact, located in several European countries).

There may also be restrictions, which vary by country, as to whether you can use a name that someone else is already using. Usually, you are allowed to use a business name provided it is not in the same industry sector as another business using the same or very similar name.

Remember also that if you want to use a 'controlled' name you will have to get permission from the relevant authorities. These too vary from one jurisdiction to another, but typical controlled names are 'International', 'Bank' and 'Royal'. The controls exist to prevent a business implying that it is something that it is not.

And, of course, a website address must be unique. Given that so many website addresses have been bought speculatively by so called 'cyber-squatters', you may

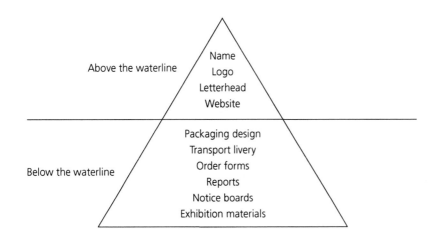

Figure 1.4.2

The corporate communications iceberg

have to look quite hard for a name if you are determined that your website address must be the same as the name of the business.

Remember also that there are regulations affecting what information you must give on your business stationery. If you are a business registered for Value Added Tax (VAT) within the European Union, for example, your VAT number must appear on all your invoices. The appropriate government department will be able to advise you.

Finally, corporate communications guru Wally Olins recommends that the ideal business name should reflect:

- who you are
- what you do
- how you do it.

Case Study

Moonpig is a business with an unusual name. If you knew nothing about it, you might guess that it was in the space or agricultural industries. Log onto its website and you will be greeted by a grinning pig suspended in space over a full moon. In fact, Moonpig is in the greetings cards business, and its competitors have more conventional names such as Clinton Cards, WH Smith, Marks and Spencer and so forth.

Moonpig will customize any one of hundreds of cards in its database with your own personalized greetings, print it and send it to the recipient anywhere in the world.

Originally, founder Nick Jenkins chose the name Splat! but decided that Moonpig was more memorable and had greater potential to be exploited visually. Moonpig was a nickname that Nick had somehow acquired at school (he prefers not to go into details). It might be a humorous name, but it has a serious purpose. Moonpig specializes in humorous cards, and is a website suited to those who are not easily offended. Nick also felt that Moonpig conveyed the surreal, off-beat quality of much of what he was offering. It is definitely not Acme Card Company.

The holding company for the business is called Altergraphics, however. His investors proved strangely reluctant to write a cheque to an organization called Moonpig!

Intellectual property

Protecting your proprietary position adds a great deal to your credibility, especially if you are selling through an intermediary. After all, if it appears to be difficult or illegal to copy the design, look and feel of what you are selling, the better the chance of securing and retaining your customer base and future revenue streams. Note the use of the word 'appears'.

As a minimum, you should register your company name and website address as soon as you start using them. You can also consider trademark registration, which protects what something is called, for any products or services to which you have given a name. If you have written any original work down on paper or on a computer file (for instance, a brochure describing your product/service), then you own the copyright to it and you can immediately claim that right simply by using the copyright symbol. Even this, creates an impression that what you have is in some way 'special'.

If you have designed something which has a unique look, then you may be able to apply for design registration. And, if you have a novel idea then you may be able to patent it.

Some products may be covered by two or more categories. For example, the mechanism of a clock may be patented while its appearance may be design-registered. Each category requires a different set of procedures, offers a different level of protection and extends for a different period of time.

They all have one thing in common, though: in the event of any infringement your only redress is through the courts, and going to law can be wasteful of time and money, whether you win or lose (although insurance protection can help in this process).

A patent agent – and they are easily found in any major city – will rapidly tell you which elements of your business idea are able to be protected by law. You can also find out more by looking at the website for the patenting authority in the country where your business will operate. The UK government Patent Office website www.patentoffice.gov.uk is particularly useful.

Pricing

In our experience, the most frequent mistake made by new venture founders when they set a selling price for the first time is to pitch it too low. This mistake occurs:

- either through failing to understand all the costs associated with making and marketing your product (these are nearly always higher than first estimated)
- or through yielding to the temptation to undercut the competition at the outset.

Both these errors usually lead to fatal results, so in preparing your business plan you should guard against them. Below are some guidelines to help you.

1 Costs Clearly, you need to price in order to not only cover the direct costs of producing, selling and delivering your product/service, but also to contribute to overheads such as rent and rates. So, in setting your prices, it is always a good idea to have a thorough understanding of your costs.

Detailed guidance on establishing your costs is given in the next chapter. It is enough to say here that you will need to know what your fixed costs will be (rent, rates, heating, marketing, and so on) and what contribution your product/service will make from each sale, after deducting direct material and labour costs of each item. In this way, you can calculate how many items you need to sell to cover your fixed costs (again, this is explored in detail in the next chapter).

Case Study

In mid-2001, Nick Jenkins found himself on the verge of running out of money. The initial costs of launching the business had proved much higher than he was expecting, and he urgently needed to raise more investment. One of his earlier investors, David Noble, was an experienced retailer. At this time, Moonpig was charging a customer £1.99 to print and send a greetings card. The gross margin at this price was not sufficient to cover the full costs. Nick felt that if the price were raised customers would simply not pay. David was strongly of the view that this was a market that was not price-sensitive. Eventually, David had his way, and the price was raised to £2.99. There was no adverse effect on sales whatsoever – in fact, the curve on the graph continued to rise. But, from that day on the business started to make money.

2 Customer or consumer perception   Pricing is an area of 'value judgement'. But, customers' opinion of values may have little or no relation to costs. In France, Perrier originally tied its price for a standard bottle of water to the price of the newspaper *Le Figaro*, as its target customers, health-conscious middle-aged consumers, frequently bought the two items simultaneously. A later generation in the UK, concerned at tap water quality, was willing to pay the price of equivalent bottles of soft drinks for a basic product still simply being pumped from the ground, but now presented in an amusing French 'luxury goods' fashion format. A high relative price undoubtedly contributed to this new image for the same basic product.

The perceived image you wish to create for your company's product or service is, therefore, an important element in the pricing decision. Your choice of channel of distribution is also important, since your selling price will have to allow for the image and margins of any intermediaries.

3 Competition and capacity   Clearly, you have to take account of what your competitors charge. Remember, however, price is the easiest element of the marketing mix for an established company to vary. If you cut prices, your competitors can normally follow you rapidly. Matching you on quality, on the other hand, typically takes much longer. Unfortunately, in the time that it takes customers to find out about the lower quality of your competitors' offerings, you could be out of business.

Equally, your capacity to 'produce' your product or service, bearing in mind market conditions, will also influence the price you set. Typically a new venture has limited capacity at the start. A valid entry strategy could be to price just high enough to fill your capacity, rather than so low as to swamp you with orders.

Case Study

One of the great advantages of being an internet retailer is that you can see from moment to moment exactly what prices your fellow internet competitors are charging. You can also update your prices almost instantly, to manage stock levels and, if necessary, match or undercut the competition.

4 Margins and markets Even today, many companies price their goods or services basically by reference to costs:

- either using a cost plus formula (such as raw materials plus 50 per cent)
- or through a cost multiplier (such as three times material costs).

When advanced economies were primarily based on manufacturing, it was easy to recommend the well-established rule of thumb that a business should aim to achieve a gross margin of at least 40 per cent (sales price less the direct materials and labour used to make the article, the resulting margin expressed as a percentage of the sales price). This 'magic' number was no more than the result of observation, that with margins of less than 40 per cent, few manufacturing companies would have enough money left to cover their overheads, reinvest in the business and service the cost of finance.

Today, it is much more difficult to give general advice, since, in most developed economies, manufacturing has shrunk while the service sector has grown. In many service businesses, allocating costs and hence identifying the margin structure is much more open to debate. What we would advise, therefore, is that you should bear in mind two important points when setting your prices:

- At what price level do you have a sustainable business in which you can re-invest for the future?
- Where do you wish to position yourself in the market?

Your competitive analysis will give you some idea as to what the market will bear. We suggest you complete (and modify if necessary) Table 1.4.3 to give yourself confidence that you can match or improve upon competitors' prices. At the very least, you will have arguments to justify your higher prices to your customers and, also importantly, your future employees.

Promotional materials

Very few start-up businesses have the size of budget that allows them to fund a major campaign of advertising on television or in the press. Even if the funds are available, this is usually an inappropriate route to take. Advertising is, after all, as Tim Bell, formerly chief executive of Saatchi & Saatchi famously observed, 'simply an expensive way for one person to talk to another'. It is much more likely that you will know who your first few target customers are, and will try to sell to them directly.

Table 1.4.3	*Product attributes*	*Rating score (worse –3, –2, –1; same 0; better +1, +2, +3*
Product comparison with competitors	Design performance	
	Packaging	
	Presentation/appearance	
	After-sales service	
	Availability	
	Delivery	
	Colour/flavour	
	Odour/touch	
	Image	
	Specification	
	Payment terms	
	Other	
	Total	

We recommend that you adopt a 'cost/benefit' approach to your early promotional efforts. You might, for example, mail 5000 potential targets at a cost of £2500. Assume that you receive a response rate of 1 per cent, that is 50 replies, and that these translate into 25 sales with an average gross margin of £500. You now have some useful benchmarks against which to measure subsequent promotions:

- a cost per mailing of £0.50 (£2500/5000)
- a response rate of 1 per cent (5000/50)
- a cost per enquiry of £100 (£5000/50)
- a sales conversion rate of 50 per cent (50/25)
- a total cost per conversion of £200 (£5000/25)
- and a yield per sale of £300 (£500 gross margin – £200 sales cost).

There is a vast array of promotional techniques like the direct mail example just described. These range from business cards to entries in the *Yellow Pages*, leaflets, brochures, press releases, giveaways, posters, promotional items, such as pens, websites and so on. Here, we will concentrate on the three we think most important for the starter company: promotional literature, public and press relations, and exhibitions.

1 Promotional literature (leaflets, brochures, letters and websites) Promotional literature is the most practical way for a new business to communicate with its potential customers. It has the merits of being relatively inexpensive, simple and quick to put into operation, it can be concentrated into any geographic area, it can be mailed, emailed or distributed by hand, it can be displayed on a website, and, finally, it is easy to monitor results.

The discipline of composing something that effectively communicates what you are selling is a valuable exercise in itself, since it forces you to re-examine your marketing message from the customer's viewpoint. What are the benefits exactly? New ventures which are based on a product, especially, a technically complex one, often find this very challenging: there is always a temptation to 'drown' the potential customer in so much information that the essence of the proposition is lost.

Case Study

It was while watching a rugby game in Cardiff, Wales, that Nick Opperman's thoughts began to crystallize. Previously, he had been struck by the idea that there could be a business in giving away radios in the streets, so that people could keep up with the news. However, he had never seen a way to make this a paying proposition. The rugby match made him see the opportunity in a different light. All of us, he thought, have been sitting at a football or rugby game wondering why the game was stopped, who was the player with the ball, and so on. Why not provide spectators with a radio tuned specifically for the event that would allow them to get the same level of information as someone sitting at home in front of their TV?

From this idea, the SoundDec® earpiece radio was born. To create a cheap, pre-tuned, high-quality radio that looked good and fitted snugly into someone's ear, proved a much bigger technical challenge than he ever foresaw. Finally, he and his team launched their new product in the spring of 2002, through their company, Sound Decisions Ltd.

Nick decided that the most likely way to sell and market the radio was to sell to event organizers and sponsors who could put their logo on the radio and then either sell the radio to spectators or include it in the ticket price. To explain the features and benefits of the SoundDec® earpiece radio to event organizers and sponsors, Nick drafted the following description which can be seen in Figure 1.4.3.

Even if your business idea does not involve the internet as a sales or distribution channel, a website can also be a very useful promotional tool. At the simplest level, the site can act as an 'online brochure' containing similar information to your offline promotional literature. The big advantages of websites over static literature are that

- It's far easier and cheaper to make changes to a website than to reprint hardcopy literature.
- A website allows you to capture customer information by inviting people to email you with enquiries, comments and suggestions.
- No one knows how big (or small) you are on the web.

Many people ask 'but how do we drive traffic to the website?' The easiest and most obvious way, is to make sure that your website address is printed on every piece of stationery (business cards, letters, invoices, packaging) and in every other piece of promotional literature. In this way, you can use other promotional activity to direct people to your site where they can find out more – and you can

Figure 1.4.3

Extract from Sound
Decisions sales
documents to
explain features and
benefits of their
radio

Sound Decisions Ltd.

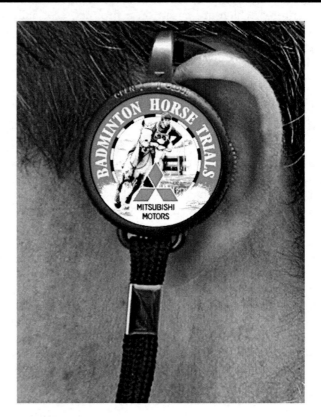

EVENT RADIO – A PROMISE UNFULFILLED...

Event radio is not a new idea – a well-developed broadcast infrastructure industry has grown up in the last ten years – however the spread of radio at events has faltered. Analysis highlights one fundamental reason as the lack of a decent radio receiver designed specifically for use at events.

...UNTIL THIS UNIQUE SOLUTION: EaRadio™

Utilising the latest chip technology Sound Decisions have developed EaRadio™, a novel radio with features conceived solely to meet the needs of event radio. It is cheap, attractive, immensely comfortable to wear and has near-perfect, pre-tuned, audio quality. The only control is that of volume and the unit has a large brandable area on both the outer casing and lanyard.

This radio, combined with the comprehensive and professional broadcast systems operated by the event enhancement companies who are working in association with Sound Decisions, will allow event organisers to offer a better deal to the spectator and sponsors.

- At last the spectator is no longer discriminated against when compared to the TV viewer – he can receive expert commentary and information regarding the event he is paying to watch.
- For the sponsors there are new branding and promotional opportunities through the sponsorship of the event radio station and the supply of radios (logos & messages on the radios and the lanyards that hold them), as well as the potential of advertising across the broadcast content.

What price can be put on the goodwill generated in the hearts and minds of the spectators when a sponsor either gives them or subsidises an information flow for the duration of an event?

THE EaRADIO™ IN USE

The EaRadio™ is a self-contained unit. All the state-of-the-art electronics are located within the outer shell casing. The antenna is hidden within the lanyard, allowing excellent reception whilst avoiding the need for a whip-aerial which might foul on headgear.

When not on the ear, the EaRadio™ hangs around the neck suspended by its lanyard. In this respect the device is 'use-or-ignore' and does not detract from spectator enjoyment.

The hinged arm lodges comfortably behind either ear. There are no earphone leads that might tangle in clothing.

ALMOST ALL EVENTS CAN BENEFIT...

Some event types lend themselves to event radio more obviously than others. Objectively, there are a few determining criteria that establish which events are likely to benefit most; those ...

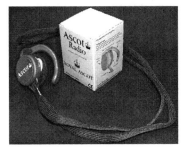

- where much of the action takes place out of sight of the spectator (e.g. motorsports, three-day eventing, golf, yachting etc.),
- where traditional public address is difficult due to ambient noise or distance (e.g. airshows etc.),
- where traditional public address is simply not acceptable (e.g. golf, cricket, snooker etc.),
- where spectators are demanding added-value for their entry fee,
- where the spectators can see the action, but want to know what is going on at associated events (e.g. rugby and football league matches),

- where expensive displays, such as TV monitors or 'jumbotrons', are currently available to spectators but without an audio stream (e.g. horse racing, rugby and football league matches etc.),
- where traditional commercial radio stations could access a captive audience whilst adding value to their attendance (e.g. the Boat Race, London Marathon, Notting Hill Carnival etc.).

... WITH INCREASED PROFITS

Such a variety of different applicable event types leads to a plethora of potential revenue streams available from event radio. For some events EaRadio™ might be retailed at the concession stands, at others a principal sponsor could cover some or all of their cost. The radios could be cover-mounted on programmes. Contributions could be made to charity for each unit purchased or recycled in bins made available.

Sound Decisions offer a customisable turn-key service at events whereby they can manage the sale of radios (utilising their own staff and sales kiosks), the procurement of RSL radio licences, the hire of a broadcast station and the production and transmission of content.

Whilst most event radio utilises discrete short-term radio-frequency licences (RSLs) to provide a unique and dedicated radio station, there are times when a commercial radio station might wish to brand and distribute EaRadio™ units. These would be tuned solely to their frequency and listeners would be 'captive' to that station both during and after the event.

find out a little about them! It may even be possible to do away with an offline brochure and replace it with the website.

You can also register your site with the various search engines and attempt to develop links from other sites. There is a whole industry (some would say a 'black art') around ensuring that your site comes near the top of search engines and it may be worth taking advice from a web designer or marketing agency if you believe that this is an important part of your promotional mix. Alternatively, you can pay the search engines for what are called 'sponsored links'. These are the listings which appear to the side or above the main list of websites generated by a search. You can bid on words that describe your product/service, where you are offering to pay the search engine so much money for each user who clicks through to your site from the sponsored link. The more you bid, the higher up the listing you'll come when a user enters that word in to the search engine. The amount you need to bid to obtain a reasonably high spot on the list will depend on the size of the industry in which your business operates and, hence, the level of competition for the links.

2 Public and press relations (PR)   It is a little-known fact that, for every one person who reads a newspaper advertisement, ten people will, on average, read the article next to it. Editorial – as non-advertising text is called – has some significant advantages over advertising:

- Research consistently shows that it is more likely to be read by your target audience.
- It is also likely to be taken more seriously, since it is no secret that advertising is paid for.
- Favourable references to your business from a respected journalist can have a massive and immediate impact on sales (restaurant reviews are a well-known instance of this).

On the other hand, unlike advertising, where you can be certain of appearing because you have paid for the space, journalists and their editors control what they write. You may devote hours to cultivating a particular publication and journalist only to find that your business gets a brief mention, or even no mention at all.

Journalism is fundamentally about identifying and creating stories. These may be human interest stories, or stories about a new scientific or technical advance, but it is stories which engage the interest of readers. If your new business idea, or some aspect of it has some interesting 'new news', then there is a fair chance that someone, somewhere, will write about it.

How can you maximize your chances of getting media coverage? Like so much in business, it starts with research. If you know your target market, it is usually not difficult to identify magazines, TV or radio programmes which are relevant to their interests. It is but a short step to locating the journalists who specialize in these areas. If you feel you are not the kind of person who can 'cold call' a journalist with a story, there are PR agencies in all industrial sectors who will do so on your behalf – but, like market research and advertising agencies, they charge for their services.

Case Study

Many people are inclined to view Friday 13th as an inauspicious day. For Peter Rankin, Friday 13th December 2002 turned out to be one of the best days of his life. Rankin had started his career in advertising, specializing in handling direct advertising accounts. In his early thirties, he opted to go to business school and broaden his commercial knowledge. At the back of his mind was also the thought that business school might be a fruitful environment in which to explore new business ideas.

Halfway through his MBA, Rankin came across some information which made him sit up and think. He had always been interested in communications technology and, while web-surfing, was surprised to find that wireless closed circuit TV (CCTV) technology was much, much cheaper than he thought. Instead of costing several hundred pounds, a system that allowed you to plug a SCART lead into the back of a TV or VCR, linked wirelessly to a camera outside the front door, could be bought for less than £100. It was also easy to install and operate. Rankin bought some equipment and tried it out. He was impressed. To find out if it was the pizza delivery man or the neighbourhood mugger ringing your front door bell, all you needed to do was change channels on your TV.

Having managed to sell some equipment to fellow penniless MBA students, who were equally impressed, Rankin decided to take the plunge. Before his course was finished, he had undertaken extensive market research, completed a business plan, raised some money and commissioned a website. He enlisted his brother to help him with sales and, within a few months, he was in business.

Despite his research, he was unsure which segment was the right one to target. There were so many applications for CCTV. It could be sold as a baby monitoring device, for security in the home, for security in the office, for remote monitoring of second homes (via a PC), to monitor your car in the street, and so forth. The versatility was itself a problem: try to encompass all the benefits and applications, and the sales message risked becoming confused and diluted. The key feature, however, was that for all applications, the user could install it quickly and easily.

He decided to try and let the 'market speak', through using his website and the most popular internet search engines to sell to the public at large. Sales trickled in, but more slowly than he expected. Then came the big break. Rankin had always prided himself on his network of contacts and actively sought to maintain and expand these. In early December, through a friend of a friend, he was contacted by a researcher from a popular daytime TV show. The show was doing a feature on Friday 13th on nannies who abuse children and how CCTV had allowed one family to prevent this from happening. Rankin's name and that of his company, iViewCameras, had been given to the researcher as an expert in the field of CCTV. She had visited the company's website and been impressed by their obvious knowledge of the market. Would he like to contribute to the programme?

Rankin is a self-confessed 'non-techie', but for two days he immersed himself in finding out everything there was to know about CCTV. He spent hours with his brother practising product demonstrations. The rehearsal for the show went like a dream and in the live broadcast he was given six minutes to present different types of low-cost CCTV systems and explain their features and benefits, in front of several million viewers. (The broadcast was later made available to download from the website, www.iviewcameras.co.uk.) From that day on, the office phone lines were ringing continuously, and the website was swamped. As Rankin put it 'As an ex-advertising man, I know that you can't buy that kind of publicity – and, if you could, it would cost an awful lot more money than we have!'

If you intend to try this for yourself, here are some guidelines for creating a press release to send to journalists.

To be successful, a press release needs to get attention immediately and be quick and easy to digest. Studying and copying the style of the particular journals (or other media) you want your press release to appear in will make it more likely that your press release gets noticed.

- *Layout*: The press release should be typed on a single sheet of paper. Use double spacing and wide margins to make the text both more readable and easy to edit. Head it boldly 'Press Release' or 'News Release' and date it.
- *Headline*: This must persuade the editor to read on. If it does not attract interest, it will be quickly 'spiked'. Editors are looking for topicality, originality, personality and, sometimes, humour.
- *Introductory paragraph*: This should be interesting and succinct and should summarize the whole story – it might be the only part published.
- *Subsequent paragraphs*: These should expand and colour the details in the opening paragraph. Most stories can be told in a maximum of three or four paragraphs. Editors are always looking for 'fillers', so short releases have the best chance of getting published.
- *Contact*: List at the end of the release the name, telephone number and email address of a contact for further information.
- *Style*: Use simple language, short sentences and avoid technical jargon (except for very specialized technical magazines). Again, write in the style of the magazine to which you are sending the article.
- *Photographs*: These can be either black and white or colour, depending on your target publication. If you are in doubt, telephone first to find out what is preferred. Don't staple them to the release (photographs with holes are unpublishable).
- *Follow-up*: Sometimes a follow-up phone call to see if the editor or journalist intends to use the release can be useful – but you must use your judgement on how often to do so.

Find out the name of the editor or relevant writer/reporter and address the envelope to him or her personally. Look for a way to extend the relationship by, for example, inviting them to the 'opening' of your new business premises.

The press release is not a 'sales message' but a factual story. Too many small companies, in their enthusiasm for their products, overlook this difference between sales literature and a press release, which explains why only 6 per cent of press releases sent out are printed, and 94 per cent are not!

3 Exhibitions As a means of gathering market research data on competitors, exhibitions and trade fairs are extremely valuable. Many industries, such as the furniture, electronics and publishing industries, traditionally do most of their business to business buying and selling at these events. If you are targeting this kind of industry, exhibiting at a trade fair can also be a useful way of establishing the acceptability of your product or service quickly and relatively inexpensively. Trade enquiries can be turned into a convincing argument in support of your case for financial backing.

Distribution and selling methods

The basic concepts involved in how you will sell and distribute (e.g. directly or through a third party) have been addressed in the early part of this chapter. Here, we would draw your attention to the point that your entry distribution channels are not necessarily the channels that will feature most in your 'steady state' business. You may have to persuade a third-party to take your products by undertaking some initial personal selling, to prove that there is demand for your products. This is typically the case in the fashion industry, where struggling designers frequently have to spend some time on the road themselves, and also in the soft drinks industry. Smaller beverages companies normally find their way onto supermarket shelves by first selling their brands in 'out of home' channels, such as sport and social clubs, bars, cafes and so on, where consumer demand is built. If really successful, they will find that supermarket buyers approach them, not the other way round. Your business plan should clearly explain which channel and which selling method you have chosen, to help the differentiation and success of your business.

The internet has opened up a whole new sales and distribution channel which may be appropriate for you to consider. When the internet frenzy was at its peak, the phrase 'this time it's different' was heard over and over again – some would say that these are the four most expensive words in history. However, one of the lessons from those like InternetCamerasDirect and Moonpig who have made a success of the internet as a sales and distribution channel, is that, although the internet has certain very useful features which other channels do not (e.g. the ability to track what customers look at), in many ways, it should be managed just like any of the more traditional channels.

Premises

Many entrepreneurs start their businesses from their own homes. ChocExpress started from Angus Thirlwell's house and InternetCamerasDirect's first office was Nigel Apperley's dining room! The stage at which separate business premises are needed will be dependent on the nature of the business (e.g. a manufacturing business is likely to need premises from the outset whereas a professional services business such as a consultancy may not) and the rate of growth. Nevertheless, at some point, the time will come when you need to find business premises for yourself and others to work in.

At this point, it is important to think carefully about what type of premises are most appropriate for your business and where they should be to give it the best chance of success. Should you be near your customers? Or is it more important to be near key suppliers? How attractive will the location be to existing and new staff and is there a good flow of potential new recruits with the right skills? Is it important to be part of a network of similar businesses (e.g. barristers' chambers, technology parks)?

For instance, when Jeff Bezos originally had the idea for Amazon, he and his wife were living in New York. However, they decided to move to the other side of the US to base the business in Seattle since Seattle was the centre of the existing US book distribution industry and there would be a ready supply of highly skilled IT people by virtue of the proximity to the Microsoft worldwide headquarters and other major IT businesses.

One of your key decisions will be whether to lease or buy. Purchasing premises outright frequently makes sense for an established, viable business as a means of increasing its asset base. But, for a start-up, interest and repayments on the borrowings will usually be more than the rental payments. On the other hand, leasing can also be a trap; a lease rental of, say, £25 000 a year may seem preferable to a freehold purchase of, say, £250 000. But remember, in many countries, if you sign and give a personal guarantee on a new long-term lease (which you will almost certainly be asked to do), you will remain personally responsible for payments over the whole life of the lease. Landlords are as reluctant to allow change in guarantors as they are to accept small business tenants without personal guarantees.

There is also an argument that if you intend to spend any money on converting or improving the premises, doing so to leased property is simply improving the landlord's investment and wasting your money. You may even be charged extra rent for the improvements, unless you ensure that tenant improvements are excluded from the rent reviews.

In recent years, finding suitable premises for new businesses has been greatly helped by two trends:

- the emergence of serviced office suites, which you can rent for as little as a quarter-year or even one month
- the growth in science and business parks, many of which have start-up or 'incubator' units for new businesses.

Since there are so many of these now, and they are in competition with each other to attract tenants, it is worthwhile investing some time and energy in exploring what is available in the area in which you want to locate.

Business premises also have to conform to planning, licensing and health and safety requirements. Some of these will vary depending on the type of business you intend to run from the premises (e.g. if you are handling food).

New retailing businesses deserve a few specific words. If you are a retailer and you intend to have traditional retail space, then the premises that you choose and the way that you decorate them will be factors in differentiating your service or product from your competitors. They should be in accord with each of the other elements of the marketing mix you have chosen.

Whichever option you choose for your first premises, we would stress that property issues are rarely completely straightforward and you should take appropriate advice from a commercial property specialist, typically a lawyer or a property surveyor.

Chapter summary

In this chapter, we have considered three major questions relating to your market.

We first looked at your business model, or in plainer language, what are you going to do, for whom, and who is going to pay you for it? Almost certainly you will need to focus on addressing either the consumer or the business-to-business market, to avoid the danger of spreading your resources too thinly.

We then moved on to consider how to reach the end customer or, in marketing terminology, the route to market. This decision is driven chiefly by two factors:

- the opportunity, or necessity, to share risk and reward with someone already selling to your target markets
- the structure of your market (i.e. whether the most appropriate way to reach your target user group is pre-determined by the way that the market is organized).

In reaching a decision about the most appropriate route to market, you will need to satisfy yourself that you understand, and have the capability to meet, the needs of

- both the buyer and the user (if these are different) within your target market
- both the buyer and any intermediary you sell to in order to reach your final user.

Finally, we looked in detail at marketing strategy. Within this area, we first considered market segmentation since very few start-ups can, or should, attempt to serve mass markets. We reviewed alternative overall marketing strategy and concluded that new ventures should concentrate on being better and different, that is following focus or differentiation strategies. Undercutting established competitors is a dangerous game and is rarely the basis for building a sustainable business. Finally, we looked at the most appropriate mix of marketing activities for start-ups including product/service definition, business names, intellectual property, price, promotional materials, distribution and selling methods and premises. The weight which you accord to each of these in your marketing mix varies with the product or service. You should, however, seek to integrate the various elements so that your business presents a consistent picture to the world.

Assignments

Business model
1. What is your business model? What will you do, for whom and who is going to pay? In particular, are you customers individual consumers or are they other businesses?

Route to market
2. Will you sell directly to your end customer or through a third party?
3. Is your product/service bought by the end user or by someone else on their behalf? If the latter, who are they?
4. If you sell through an intermediary, what are the specific needs of both the end user and the intermediary? Can you meet both these sets of needs?

Marketing strategy

5. List and describe your first target customers and the market segment they represent.

6. What are your main competitors' weaknesses and how will your product/service be distinctive and better?

7. Identify the main features of your product/service and 'translate' these into benefits for your customers. Write a succinct and compelling description of your product/service.

8. What is your company name and logo? Consider whether you should have any proprietary protection on your business name or product/service.

9. What will be your pricing policy relative to competitors and bearing in mind your capacity to meet demand? Does this pricing support your overall market positioning?

10. Consider what promotional material you will need at launch. Write an example of a piece of promotional literature (e.g. a brochure or a press release) for your product/service.

11. What distribution and selling methods will you use at launch? Remember these might not be the same as the ideal methods that you will aim for once the business is established.

12. Do you need business premises from the start? If so, write down your requirements (e.g. specific location, size, activities which will be performed there) and discuss these with a local commercial property agent in order to get a feel for availability, rents and other issues.

13. Review all your decisions regarding marketing and ensure that you have a coherent and consistent message.

Suggested further reading

Adcock D., R. Bradfield, A. Halborg and C. Ross (1995) *Marketing: Principles and Practice*, London: Pitman.

Bhidé, Amar V. (2000) *The Origin and Evolution of New Businesses*, New York: Oxford University Press.

Porter, Michael E. (1998) *Competitive Strategy*, New York: Free Press.

5 Can you make a profit?

Introduction and objectives

Your big idea looks as though it has a market. You have evaluated your skills and inclinations and believe that you can run this business. The next crucial, question is – will it make you money? It is vital that you establish the financial viability of your idea before you invest money in it or approach outsiders for backing. You need to carry out a thorough, workmanlike appraisal of the business's financial requirements. If these come out as unworkable, you can then rethink, without having lost anything. If the figures look good, then you can go ahead and prepare cash flow projections, a profit and loss account and a balance sheet, and put together the all-important business plan.

By the end of this chapter, you should have a clear understanding of:

- How to forecast the likely sales volume.

- How to estimate the costs associated with starting up and running the business from day to day.

- How to calculate the all-important break-even point for your business.

- How to set the price for your product or service so that you can make a profit.

- How to assess the cash and profit required for the business not just to survive, but also to thrive, and thus calculate the amount of capital you require to get started.

- The various sources of funding available to a new business, and the reasons for choosing one source over another taking account of the financial risks.

Forecasting sales

While all forecasts may turn out to be wrong, it is important to demonstrate in your strategy that you have thought through the factors that will impact on performance. You should also show how you could deliver satisfactory results even when many of these factors work against you. Backers and employees alike will be measuring the downside risk, to evaluate the worst scenario and its likely effects, as well as looking towards an ultimate exit route.

Here are some guidelines to help you make an initial sales forecast.

Credible projections

Your overall projections will have to be believable. Most lenders and investors will have an extensive experience of similar business proposals. Unlike you, they will have the benefit of hindsight, being able to look back several years at other ventures they have backed, and see how they fared in practice as compared with their initial forecasts.

You could gather some useful knowledge on similar businesses yourself by researching company records. In most countries, companies are legally obliged to publish accounts and these accounts are available for anyone to examine. These public accounts are usually available either in hard copy (for example, in the UK from Companies House) or via online databases. You can also find extremely useful and valuable data by talking with the founders of similar ventures, who will not be your direct competitors.

Market share

- How big is the market for your product or service?
- Is it growing or contracting?
- At what rate?
- What is the economic and competitive position?

These are all factors which can provide a market share basis for your forecasts. An entry market share of more than a few per cent would be most unusual. But, beware of turning this argument on its head. Unsubstantiated statements such as, 'In a market of £1 billion per annum, we can easily capture 1 per cent, which is £1 million a year' will impress no investor.

Customers

How many customers and potential customers do you know who are likely to buy from you, and how much might they buy? Here you can use many types of data on which to base reasonable sales projections. You can interview a sample of prospective customers, issue a press release or advertisement to gauge response, and exhibit at trade shows to obtain customer reactions.

If your product or service needs to be on an approved list before it can be bought, then your business plan should confirm you have that approval or at least show how you will get it.

You should also look at seasonal factors that might cause sales to be high or low at certain periods in the year. This will be particularly significant for cash flow projections. You should then relate your seasonal, customer-based, forecast to your capacity to make or sell at this rate. Sometimes your inability to recruit or increase capacity may limit your sales forecasts.

Rules of thumb

For some types of business, there are rules of thumb that can be used to estimate sales. This is particularly true in retailing where location studies, traffic counts, and population density are known factors.

Desired income

This approach to estimating sales embraces the concept that forecasts may also accommodate the realistic aims of the entrepreneur. Indeed, you could go further and state that the whole purpose of strategy is to ensure that certain forecasts are achieved. In a mature company with proven products and markets, this is more likely to be the case than with a start-up. Nevertheless, an element of 'How much do we need to earn?' must play a part in forecasting, if only to signal when a business idea is not worth pursuing.

Estimating costs

When you first start out in your business, you will almost inevitably have some initial start-up costs but there are no revenues from sales coming in. These costs might include things like equipment, first payments on premises, fixtures and fittings, preparing your initial marketing materials, initial stock, the cost of registering the company, etc. Later in this chapter, we will see how these are handled in terms of a pre-trading cash flow statement. At this point, we are more interested in how costs affect profitability.

Therefore, the key distinction is between *fixed costs* and *variable costs*. The key point is that you cannot simply add them together to arrive at total costs until you have made some assumptions about sales (see break-even analysis below).

Fixed costs are those costs which do not change, however much you sell. For example, if you are running a conventional shop, the rent and the rates are relatively constant figures, quite independent of the volume of sales. On the other hand, the cost of the products sold from the shop is completely dependent on volume. The more you sell, the more it 'costs' to buy stock. The former of these costs is called 'fixed' and the latter, 'variable'.

Let's take variable costs first. Given that these costs are by definition related to the amount you sell, your sales forecasts form the key starting point for estimating them. For example, if you intend to run a restaurant and you forecast that you will sell 100 dinners, you will have to buy a fairly predicable quantity of ingredients beforehand. So, the key items of variable cost are likely to be:

• bought-in stock or raw materials

- direct labour (note: this is only that labour which varies with the number sold)
- packaging
- direct selling costs (e.g. a commission paid on each unit sold)
- delivery.

Fixed costs, or overheads, are likely to be of more numerous different types and might include things like:

- rent and rates (or loan repayments) on premises
- leasing (or depreciation) of major items of equipment (note: this could include equipment such as cars, commercial vehicles, computers and telephone systems as well as machinery used in production)
- heat, light and power
- labour (which does not vary with the number sold)
- marketing and promotion
- telephone call charges
- postage and stationery
- insurance
- legal services
- accountancy services
- consultancy
- bank charges and interest
- software licences and maintenance charges
- travel and subsistence expenses
- training and staff development
- memberships and subscriptions
- fixtures, fittings, furniture.

The list is of course not necessarily exhaustive.

In estimating each of these different types of costs, we suggest the following guidelines:

- Ensure that you have identified all the costs involved in making and marketing your product/service and in running your business.
- Where items are to be bought in, obtain several quotations (at least three), preferably in writing. This will not only provide peace of mind for you in knowing that you have obtained a good price, but will also give you credibility in the eyes of any external parties (e.g. banks, investors) who you are trying to convince that you can run this business successfully.
- Try to compare the estimates you arrive at with other similar businesses. For variable costs, this is likely to mean other businesses in the same industry. However, some of the fixed costs such as rent, rates, heat, light etc. are fairly consistent across industries. You can look at other businesses' published accounts and ask around your own contacts.

- If, initially, you intend to run the business from your home, don't fall in to the trap of believing that you will have no additional costs. Your phone bill will increase (or your business will fail), in winter the heating will be on for most of the day, and you will need somewhere to file all your paperwork!

- If you show your numbers to an external party, such as a bank or a potential investor, they are likely to be more interested in the assumptions you have made and the ways in which you have come to your estimates, rather than the absolute numbers themselves. The more justification for your estimates that you can provide, the more credible you will appear and the more likely they are to back you. If they find even the smallest discrepancy in your workings, or if you can't explain how you have come to a particular figure, they are likely to conclude that you can't be trusted with their money.

- With regard to labour costs, in addition to the salary or wages that you are going to pay the employee, you also need to allow for any additional costs to you as the employer. These might include an employers tax contribution (such as National Insurance in the UK), pension contribution, bonus, and any other items in the employment package which you have not allowed for elsewhere.

- Remember to allow for money to pay yourself. In reality, many entrepreneurs do not pay themselves for a period immediately after starting up. However, in putting together your estimates, you should allow for a reasonable and justifiable payment (either through salary or dividend) for yourself. Otherwise, the business is little more than a hobby.

Calculating your break-even point

The break-even point is the stage when a business starts to make a profit. Identifying the break-even point may sound simple – indeed it should be. Nevertheless, many businesses, both early stage and more mature, fail to use this important and powerful idea.

One of the main reasons businesses fail in the early stages is that too much start-up capital, which is already probably in short supply, is used to buy fixed assets. While some equipment is clearly essential at the start, other purchases could be postponed. This may mean that 'desirable' and labour-saving devices have to be borrowed or hired for a specific period. This is obviously not as convenient as having them to hand all the time. But if, for example, photocopiers, fax machines, and computers, and even delivery vans, are bought into the business, they become part of the fixed costs.

The higher the fixed costs, the longer it usually takes to reach break-even point and profitability. And time is not usually on the side of the new business: it has to become profitable relatively quickly or it will simply run out of money and die.

We mentioned earlier that you cannot simply add fixed and variable costs together to get total costs, since variable costs are dependent on sales. Break-even analysis is a tool for combining fixed costs, variable costs and sales volumes so that you can calculate when you are likely to start making money. It is an important and powerful tool to be used both in preparing a business plan and in the day-to-day running of a business.

Breaking even

Let's take an elementary example: a business plans to sell only one product and has only one fixed cost, the rent. In Figure 1.5.1, the vertical axis shows the value of sales and costs in thousands of pounds and the horizontal shows the number of 'units' sold. The second horizontal line represents the fixed costs, those that do not change as volume increases. In this case it is the rent of £10 000. The angled line running from the top of the fixed costs line is the variable cost. In this example, we plan to buy in at £3 per unit, so every unit we sell adds that much to our fixed costs.

Only one element is needed to calculate the break-even point – the sales line. That is the line moving up at an angle from the bottom left-hand corner of the chart. We plan to sell at £5 per unit, so this line is calculated by multiplying the units sold by that price.

The break-even point is the stage at which a business starts to make a profit. That is when the sales revenue begins to exceed both the fixed and variable costs. The chart shows our example break-even point at 5000 units.

A formula, deduced from the chart, will save time for your own calculations.

$$\text{Break-even profit point (BEPP)} = \frac{\text{fixed costs}}{\text{selling price} - \text{unit variable costs}}$$

$$= \frac{10\,000}{£5 - £3} = 5000$$

Capital intensive versus 'lean and mean'

Look at these two hypothetical new businesses. They are both making and selling identical products at the same price, £10. They plan to sell 10 000 units each in the first year.

The owner of Company A plans to get fully equipped at the start. His fixed costs will be £40 000, double those of Company B. This is largely because, as well as his own car, he has bought such things as a delivery van, new equipment and a

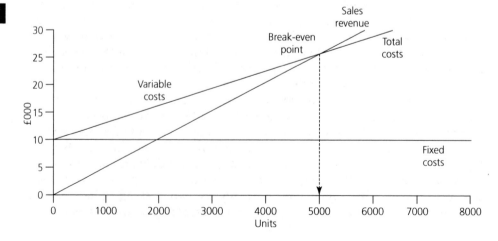

Figure 1.5.1

Break-even chart

photocopier. Much of this will not be fully used for some time, but will save some money eventually. This extra expenditure will result in a lower unit variable cost than Company B can achieve, a typical capital-intensive result.

Company B's owner on the other hand, proposes to start up on a shoestring. Only £20 000 will go into fixed costs, but of course, her unit variable cost will be higher, at £4.50. The variable unit cost will be higher because, for example, she has to pay an outside carrier to deliver, while A uses his own van and pays only for petrol.

So the break-even charts will look like those in Figures 1.5.2 and 1.5.3.

From the data on each company you can see that the total costs for 10 000 units are the same, so total possible profits if 10 000 units are sold are also the same. The key difference is that Company B starts making profits after 3636 units have been sold. Company A has to wait until 5333 units have been sold, and it may not be able to wait that long.

This is a hypothetical case; the real world is littered with the corpses of businesses that spend too much too soon. The marketplace dictates the selling price and your costs have to fall in line with that for you to have any hope of survival.

Case Study

Nick Jenkins's Moonpig, the internet retail outlet for greeting cards, used a new digital print technology to print each card to demand. After the initial sunk development costs of £50 000, almost all costs will be variable. By keeping fixed costs low, break-even could theoretically be reached at sales of only 75 000 cards.

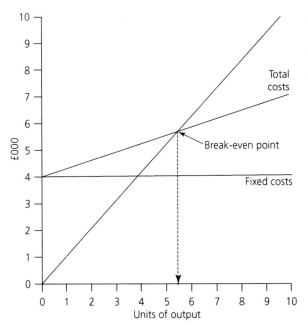

Data	£
Unit variable cost	2.50
Fixed costs	40 000.00
Variable costs	25 000.00
Total costs	65 000.00
Selling price	10.00

Break-even point =

$$\frac{40\,000.00}{10.00 - 2.50} = 5333 \text{ units}$$

Profits at maximum volume	33 000.00 (Sales revenue − Total cost)

Figure 1.5.2

Company A: capital intensive

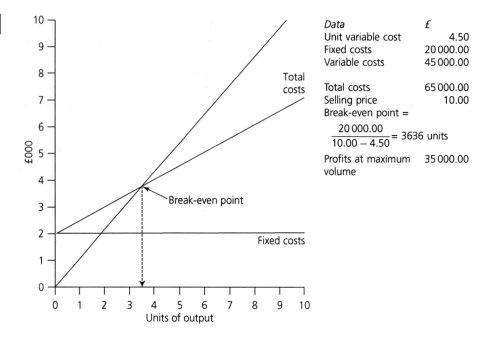

Figure 1.5.3

Company B: lean
and mean

Data	£
Unit variable cost	4.50
Fixed costs	20 000.00
Variable costs	45 000.00
Total costs	65 000.00
Selling price	10.00

Break-even point =

$$\frac{20\,000.00}{10.00 - 4.50} = 3636 \text{ units}$$

Profits at maximum volume	35 000.00

Profitable pricing

To complete the break-even picture, we need to add one further dimension – profit. It is a mistake to think that profit is an accident of arithmetic calculated only at the end of the year. It is a specific quantifiable target that you need to set at the outset.

Let's go back to our previous example. You plan to invest £10 000 in fixed assets in a business, and you will need to hold another £5000 worth of stock too – in all say £15 000. You could get £500 profit by just leaving it in a bank or building society. So, to allow for the risks of setting up your own business, you will expect a greater return of, say, £4000. Now, let's see when you will break even.

The new equation must include your 'desired' profit so it will look like this:

$$\text{Break-even profit point (BEPP)} = \frac{\text{fixed costs} + \text{profit objectives}}{\text{selling price} - \text{unit variable costs}}$$

$$= \frac{10\,000 + 4000}{£5 - £3} = 7000 \text{ units}$$

We now know that to reach our target we must sell 7000 units at £5 each and have no more than £10 000 tied up in fixed costs. The great strength of this equation is that each element can be changed in turn on an experimental basis to arrive at a satisfactory and achievable result. For instance, suppose you decide that it is unlikely you can sell 7000 units, but that 6500 is achievable. What would your selling price have to be to make the same profit?

Using the BEPP equation you can calculate the answer:

$$BEPP = \frac{\text{fixed costs + profit objectives}}{\text{selling price − unit variable costs}}$$

$$6500 = \frac{10\,000 + 4000}{6500} = £2.15$$

$$£x = £2.15 + 3 = £5.15$$

If your market will bear a selling price of £5.15 as opposed to £5 all is well; if it won't, then the ball is back in your court. You have to find ways of decreasing the fixed or variable costs, or of selling more, rather than just accepting that a lower profit is inevitable.

From the particular to the general

The example used to illustrate the break-even profit point model was of necessity simple. Few, if any businesses sell only one or two products, so a more general equation may be more useful if your business sells hundreds of products as, for example, a real shop does.

In such a business, to calculate your break-even point you must first establish your gross profit. If you are already trading, this is calculated by deducting the money paid out to suppliers from the money you received from customers. If you are not yet trading then researching your competitors will give you some indication of the sort of margins you should aim for.

For example, if you are aiming for a 40 per cent gross profit, your fixed costs are £10 000, and your overall profit objective is £40 000, then the sum will be as follows:

$$BEPP = \frac{\text{overheads}}{\text{gross profit margin}} = \frac{10\,000 + 4000}{40\%}$$

$$= \frac{14\,000}{0.4} = £35\,000$$

So, to reach your target you must achieve a £35 000 turnover. (You can check this out for yourself: look back to the previous example where the BEPP was 7000 units, and the selling price was £5 each. Multiplying those figures out gives a turnover of £35 000. The gross profit in that example was also two-fifths, or 40 per cent.)

If you find that you need help transposing the facts and figures of your business on to a break-even chart or any of the other financial statements, contact a qualified accountant.

A worked example

Let us now look at how you could use break-even analysis and quickly evaluate the financial desirability of your own business idea.

The information below is for a hypothetical business, Luke's Plumbing. Luke's expected sales are £75 000 in the first six months. By using his knowledge of break-even analysis, Luke can see that he needs to achieve sales of £9167 each month to cover all his costs. If he does reach his target of £75 000, then he can expect to make £6000 profit over the six months. If this level of profit does not meet Luke's business objectives then he needs to review his pricing and costing strategies using the method described under the heading 'profitable pricing' above.

Luke's plumbing: six-month financial projection

1. Calculate gross profit

Projected sales	£75 000
– Direct costs:	
purchases (material costs)	£32 500
labour costs	£20 000
= Gross profit	£22 500 (A)

2. Calculate gross profit margin

$$\frac{\text{Gross profit (A) £22 500}}{\text{Sales £75 000}} \times 100$$

= Gross profit margin £30 (B)

Note: For simplicity all figures shown are exclusive of VAT

3. Calculate overheads

Indirect costs:

Business salaries (including your own drawings)	£ 6000
+ rent	£ 2000
+ rates	£ 500
+ light/heating	£ 500
+ telephone/post	£ 500
+ insurance	£ 500
+ repairs	£ 2000
+ advertising	£ 1500
+ bank interest/HP	£ 1500
+ other expenses (e.g. depreciation of fixed assets)	£ 1500
= Overheads	£16 500

4. Calculate actual turnover required to break-even

$$\frac{\text{Overheads (C) £16 500}}{\text{Gross profit margin (B) 30\%}} \times 100$$

5. Calculate the monthly target to break-even

$$\frac{\text{Break-even sales (D) £55 000}}{6}$$

6. Profits accumulate in favour of the business once the break-even point has been reached. As overhead costs have been provided for in the break-even calculation, profits accumulate at a rate of 30 per cent (i.e. the gross margin percentage) on projected sales over and above the break-even figure.

In the case of the example, this is:

Projected sales	£75 000
– Break-even sales (D)	£55 000
% Gross profit margin (B)	30%
= Profit (for 6 months)	£ 6000

These figures can be affected by:

- actual level of sales achieved
- increase/decrease in gross margin
- increase/decrease in overheads.

Cash flow versus profit

Your business plan must show your clear appreciation that profit is not cash and cash is not profit. In the short term, a business can survive even if it is not making a profit as long as it has sufficient cash reserves but *it cannot survive* without cash even though it may be making a profit. The purpose of the cash flow projection is to calculate how much cash a business is likely to need to accomplish its objectives, and when it will need it in the business.

These projections will form the basis of negotiations with any potential provider of capital. Let us look at the following example to illustrate this point.

Case Study

The Kensington Quick Fit Exhaust Centre has just started up, employing a young apprentice. They have to stock a basic range of spares for most European and Japanese cars. In January, they fit 100 exhaust systems at an average cost of £75 each to the customer, making total sales for the month of £7500. These exhausts have cost Kensington on average £35 each to buy, and their total wages bill was £300. The company's position is as follows:

	£
Materials	3500
Labour	300
Total direct cost	3800

The gross profit in the month is £3700 and, after making provision for other business costs of £500 for heat, light, rates, insurances etc., Kensington Quick Fit has made a profit of £3200.

However, the proprietor is a little concerned that although he is making a good profit his bank balance is not so healthy; in fact it is worse than when he started. An examination of his operations reveals that, when he buys in his exhaust systems, his suppliers impose a minimum order quantity of 150 units, and since he needs two suppliers – one for the European car systems and one for the Japanese cars – he has to buy in 300 units at a time. He does, however, make sure that he has sufficient cash for his other outgoings before ordering these 300 units.

At the end of the month he has spent the following cash sums to meet his January sales:

	£
Materials	10 500
Labour	300
Total direct cost	10 800

During the month he has received cheques for £7500 and made a profit of £3500 but his cash at the bank has gone down by £3300, and he still owes £500 for the other business expenses.

He does have 200 exhaust systems in stock at a cost of £7000, which accounts for his poor cash position, but these can only be converted into cash when they are fitted to customers' cars.

Kensington's proprietor was aware of the situation as he closely monitored the timing of the outflow of cash from the business and the inflow of cash from his customers, and he knew that the temporary decrease in his bank balance would not stop his business surviving. However, there was no escaping the fact that although his business made a profit in the month of January the most immediate result was that his bank balance went down!

The bare essentials

In practical terms, the cash flow projections and the profit and loss account projections are parallel tasks which are essentially prepared from the same data. They may be regarded almost as the 'heads' and 'tails' of the same coin – the profit and loss account showing the entrepreneur the profit/loss based on the assumption that both sales income and the cost of making that sale are 'matched' together in the same month; and the cash flow statement looking at the same transactions from the viewpoint that in reality the cost of the sale is incurred first (and paid for) and the income is received last, anywhere between one week and three months later.

Obviously, the implications for a non-cash business of this delay between making the sale and receiving the payment and using a service/buying goods and paying for them are crucial, especially in the first year of the business and when your business is growing quickly.

Pre-trading cash flow forecast

Cash flow projections are made on the assumption that the business is operating at optimum efficiency from the outset. This in all probability is a simplistic view. New businesses will have a period when set-up costs are being incurred but no revenue from sales is coming in. Under these circumstances, your business plan should include a pre-trading cash flow forecast. Frogurt, a frozen yoghurt business started by three young university graduates, did this in their business plan.

Frogurt: Pre-trading cash flow forecast

£ Month:	1	2	3	TOTAL
Cash inflows				
Capital introduced	12 000	–	–	12 000
Loans	–	30 500	–	30 500
Total inflows	12 000	30 500	0	42 500
Cash outflows				
Fixtures and fittings	6 000	7 000	7 000	20 000
Stock	–	–	4 500	4 500
Machine purchases	–	17 000	–	17 000
Total outflows	6 000	24 000	11 500	41 500
Outflows/inflows	6 000	6 500	–11 500	1 000
Balance brought forward	6 000	12 500		
Balance carried forward	6 000	12 500	1 000	1 000

Sources of start-up finance

The different types of money

Your cash flow projections will provide a good idea of how much money your business will need, when it is required and for how long.

The next step is where to go and find this finance. Before considering possible sources of finance, you should categorize your needs into fixed or working capital. Fixed capital is money tied up in things the business intends to keep over longer periods of time, such as property, equipment, vehicles, etc. Working capital is the money used to finance the day-to-day operations. The stock, for example, and any money required to finance your customers until they pay up, are elements of working capital, as are all other running costs and overheads.

Your own capital

Obviously, the first place to start is to find out exactly how much you have to invest in the business. You may not have much in ready cash, but you may have valuable assets that can be converted into cash, or used as security for borrowing. The difference between your assets and your liabilities is your 'net worth'. This is the maximum security that you can offer for any money borrowed, and it is hoped that the calculations below will yield a pleasant surprise (see Tables 1.5.1 and 1.5.2).

External funds

There are a number of different types of external money which a new business can tap into. Debt is money borrowed most usually from a bank and which one day you will have to repay. While you are making use of borrowed money you

Table 1.5.1	Type of capital	Business needs	Financing method
Matching finance to business needs	Fixed capital	Acquiring or altering a property; buying equipment, such as cookers, ovens, photocopiers, or vehicles; the franchise fee and other 'start-up' package costs such as training	Your own capital; term loans; hire purchase; leasing; sale and leaseback; venture capital; government loan guarantee scheme; mortgage loan
	Working capital	Raw materials or finished goods; money to finance debtors; dealing with seasonal peaks and troughs, loan guarantee scheme expansion or unexpected short-term problems; paying royalties	Your own capital; bank overdraft; factoring; trade credit; government

Table 1.5.2	Assets £	Liabilities £
Your net worth	Cash in hand and in the bank, building society, national savings or other deposits	Overdraft
	Stocks and shares	Mortgage
	Current redemption value of Insurances	Other loans
	Value of home	Hire purchase
	Any other property	Tax due, including capital gains
	Motor car(s) etc.	Credit cards due
	Jewellery, paintings and other marketable valuables	Garage, local shop accounts due
	Any money due to you	Any other financial obligations
	Value of existing businesses	
	Total assets	Total liabilities
	Net worth = Total assets = Total liabilities: £	

will also have to pay interest on the loan. Equity is the money put in by shareholders, including the owner, and money left in the business by way of retained profit. You don't have to give the shareholders their money back, but they do expect the directors to increase the value of their shares, and if you go public they will probably expect a stream of dividends too. If you don't meet the shareholders' expectations then they won't be there when you need more money – or if they are powerful enough they will take steps to change the board.

There are also a whole range of other financing options including overdrafts, invoice factoring, invoice discounting, hire purchase and leasing.

Grants are also available in some circumstances to help the government of the day, or increasingly the European Union, achieve its own objectives. If their aims are in line with your own, their grants can be a useful help. But, the strategy calling for the cash must be capable of standing on its own.

To most of us, raising external money is synonymous with a visit to our local bank manager. Though not the only source of finance, the banks are a good starting point. The 'high street banks', in every country, are in serious competition with each other for new business. It is as well to remember that bank managers are judged on the quantity and quality of their lending and not on the deposits they take. If they cannot successfully lend, they cannot make a profit for the bank.

For most satisfactory new business propositions the clearing bankers would normally be happy to match pound for pound the money put up by the owner, i.e. 1:1 gearing. They will also recommend a 'package' of funds – part term loan, part overdraft and perhaps part government loan guarantee – that best suits the type of business you are interested in starting up. For example, if the business you are considering is a service, requiring few physical assets, serving cash customers and expecting to break even in the first year, then you may be advised to take a small term loan and a larger overdraft facility. This will give you the money you need to start, without upsetting the long-term security of the business. The converse relationship between loan capital and overdraft may be prudent if you are considering a 'capital-intensive' business such as a restaurant.

The banks offer a wide range of services in their own right. Through wholly or partially owned subsidiaries, they cover virtually every aspect of the financial market. As well as providing funds, the clearing banks have considerable expertise in the areas of tax, insurance and financial advice generally.

Overdrafts

Bank overdrafts are the most common type of short-term finance. They are simple to arrange: you just talk to your local bank manager. They are flexible, with no minimum level. Sums of money can be drawn or repaid within the total amount agreed. They are relatively cheap, with interest paid only on the outstanding daily balance. Of course, interest rates can fluctuate, so what seemed a small sum of money one year can prove crippling if interest rates jump suddenly. Normally, you do not repay the 'capital': you simple renew or alter the overdraft facility from time to time. However, overdrafts are theoretically repayable on demand, so you should not use short-term overdraft money to finance long-term needs, such as buying a lease, or plant and equipment.

Term loans

These are rather more formal than a simple overdraft and cover periods of up to 3, 3 to 10 and 10 to 20 years respectively. They are usually secured against an existing fixed asset or one to be acquired, or are guaranteed personally by the directors (proprietors). This may involve you in some costs for legal fees and arrangement or consultants' fees, so it may be a little more expensive than an overdraft, but unless you default on the interest charges you can be reasonably confident of having the use of the money throughout the whole term of the borrowing.

The interest rates on the loan can either be fixed for the term or variable with the prevailing interest rate. A fixed rate is to some extent a gamble, which may work in your favour, depending on how interest rates move over the term of the loan. So, if general interest rates rise, you win, and if they fall, you lose. A variable rate means that you do not take that risk. There is another benefit to a fixed rate of interest. It should make planning ahead a little easier with a fixed financial commitment; with a variable overdraft, a sudden rise can have disastrous consequences. The banks have been quite venturesome in their competition for new and small business accounts. One major clearer had a scheme which offered free banking to new businesses for one year – even if they were overdrawn – provided the limit had been agreed. The key innovation in such schemes is that the loan will be subordinated to other creditors, with the bank repaid before the shareholders but after all the other creditors if the company fails. In return for this risk, they are likely to want an option on up to 25 per cent of the company's capital.

Government loan guarantee schemes for small businesses

Some governments offer loan schemes to small firms who might otherwise find themselves turned down by their bank. To be eligible for such a loan, your proposition generally must have been looked at by an approved bank and considered viable, but should not be a proposition that the bank itself would normally approve. You can be a sole trader, partnership or limited company wanting funds to start up. The bank puts your application on to the relevant government department, using an approved format. This takes the form of an elementary business plan, which asks for some details of the directors, the business, its cash needs and profit performance, or projection of the business. There are no formal rules on size, number of employees or assets, but large businesses and their subsidiaries are definitely excluded from the scheme as are some business sectors, which vary from country to country dependent on the economic goals in force at the time.

Borrowing from family and friends

Those close to you can often lend you money or invest in your business. This helps you avoid the problem of pleading your case to outsiders and enduring extra paperwork and bureaucratic delays. Help from friends, relatives, and business associates can be especially valuable if you've been through bankruptcy or had other credit problems that would make borrowing from a commercial lender difficult or impossible. Their involvement brings a range of extra potential benefits, costs and risks that are not a feature of most other types of finance. You need to decide if these are acceptable.

Some advantages of borrowing money from people you know well are that you may be charged a lower interest rate, may be able to delay paying back money until you're more established, and may be given more flexibility if you get into a jam. But, once the loan terms are agreed to, you have the same legal obligations as you would with say a bank or any other source of finance.

In addition, borrowing money from relatives and friends can have a major disadvantage. If your business does poorly and those close to you end up losing money, you may well damage a good personal relationship. So in dealing with friends, relatives, and business associates, be extra careful not only to establish clearly the terms of the deal and put it in writing but also to make an extra effort to explain the risks. In short, it's your job to make sure your helpful friend or relative won't suffer a true hardship if you're unable to meet your financial commitments.

Many types of businesses have loyal and devoted followers, people who care as much about the business as the owners do. A health food restaurant, a specialist bookstore, or an art gallery, for example, may attract people who are enthusiastic about lending money to or investing in the business because it fits in with their lifestyle or philosophy. Their decision to participate is driven to some extent by their feelings and is not strictly a business proposition. The rules for borrowing from friends and relatives apply here as well. Put repayment terms in writing, and don't accept money from people who can't afford to risk it.

Venture capital

Many entrepreneurs see venture capital (VC) as the answer to their start-up funding requirements. The profile of VC has been particularly heightened since the internet and technology booms, where many of the high profile start-up businesses were financed by VC money.

Formal venture capital is provided by venture capital firms (VCs) who are investing other people's money, often from pension funds, and seek to achieve large returns by investing in businesses with the potential to grow and develop into major businesses of tomorrow. These returns are only available to the VC if the business in which they have invested grows very rapidly and is sold or floated. Therefore, these investments are for the medium to long term: in general, VCs would expect their investment to have paid off within seven years. And the only way for them to get the return on the investment is to exit, i.e. for the business to be sold or floated.

On the other hand, investments in private firms, particularly, at very early stages, are also very risky and the VC firm will take a number of steps to try to reduce this risk. Firstly, VCs know that they will win some and lose some. So, they must manage portfolios of investments. Typically, in a VC's portfolio, two in every ten investments they make are total write-offs, six perform averagely well at best, and there are two real stars. So, these two stars have to cover a lot of duds. For this reason, VCs have a target rate of return of more than 30 per cent to cover this poor hit rate.

Secondly, VCs will expect to play an active part in the management of the business. This will typically be by means of a non-executive director position on the board. In this way, they can influence decisions affecting the business and their investment.

Thirdly, VCs will focus on particular industry segments (e.g. IT, bio-technology) so that they develop expertise, knowledge and networks which will help them and their investee companies be more successful.

Fourthly, VCs know that pure start-ups are the most risky investments of all. Therefore, whilst VC is big business, the value of funds invested in early stage companies has remained modest, even after the technology booms, at just a few per cent of all the funds invested. While this is mainly attributable to the risk–reward relationship, the due diligence and transaction costs involved in investing small amounts in early stage businesses are similar to those associated with large investments, and so they are far higher per unit of funds invested. This is also the reason why VC firms will not usually be interested in making investments of less than about £1 million, and often more.

Finally, VCs go through a process known as 'due diligence' before investing. This process involves a thorough examination of both the business and its owners, past financial performance. Accountants and lawyers subject all the directors' track records, and the business plan, to detailed scrutiny. Directors are then required to 'warrant' that they have provided *all* relevant information, under pain of financial penalties. The cost of this process will have to be borne by the business raising the money, but will be paid out of the money raised, if that is any consolation.

So, in order to attract VC money, you and your start-up venture would need to:

- be prepared to sell or float the business in at the most seven years
- demonstrate potential for very rapid growth
- be able to show a rate of return to the investor of at least 30 per cent
- be looking for investment of at least £1 million
- be prepared to lose some control to the VC who will want to influence strategy
- be in a sector where these rates of growth and returns are achievable, e.g. IT, bio-technology.

So, despite the temporary furore during the internet boom, the reality is that VC money is appropriate for only a very small proportion of start-up businesses.

If you and your start-up venture satisfy the criteria above, and you believe that you fall in to that very small proportion of start-ups which might be of interest to a VC, then how should you go about trying to find VCs who might be interested? You could go to the venture capital trade association in your country (e.g. British Venture Capital Association www.bvca.co.uk and European Venture Capital Association www.evca.com both have online directories giving details of hundreds of venture capital providers), identify VCs who invest in your industry sector and send them your business plan. However, this approach rarely works. VCs are far more likely to invest in businesses which have been brought to their attention by someone they already know and trust. So, you would be far better advised to try to get a referral. This might be through your bank, your accountant, your solicitor, a successful entrepreneur, etc.

Business angels

The term 'angel' was first coined, in business parlance, to describe a private wealthy individual who backed a theatrical production, usually a play on Broadway or in London's West End. By their very nature, such 'investments' were highly speculative in nature as shows tend to either soar or bomb.

Business angels are a similar breed. They are informal suppliers of risk capital to new and growing businesses, often taking a hand at the stage when no one else (e.g. VC firms) will take the chance. But, whilst they often lose their shirts, they sometimes make serious money. One angel who backed the business software development company, Sage, with £10 000 in their first round of £250 000 financing, saw the value of his stake rise to £40 million.

Business angels often provide help and guidance to their 'clients', and may on average spend ten hours a week in working with each of their investments.

In the US, UK and the rest of Europe authoritative studies estimate that the total investment provided by business angels is between two and five times greater than that from the formal venture capital industry. In truth, no one knows with any certainty the amount of capital business angels either have or are prepared to invest. One reason for this is that they are quite difficult to find.

One way of increasing the chances of finding an angel is through business angel networks (BANs), in which groups of angels cluster together to pool investments and expertise. One effect of this is to bring larger sums of money to bear. On their own, an individual angel is unlikely to put up more than £50 000. That sum is hardly likely to make a great impact on the total sum needed to get a high-tech or internet venture off the ground. But, grouped together in syndicates, angels can and do put millions into new ventures.

So, what do angels look like and what are they looking for? Here are a few pointers:

- Business angels are generally self-made, high net worth individuals, with entrepreneurial backgrounds. They are 99 per cent male. Most are in the 45–65 year age group and 19 per cent are millionaires.

- Typically, business angels invest 5–15 per cent of their investment portfolio in this way. An example supporting these statistics is Robert Wright, a Cranfield MBA, who founded a small UK airline, City Flyer Express, and became a business angel when he sold out to British Airways for £75 million in 1999. He has built up a portfolio of six investments and has committed less than £1 million to his angel activities. Two of his investments are in the high-tech area, and one of those being run by two other Cranfield MBAs.

- A business angel's motivation is, first and foremost, financial gain through capital appreciation, with the fun and enjoyment of being involved with an entrepreneurial business an important secondary motive. A minority are motivated in part by altruistic considerations, such as helping the next generation of entrepreneurs to get started, and supporting their country or state.

- Business angels invest in only a very small proportion of investments that they see: typically at least seven out of eight opportunities are rejected. More than 90 per cent of investment opportunities are rejected at the initial screening stage.

- Around 30 per cent of investments by business angels are in technology-based businesses.

- The majority of business angels invest in businesses located in close proximity to where they live – two-thirds of investments are made in businesses located within 100 miles of their home or office. They are, however, prepared to look further afield if they have specific sector-related investment preferences, for instance if they are technology investors.

- Most angels vigorously avoid investing in industries they know nothing about.

- Angels fundamentally back people rather than propositions. An avid angel who is involved in at least 40 companies, insists, 'I also bet on the jockey, not just the horse'.

- Business angels are up to five times more likely to invest in start-ups and early stage investments than venture capital providers in general.

A mix of funds

In practice, most start-up business will use a mixture of funds from a variety of sources to get off the ground and underway. Moonpig's funding sources (see table below) are typical of the range of funds used, including the founder's own money, cash from friends, business angels, money in kind from suppliers and bank facilities.

Case Study

Table 1.5.3

Moonpig's raising of capital and capital structure

Time	Investor	Total amount committed by investor	Approximate share of equity
End of 1999	Nick Jenkins	£160 000	85%
	Paperlink	Designs provided	15%
July–Aug 2000	Nick Jenkins	£375 000	60%
	Paperlink	Designs	12%
	Angel Funding	£500 000	19%
	Friends	£125 000	9%
Dec 2000	Nick Jenkins	£600 000	42%
	Paperlink	Designs	6%
	Angel Funding	£500 000	11%
	Friends	£125 000	8%
	South African Bank	£750 000	33%
July 2001	Nick Jenkins	£800 000	42%
	Paperlink	Designs	3%
	Angel Funding	£500 000	35%
	Friends	£125 000	6%
	New Investor	£200 000	14%

Funding for buying a business

Buying an existing business, in part or in whole, frequently has unique funding issues, that can both narrow your funding options and make it easier to raise outside money. Investors and banks are almost always more attracted to an established business with a proven track record, rather than the uncertainties afforded by a new venture in unproven hands. On the other hand, existing businesses have assets and liabilities, key relationships, employees and existing shareholders. All of these may create issues for you when valuing the business and completing the legal arrangements. For this reason, obtaining specialist advice is highly recommended.

In general, if the business you are seeking to buy has reasonable projected future cash flows, then you should be able to borrow a significant proportion of the money you need to buy the business. Of course, you will then have to allow for the repayments of the loan as part of your break-even, profit and loss and cash flow calculations.

Case Study

When Christopher Young was invited to lead a management buy-in (MBI) of The IMPACT Programme, a commercial networking and training organization for chief information officers (CIOs) and IT directors of large companies, it came with a great deal of history. IMPACT was originally formed by the National Computing Centre (NCC) in the UK. IMPACT had been bought by the major international accounting firm, KPMG, and then subsequently, by its management. At the time that Christopher first looked at the business, IMPACT had 230 individual members from 85 blue chip companies and had been commercially successful with programmes designed to help member companies deal with the Year 2000 problem.

The two largest shareholders were the managing director and the programme director. Between them, these two individuals held much of the key knowledge and many of the important relationships. However, as the Year 2000 work began to dry up, they had different views about the future strategy of the business and were finding it increasingly hard to work together. Business performance deteriorated rapidly resulting in the business running at a loss by the end of 2000.

There were also a number of minority shareholders. As both the finances and the situation between the managing director and the programme director deteriorated, these shareholders became more and more con-

cerned. One of the minority shareholders, who was a friend of Christopher's, still believed that the business, and its long list of blue chip customers, had potential which the right management team could exploit. He contacted Christopher to invite him to be part of an MBI team with Christopher as MD and the minority shareholder as CEO.

The balance sheet at the time was in a parlous state. Shareholders' equity was a negative number and there were substantial financial obligations on the liability side. Establishing the value of the company was not easy.

It was also clear that, despite the difficulties, the current managing director and programme director would need to be retained after the MBI because of their knowledge and relationships with customers. In order to persuade them to stay, they would have to be given smaller amounts of shares in the new MBI company and, of course, meaningful salaries.

Valuing the business, managing the expectations of the existing minority shareholders, retaining the existing directors, raising the money and structuring the equity in the new company to satisfy all of these parties and the incoming MBI team, were major issues. Resolving these issues while maintaining the real value in the business, was a complex and difficult task which took several months to achieve and required expert negotiation and good legal advice.

Chapter summary

Clearly, any new business venture has to be financially viable. It is essential that you establish the financial viability of your idea before you invest your own time and money in it or approach outsiders for backing. In this chapter, we have looked at how to estimate the sales volumes and likely costs of the business. We've considered how to calculate break-even and how to set prices in order to ensure the level of profit required. If these figures look good, then you can go ahead and produce profit and loss and cash flow projections. The cash flow projection is particularly important since it indicates the amount of capital you will require to get the business going. Once you know how much funding you require, you then need to consider the various sources of funding available to start-up businesses which we have reviewed.

If you work through all the assignments up to and including those at the end of this chapter, and your venture still looks feasible, then there's a good chance that it got some potential to become a successful business. The key activity now should be to put together a business plan for starting up. The output from the assignments for Chapters 2, 3, 4 and 5 will provide you with most of the information you require for such a business plan.

Assignments

1. Forecast your sales volumes for each month during the first year of trading using as many different approaches as you can. Consolidate the various forecasts into a single set of figures which you feel confident about being able to achieve. Carefully record your assumptions.

2. Identify all the items of cost of starting up and of running the business from day to day. Remember to differentiate between fixed costs and variable costs. Estimate the cost for each item, by obtaining at least three estimates where possible and by comparing with other businesses. Again, carefully record your assumptions.

3. Calculate your expected break-even point. Consider whether you can switch some of the fixed cost items to variable costs in order to achieve break-even earlier.

4. Use your break-even analysis to assess the impact of three different pricing strategies.

5. Prepare a monthly cash flow forecast covering the pre-trading period and foreward until your cumulative cash flow becomes positive.

6. Prepare a monthly profit and loss projection for years one to three. Are the profits satisfactory?

7. Work out how much money you need to get started. Which source(s) of capital do you think will be most appropriate for your needs and why?

Suggested further reading

Barrow, Colin (2001) *Financial Management for the Small Business*, 5th Edition, London: Kogan Page.
Barrow, Colin (2003) *The Complete Small Business Guide*, Oxford: Capstone Reference.

6 What is the most appropriate legal form for your business?

Introduction and objectives

In all countries, there are a number of legal forms for businesses. At the outset of your business venture you will have to decide which legal form your business will take.

The form that you choose will depend on a number of factors: commercial needs, financial risk and your tax position. Ultimately, the legal form you choose for your start-up is as much to do with your own personality as with the finer points of law and taxation.

Whilst there are some variations from country to country, in general there are three main forms that a business can take: sole trader, partnership and limited company.

By the end of this chapter, you should have a good understanding of these three main legal forms and we will also briefly touch on co-operatives. As a result, you should be in a position to decide which is the most appropriate legal form for your business.

Sole trader

If you have the facilities, cash and customers, you can start trading under your own name almost immediately. This form of business is known as 'sole trader'.

A small number of trades have to obtain approval from the authority which governs and regulates them before business can actually commence. In Germany, for example, approval is mandatory before any crafts trade is started. The trade has to be registered on the Roll of Craftsmen maintained by the Chamber of Craft for the region. The trade has to be in the hands of a master craftsman before it can be registered on the Roll of Craftsmen. There are only a few exemptions from the requirement to take the master's proficiency examination. Apart from this, trades can be practised completely freely. In particular, most commercial trades (wholesale and retail) are unregulated. Obviously, certain particular trades are subject to a series of special regulations before they can be practised.

As a sole trader, unless you intend to register for Value Added Tax (VAT), there are few rules about the records you have to keep. You may have to register for

VAT immediately if you expect your turnover in the first quarter to be higher than the local threshold figure. (In France, for example you may have to register if your turnover looks likely to reach €30 000 in your first year, whilst in the UK you could keep out of the VAT net until your turnover approached €80 000. These are approximate figures. The actual figures change from year to year and have some variations between business sectors.) There is unlikely to be a requirement for an external audit or for financial information on your business to be available to the public at large. Nevertheless, you would be prudent to keep good books and to get professional advice, as you will have to declare your income to the relevant tax authority. Without good records, you will lose in any dispute over tax.

On the downside, sole traders are personally liable for the debts of the business and, in the event of the business failing, the owner's personal possessions can be sold to meet the debts.

In addition, a sole trader does not have access to equity capital, which has the attraction of being risk-free to the business. He or she must rely on loans from banks or individuals and any other non-equity source of finance.

Partnership

There are very few restrictions to setting up in business with another person (or persons) in partnership. Many partnerships are entered into without legal formalities and sometimes without the parties themselves being aware that they have entered a partnership. All that is needed is for two or more people to agree to carry on a business together, intending to share the profits. The law in most countries will then recognize the existence of a partnership.

Most countries have some, often several forms of partnership. French law, for example, recognizes three forms of partnerships: general partnerships (*société en nom collectif*), limited partnerships (*société en commandite*) and limited partnerships with publicly distributed equity participations (*société en commandite par actions*).

Most of the points raised when considering sole tradership apply to partnerships. Most importantly, all the partners are personally liable for the debts of the partnership, even if those debts were incurred by one partner's mismanagement or dishonesty without the other partner's knowledge. Even death may not release a partner from his or her obligations, and in some circumstances his or her estate can remain liable.

Unless you take 'public' leave of your partnership by notifying your business contacts and advertising retirement you will remain liable indefinitely. So, it is vital before entering a partnership to be absolutely sure of your partner and to take legal advice in drawing up a partnership contract. The contract should cover the following points:

- *Profit sharing, responsibilities and duration*: This should specify how profit and losses are to be shared, and who is to carry out which tasks. It should also set limits on partners' monthly drawings, and on how long the partnership itself is to last (either a specific period of years or indefinitely, with a cancellation period of, say, three months).

- *Voting rights and policy decisions*: Unless otherwise stated, all the partners have equal voting rights. It is advisable to get a definition of what is a policy or voting decision, and how such decisions are to be made. You must also decide how to expel or admit a new partner.

- *Time off*: Every partner is entitled to his share of the profits even when ill or on holiday. You will need some guidelines on the length and frequency of holidays, and on what to do if someone is absent for a long period for any other reason.

- *Withdrawing capital*: You have to decide how each partner's share of the capital of the business will be valued in the event of any partner leaving or the partnership being dissolved.

- *Accountancy procedure*: You are not obliged either to file accounts or to have accounts audited. However, it may be prudent to agree a satisfactory standard of accounting and have a firm of accountants to carry out that work. Sleeping partners may well insist on it. (A *sleeping partner* is the name given to a partner who has put up capital but does not intend to take an active part in running the business.)

Limited partnership

One possibility that can reduce the more painful consequences of entering a partnership is to have your involvement registered as a limited partnership, or *Kommanditgesellschaft* (KG) as this form of legal entity is known in Germany and *Société en nom collectif* in France. A limited partnership is very different from a 'general' partnership. It is a legal animal that, in certain circumstances, combines the best attributes of a partnership and a corporation.

A limited partnership works like this. There must be one or more general partners with the same basic rights and responsibilities (including unlimited liability) as in any general partnership, and one or more limited partners who are usually passive investors. The big difference between a general partner and a limited partner is that the limited partner isn't personally liable for debts of the partnership. The most a limited partner can lose is the amount that he or she:

- paid or agreed to pay into the partnership as a capital contribution
- or received from the partnership after it became insolvent.

To keep this limited liability, a limited partner may not participate in the management of the business, with very few exceptions. A limited partner who does get actively involved in the management of the business risks losing immunity from personal liability and having the same legal exposure as a general partner.

The advantage of a limited partnership as a business structure is that it provides a way for business owners to raise money (from the limited partners) without having to either take in new partners who will be active in the business, or having to form a limited company. A general partnership that's been operating for years can also create a limited partnership to finance expansion.

Concerns about partnerships

Partnerships have three serious financial drawbacks that merit particular attention.

Firstly, if your partner makes a business mistake, perhaps by signing a disastrous contract, without your knowledge or consent, every member of the partnership must shoulder the consequences. Under these circumstances, your personal assets could be taken to pay the creditors even though the mistake was no fault of your own.

Secondly, if your partner goes bankrupt in their personal capacity, for whatever reason, their creditors can seize their share of the partnership. As a private individual, you are not liable for your partner's private debts, but having to buy them out of the partnership at short notice could put you and the business in financial jeopardy.

Thirdly, if your partnership breaks up for any reason, those continuing with it will want to recover control of the business, and those who remain shareholders will want to buy back shares; on the other side, the leaver wants a realistic price. The agreement you have on setting up the business should specify the procedure and how to value the leaver's share, otherwise resolving the situation will be costly. The traditional route to value the leaver's share is to ask an independent accountant. This is rarely cost-effective. The valuation costs money and worst of all it is not definite and consequently there is room for argument. Another way is to establish a formula, an agreed eight times the last audited pre-tax profits, for example. This approach is simple but difficult to get right. A fast-growing business is undervalued by a formula using historic data unless the multiple is high; a high multiple may overvalue 'hope' or goodwill thus unreasonably profiting the leaver. Under a third option, one partner offers to buy out the others at a price he specifies. If they do not accept his offer, the continuing partners must buy the leaver out at that price. In theory, such a price should be acceptable to all.

Case Study

Jane Edge only discovered her founding partner was defrauding her when she decided to offer shares to incentivize the company's employees. To get the company valued, she needed the audited accounts, which were not ready. Her accountant partner claimed the auditors were holding up clearing the accounts on a few 'technicalities'. When Jane contacted the auditors, they said that the company was late in producing the accounts and they had not even seen them. Eventually it was discovered that the partner had siphoned off a quarter of the businesses' assets for his own purposes.

Needless to say the partner was fired and sued successfully, though no money was recovered. Unfortunately, the employee share option scheme had to be postponed, causing two key employees to leave and set up business for themselves. The company never fully recovered from this setback.

Limited company

The main distinction between a limited company, called more transparently *société anonyme* (SA) in France, and the forms of business already discussed is that it has a legal identity of its own separate from the people who own it. This means that, in the event of liquidation, creditors' claims are restricted to the assets of the company. The shareholders are not usually liable as individuals for the business debts beyond the paid-up value of their shares.

In practice, the ability to limit liability is severely restricted by the requirements of potential lenders such as banks. They often insist on personal guarantees from directors when small, new or troubled companies look for loans or credits.

Other advantages for limited companies include the freedom to raise capital by selling shares and certain tax advantages. The disadvantages include the legal requirements for the company's accounts to be audited and for certain records of the business trading activities to be filed annually in a manner that provides access to the general public.

A limited company can be formed by two shareholders, one of whom must be a director. A company secretary must also be appointed, who can be a shareholder, director, or an outside person such as an accountant.

In most countries, a limited company (or equivalent form) can be bought 'off the shelf' from a registration agent, then adapted to suit your own purposes. This will involve changing the name, shareholders and articles of association. Alternatively, you can form your own company, using your solicitor or accountant. The cost either way will be in the low hundreds of Euros.

Co-operative

If making money is much lower on your list of priorities for starting up in business than being involved in the decisions of an ethical enterprise, then joining a co-operative or starting your own is an idea worth exploring.

Although the most commonly known co-operatives in the UK are the high street shops and supermarkets owned by the Co-operative Retail Society (or Co-op), there is another less visible, but nonetheless important, variety, the workers' co-operative. In 1844, 28 workers in northern England formed the first successful workers co-operative. They were weavers, shoemakers, cabinetmakers, tailors, printers, hatters and engineers. They called themselves the Rochdale Equitable Pioneers Society, taking their name from the town they lived in, Rochdale, 12 miles north of Manchester.

There are over 1500 workers co-operatives in the UK with over 40 000 people working in them. In the United States, there are 47 000 co-operatives generating over $100 billion in sales output. Italy is reputed to have the most co-operative businesses, somewhere in excess of 50 000, albeit mostly they are very small businesses.

There are co-operatives that sell bicycles, furniture, camping equipment, appliances, carpeting, clothing, handicrafts and books. There are co-operative wholesalers like those in the hardware, grocery and natural foods businesses. There are co-operatives that disseminate news and co-operatives for artists. There are co-operative electric and telephone utilities. There are co-operatively managed banks, credit unions and community development corporations. There are thousands of farm co-operatives, along with co-operatives that provide financing to farm co-operatives. There are subscriber-owned cable TV systems and parent-run day-care centres. There are co-operatively organized employee-owned companies, co-operative purchasing groups for fast food franchises and, of course, various kinds of co-operative housing. There are co-operatives that provide health care, such as health maintenance organizations and community health clinics. There are co-operative insurance companies. There are co-operative food stores, food-buying clubs, and discount warehouses. You get the idea. There are co-operatives in virtually every area of business you could possibly imagine.

Chapter summary

In order to get in to business, you will need to decide on the legal form that your business will take. The choice of legal form which is most appropriate for you will be dependent on commercial needs, financial risk, your personal tax position and, ultimately, your own personality.

Although legal forms vary from country to country, there are three main types each of which we have reviewed in this chapter. Table 1.6.1 summarizes the pros and cons of each of these three types

Legal form	Advantages	Disadvantages
Sole trader	Can start trading immediately Minimum formalities No set-up costs No audit fees No public disclosure of trading information.	Unlimited personal liability for trading debts No access to equity capital Low status public image When you die, so does the business.
Partnership	No audit required, though your partner may insist on one No public disclosure of trading information.	Unlimited personal liability for your own *and your partners'* trading debts (except sleeping partners) Partnership contracts can be complex and costly to prepare Limited access to equity capital Death of a partner often causes partnership to be dissolved.
Limited company	Shareholders' liabilities restricted to nominal value of shares Possible to raise equity capital High status public image The business has a legal status of its own and continues with or without the founder.	Audit required if your turnover exceeds a certain figure (varies by country) Trading information must be disclosed Suppliers, landlords and banks will probably still insist on personal guarantees from directors Can't start trading until you have a certificate of incorporation.

Table 1.6.1

Three standard business types: advantages and disadvantages

Assignments

1. Find out all the different legal forms of business in the country in which you intend to start your venture and summarize the advantages and disadvantages in a table similar to the one above.

2. Identify the criteria which are important to you and your new business in choosing between these various forms and assess each of the legal forms against these criteria.

3. Decide which legal form is most appropriate for you and your new business.

4. Undertake any legal/contractual/registration tasks which are required for the legal form which you have chosen.

The challenges of growing the business

Now that you have got the business established, what next?

To grow or not to grow?

Some entrepreneurs will be happy with having got this far – and, indeed, congratulations if you have, it is a great achievement! These entrepreneurs may feel that they have achieved everything that they set out to. They are working for themselves, running their own business, generating sufficient income to support their lifestyle and perhaps employing a small number of other people. They may have no further ambitions for the business and may be perfectly happy to run it in this way until they retire. These entrepreneurs are usually called 'lifestyle' entrepreneurs and many can be found among tradespeople (for example, plumbers, carpenters, hairdressers), people with specific skills (for example, artists, music teachers) and indeed, the traditional 'professions' (for example, solicitors, accountants, architects).

There are other entrepreneurs who are hugely ambitious and, right from the start, have a goal to build a very large business. For example, from the very beginning, Karan Bilimoria had an ambition for Cobra Beer to be available in every Indian restaurant and to become the first global Indian brand.

There are also a large number of entrepreneurs and owner-managers whose scale of ambition lies somewhere in between these two. They may be running profitable businesses with turnover in the millions while at the same time being ambitious for the business to be bigger and/or more profitable so that they would feel more secure and more fulfilled. The participants on the Business Growth and Development Programme that we have run for many years are often in this category.

Over the years, we have worked with hundreds of entrepreneurs and owner-managers on numerous programmes. For many, growth is not an optional extra: it is an imperative. The stark facts are that a growing business has a better chance of survival in a competitive marketplace.

Professor David Storey, in his comprehensive 1994 study *Understanding the Small Business Sector*, has noted that 'the fundamental characteristic, other than size per se, which distinguishes small firms from large is their higher probability of ceasing to trade'.

In other words, bigger businesses are more likely to survive. One could reasonably surmise that bigger businesses are in a better position to survive the loss of a key customer or a key member of staff, and have a wider range of products/services and more financial strength which allows them to ride out drops in demand and the ups and downs of the economic cycle. So, let's briefly consider the other factors which influence business survival and mortality.

In the UK, studies have shown that the mortality rate, as measured by de-registration for VAT, is clearly related to business age. The following graphs show that this is a common phenomenon throughout Europe and the United States where both the best- and worst-performing economies mirror each other in respect of firm's mortality characteristics, as do franchised and non-franchised enterprises.

Nearly one-third of firms cease to trade in the first three years, increasing to nearly two-thirds within 10 years (see Figures 2.0.1 and 2.0.2). The reasons for failure are many and various, but have perhaps best been summarized by Hall in *Surviving and Prospering in the Small Firms Sector*, who concluded:

> It would appear that the owners of young firms are more likely to suffer from inadequate funding, poor products and inefficient marketing. As their companies aged, however, they were more likely to be buffeted by strategic and environmental shocks for which they did not have the managerial skills to respond.
>
> (Hall 1995)

John McQueen, secretary to the Association of Bankrupts, put it more bluntly: 'My own belief is that it is a dire lack of marketing abilities together with slack pricing and buying policies [too much stock] that is the real killer to business . . . not the under capitalization myth.'

Those new start-ups which had based their business plans upon the advice of Brian Warnes, author of the 1984 classic, *The Ghengis Khan Guide to Business*, should at least have avoided the low margins trap. But, what were the characteristics of other surviving

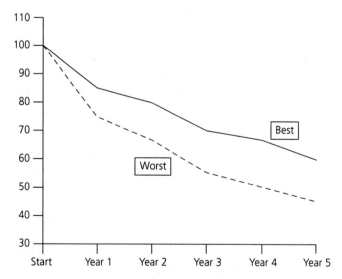

Figure 2.0.1

Survival rate of new enterprises in Europe (all countries follow the same pattern)

Source: European Observatory for SME Research (2000)

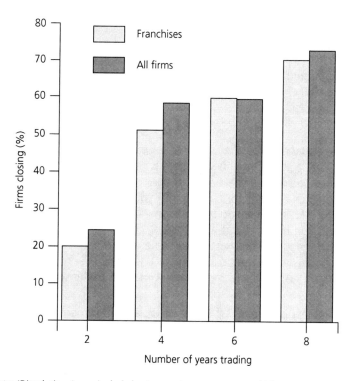

Figure 2.0.2

Business dissolution rates in USA

Note: 'Dissolutions' may include business sales, mergers, acquisitions, etc. as well as involuntary closures such as bankruptcies, failures and terminations.
Source: SBA Office of Advocacy (2001)

firms? Professor David Storey of Warwick University found evidence to support two interesting conclusions:

1. Failure rates were lowest amongst firms expressing a desire to grow, i.e. were motivated to want to grow
2. Achieving real growth required 'active market development in terms of both the identification of new market opportunities and increasing the breadth of the customer base'.

It is clear from these studies, and many others, that setting out to grow your business makes good sense – even if you do not have an ambition as grand as Karan Bilimoria's!

Perhaps wider communication of the above statistics of failure, and the consequence of not wanting to grow, would concentrate a few more minds in a positive direction. Participants in the Business Growth and Development Programme (BGP) were clearly all motivated to grow and willing to pay for the experience. Hence, perhaps, it is not that surprising to find that businesses which participate in BGP grow their sales and profit more quickly than average SMEs and that they grow more quickly after participation in the programme than they did before.

Growing businesses are also better able to attract and retain talented and ambitious people. Growing businesses are not only more exciting places to work, they are also more interesting and, dare we say it, fun enterprises to run.

But, before you set off...

Of course, no one in their right mind sets out to run an unsuccessful business but, as the above figures show, that's exactly what millions of business founders end up doing. So, before you set out on the path to growth, it's well worth making a few checks on your progress to date:

- *Are you meeting your personal goals and working to your values?* Why did you start the business in the first place? Once the business is up and running, and there are many day-to-day issues and future challenges to deal with, it's all too easy to forget about your own original reasons for getting into your own business. Equally, we all have deeply rooted values and no doubt yours are at least partly reflected in the nature of the business you have started. Once again, these can all too easily be lost in the hurly-burly of running the business. Take some time out to remind yourself of your personal goals and values on a regular basis and check that you are still fulfilling them. If you are not fulfilling them, then it may be better to do something else instead.

- *Are you meeting your business objectives?* If you ever worked in someone else's organization, the chances are that you were set a stream of tasks to achieve with associated deadlines, not all of which were achievable or realistic. On many occasions they may well have been downright contradictory. Now you are running your own business, you have the opportunity to set the pace and direction of the venture. Having some clear business objectives, with measures and timeframes against them, is very worthwhile and the achievement of them is both motivational and should help you achieve your original goals.

- *Are you making enough money?* This sounds like a daft question, but it might well be the most important one you will ask. The answer comes out of your reply to two subsidiary questions. The first is: Could you do better by investing your time and money elsewhere? If the answer to this question is 'yes', then it's time to go back to the drawing board with your business idea. The second question is: Will you make enough money to invest in growing your business? The answer to this question will only become clear when you work out your profit margins. But, the evidence that many businesses do not make enough money to re-invest in themselves is pretty clear when you see run-down premises, old, worn-out equipment and the like.

Contents of this section

Fuelling and maintaining growth, however, is seldom easy. A few lucky firms find themselves in fast-growth industries where demand, for a period, is constantly outrunning supply. But for most businesses achieving growth does not happen by accident. It happens as a result of hard work, careful planning and a strategic understanding of the market and the broader business environment.

The key elements which we see as important for companies that have survived the initial *Challenges of Getting in to Business* and now face the second stage *Challenges of Growing the Business* are:

- being in good financial health
- knowing how you win
- further developing your distinctiveness
- watching what happens around you
- having a clear and focused growth strategy
- developing a balanced management team
- making enough money and funding growth.

Each of these key elements is examined in turn in a chapter in this section.

Assignments

As before, each chapter concludes with a series of assignments which suggest work to be done in applying the ideas introduced in that chapter. If you are an owner-manager who is looking to grow and develop your business, then by working through these assignments applied to your business, you will build up most of the information you need for inclusion in a growth strategy and a business plan to implement that strategy.

If you are using this book to learn about growing businesses, but do not have a business of your own, then we suggest that you work through the assignments using one of the recurring case studies. Cobra Beer and ChocExpress (renamed Hotel Chocolat) would be good examples for use in this section and full versions of both of these cases are available on the companion website.

7   Are you in good financial health?

Introduction and objectives

One of the first things you should do before embarking on the challenges of growth is to obtain a deep understanding of the financial health of the business. An analysis of the financial performance of your business, or 'financial position audit', will help you to reveal:

- Whether there are specific areas of the business in which action needs to be taken.

- How you are performing compared to the past and compared to your competitors.

- The key levers that you need to pull in order to deliver growth.

- The main areas of risk.

- Whether there are untapped sources of internal funds to help finance the growth (see Chapter 13 for more on this).

- Some of the means by which you will measure growth.

The centrepiece for all financial position audits is an appraisal of the profit and loss account, the balance sheet and ratios that can be derived from the information contained. The case for this is simple. Typically, the figures are readily available and they are comparatively easy to handle. Similar information about other companies (e.g. your competitors) will be publicly available and, therefore, meaningful comparisons can be made.

The main way in which the financial position audit is established, and in which comparisons are made, is through the use of ratios. A ratio is simply one number expressed as a proportion of another. Travelling 150 kilometres may not sound too impressive, until you realize it was done in one hour. The ratio here is 150 kilometres per hour. If you knew that the vehicle in question had a top speed of 170 kilometres per hour, you would have some means of comparing it to other vehicles, at least in respect of their speed. In finance too, ratios can turn sterile data into valuable information in a wide range of different ways, thus helping you make choices.

In the financial field, the opportunity for calculating ratios is great – for computing *useful* ratios, not quite so great. Here we will concentrate on explaining the key ratios for a growing business. Most you can calculate yourself, some you may need your bookkeeper or accountant to organize for you. All take a little time and may cost a little money, but they do tell you a lot about what is going on.

One main value of the position audit using ratios is that it points to questions that need answers. A large difference between what actually happened and what standard was set, suggests that something may be wrong. The tools of analysis (the ratios) allow managers to choose, from the hundreds of questions that might be asked, the handful that are really worth answering. In a small and/or expanding business, where time is at a premium, this quick pre-selection of key questions is vital.

Financial ratios can be clustered under a number of headings, each of which probes a different aspect of business performance. By the end of this chapter, you should be able to calculate the key ratios under each of the following headings:

- growth
- profitability
- liquidity (and working capital)
- solvency.

In order to illustrate the calculation of the ratios, we will use a simple business, Quickeats Limited. The accounts for Quickeats for the last two years are presented at the end of this chapter (Table 2.7.2). These are much simplified accounts and not everything you would expect to see in a full set of accounts has been included – just enough to illustrate the use of the key ratios.

Measuring growth

If growth is the aim, then we must have measures for growth. Growth is most commonly expressed as the improvement in some measure expressed as a percentage of the previous period's equivalent measure. So, sales growth of 20 per cent per annum would mean that the increase in this year's sales was 20 per cent of last year's total sales.

$$\text{Sales growth} = \frac{\text{This year's sales} - \text{last year's sales}}{\text{Last year's sales}} \times 100$$

Similarly, for any other measure of growth such as profit or number of employees.

The most common measures of growth are sales and number of employees. The former is often used by entrepreneurs as a type of virility test. The latter is popular with governments. Neither of these measures is particularly useful unless profit is also taken into account.

Many businesses fall into the trap of becoming 'busy fools', growing turnover with little regard to profitability. However, healthy growth requires both sales turnover and profits being grown in proportion.

Growing businesses can be classified in to one of five types of growth as shown in Figure 2.7.1. Only two of these types have particular merit, two are potentially dangerous, and one seems to make being in business for yourself something of a pointless exercise.

- *Champions*: This term describes companies who grow both their profits and sales turnover by at least 25 per cent each year. This is a fairly small proportion of businesses, fewer than 6 per cent at the last count. This type of growth gives you a very strong position in the market with a growing sales presence and the profit to develop new products and services without recourse to borrowing.
- *Profit enhancers*: This is also a very small proportion of the total population – businesses which concentrate on growing profits but not sales. While this can be a useful position to be in, particularly since it means that you are making more money without producing more, these businesses can become vulnerable as they are typically building on a fairly static customer base.
- *Grazers*: These move forward steadily at a pace much the same as for their markets in general, rather like a boat being swept along with the tide. The danger here is that the tide may turn.
- *Unprofitable growers*: These firms sales move forward sharply, whilst their profits are either fairly static, or even going down. This is a particularly dangerous course to follow. With sales growth come all sorts of additional costs. More stock, more equipment, more staff and so forth. And these have all to be supported from a static profit base. Often just one bad debt or quality problem, causing delays in payments, is enough to sink an unprofitable grower.
- *Companies in decline*: These are going backwards by both measures. Their market positions are getting weaker, with a smaller sales base. And they are not making enough profit to do anything new. They are dying slowly.

Figure 2.7.1

Typical growth profiles of SMEs

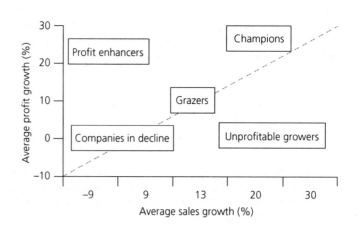

Quickeats is an example of a Champion. Profits are growing at 41 per cent, whilst sales are growing at 30 per cent. It may be instructive to position your business and your competitors on this growth chart to see how you compare.

Measuring profitability

Profitability is clearly important for nearly all businesses. At the simplest level, profit is one of the essential reasons that a business exists. Moreover, a business needs to make sufficient profit, or return, in order to:

- Give a good return to shareholders bearing in mind the risk they are taking. If the returns are less than bank interest rates, for example, then your shareholders (including, of course, yourself as the entrepreneur) will not be happy.
- Allow the business to grow.
- Keep the real value of the original capital intact after allowing for inflation.

There are two main ways to measure profitability of a business:

- profit margins
- return on capital employed (ROCE).

They are both important, but they reveal different things about the performance, and perhaps even the strategy, of the business. To fully understand what is happening in the business, you need information in both areas.

Gross profit and gross margin percentage

Gross profit and gross margin percentage are measures of the value we are adding to the products/services we are producing. To put it another way, they measure the power of the 'money making engine' of the business. The higher the percentage the greater the value we are adding. If your gross margins are not large enough, then it is very difficult to generate sufficient profits in order to grow the business.

To calculate gross profit, deduct the cost of sales from the sales.

Gross profit = sales − cost of sales

To calculate gross margin percentage, express the result as a percentage of sales.

$$\text{Gross margin} = \frac{\text{gross profit}}{\text{sales}} \times 100$$

In the case of Quickeats, the gross margin percentage in year 1 is

$$\text{Gross margin} = \frac{50\,000}{100\,000} \times 100 = 50\%$$

For year 2, the figure has moved down slightly to 48 per cent. Some possible causes of this reduction include: lower selling prices, higher material or labour costs, wastage, theft and a change in the types of products or services being sold.

Operating profit and operating margin percentage

Operating profit and operating margin are measures of how well the management is running the business.

To calculate the operating profit, we not only deduct cost of sales from sales, but we also take off expenses (other than financing charges such as interest and taxation).

Operating profit = sales – cost of sales – expenses

It is assumed that financing decisions are taken by the owners (as opposed to the management – although in many entrepreneurial businesses these are the same people) and that interest rates and taxation are set by the government and economic authorities of the day. Therefore, they are out of management control and accountability.

Once again, we then express the result as a percentage of sales.

$$\text{Operating margin} = \frac{\text{operating profit}}{\text{sales}} \times 100$$

In the case of Quickeats, the operating margin percentage in year 1 is

$$\text{Operating margin} = \frac{17\,000}{100\,000} \times 100 = 17\%$$

In year 2, this percentage is up slightly to 18.5 per cent, which is for the most part the result of total expenses only being £5000 higher (£38 000 compared to £35 000), whilst sales were £30 000 higher.

Net profit and net margin percentage

Net profit is the 'bottom line', i.e. sales less all costs. The figure can be shown before tax, often called profit before interest and tax (PBIT), or after tax. Although this may appear to be the ultimate measure of business performance, in owner-managed businesses, real performance can often be obscured by the way in which costs are recorded.

In its after tax form, which we will show here, net profit also represents the sum available either to be distributed as dividends or retained by the business to invest in its future.

$$\text{Net margin} = \frac{\text{net profit}}{\text{sales}} \times 100$$

In the case of Quickeats, the net margin percentage in year 1 is

$$\text{Net margin} = \frac{11\,880}{100\,000} \times 100 = 11.88\%$$

This would generally be considered a respectable figure, the range being anything between 5 and 25 per cent for most businesses.

In year 2, it is up to 13.51 per cent, which is largely brought about by the same reasons that led to the increase in Operating Margin. The fact that the cost of borrowing did not go up, because the growth was financed by retained profits, also helped.

Return on capital employed (ROCE)

The financial resources employed in a business are called capital. Capital can come into a business from a number of different sources including the owner's capital, other investor's capital, loans and retained profits (also known as reserves). All of these sources are commonly looking for a return on the money they invest. This return is closely analogous to the interest that you would receive if you invested your capital in a bank account.

If, for example, you had £10 000 invested in a bank and, at the end of the year, they gave you £500 interest, then the return on your capital employed would be

$$\text{ROCE} = \frac{\text{profit}}{\text{capital employed}} \times 100$$

$$= \frac{500}{10\,000} \times 100 = 5\%$$

For this reason, return on capital employed (ROCE) is one of the primary measures of performance for most businesses – and certainly for most investors.

In a business, ROCE is calculated by expressing the operating profit as a percentage of the total capital employed

$$\text{ROCE} = \frac{\text{operating profit}}{\text{total capital employed}} \times 100$$

All the different elements of capital in the business will be found on the balance sheet in the 'Financed by' section and the 'Creditors over 1 year' (i.e. long-term loans) section. Adding all the balance sheet entries in these two sections together will result in the total capital employed. Given that a balance sheet must balance, it follows that the figure for total capital employed will be equal to the sum of the balance sheet entries for fixed assets and net current assets. Net current assets is also sometimes called working capital since this is the capital which is used on a day-to-day basis to finance the working of the business.

In year 1 of our Quickeats example, the ROCE is

$$\text{ROCE} = \frac{17\,000}{10\,000 + 8910 + 10\,000} \times 100$$

$$= 59\%$$

In the second year, it is much the same at 57 per cent. By any standards, both are excellent results.

The great strength of this ratio lies in the overall view it takes of the financial health of the whole business. The ratio gives no clue as to why there is a small change in the second year, it simply provides a starting point for an analysis and an overall yardstick against which to compare absolute performance.

Return on shareholders capital (ROSC)

Shareholders are usually most interested in the net return on their capital, i.e. the return on shareholders' capital (ROSC). So, here the return would be the net profit after interest has been paid on any loans and after the taxman has had his slice, i.e. Net profit after tax and interest. The shareholders' capital is not only their initial stake, but also any retained profits in the business since, although not distributed, these also belong to the shareholders.

$$\text{ROCE} = \frac{\text{net profit after tax and interest}}{\text{total shareholders' capital}} \times 100$$

In our example, in year 1 the calculation is

$$\text{ROCE} = \frac{11\,800}{10\,000 + 8910} \times 100$$

$$= 63\%$$

Once again, this is an excellent result. For owner-managed businesses in general, this ratio can be anywhere between a few percentage points and upwards of 35 per cent. Results such as those in this example would be in the top 10 per cent.

Profit per employee

If, as in most cases, your principle 'assets' are people, and not just capital assets such as machines, then you will need to monitor what value employees are contributing. A good ratio to use for this purpose is profit per employee

$$\text{Profit per employee} = \frac{\text{net profit before tax}}{\text{number of employees}}$$

In the case of Quickeats, the ratio for year 1 is

$$\text{Profit per employee} = \frac{14\,850}{2} = \pounds7425$$

The figure drops sharply the following year to £5487. This would not be unusual, as growing businesses tend to move forward in a lumpy fashion. For a business employing say 30 people, taking on two more employees would be a relatively small step. But, for this business it represents a doubling of the workforce.

It can also be useful to calculate the sales per employee, to give you a feel for activity levels. As you can see, things at Quickeats are slowing down.

If we bring all these ratios together, we could produce a table such as the, 'Profitability at a glance at Quickeats' shown in Table 2.7.1.

We could then go on to benchmark Quickeats against others in the industry. As a result, we may conclude that our sales per employee is lower than it should be and we need to improve in this area.

However, our ROCE performance is above average. The message here is perhaps that our capital investment is paying off, using good new equipment, but we need to get a better result from our people.

Measuring liquidity

Liquidity is a measure of a business's ability to meet its current financial obligations (i.e. creditors and short-term loans such as overdrafts), known as current liabilities, as and when they fall due. These liabilities will need to be met

	Year 1	Year 2	
			Table 2.7.1
Gross margin	50%	48%	Quickeats:
Operating margin	17%	18.5%	profitability at a
Net margin	11.88%	13.51%	glance
Return on capital employed (ROCE)	59%	57%	
Return on shareholders' capital (ROSC)	63%	55%	
Profit per employee	£7 425	£5 487	
Sales per employee	£50 000	£32 500	

from cash in hand and any other resources which can quickly be converted into cash such as debtors and stock. These are known as current assets (as opposed to fixed assets which are items in which the business has invested for the longer term and cannot easily be converted into cash).

The two key measures of liquidity are the current ratio and the quick ratio (or acid test).

Current ratio

The current ratio for a business is the relationship between the current assets and current liabilities and is calculated by dividing the former by the latter.

$$\text{Current ratio} = \frac{\text{current assets}}{\text{current liabilities}}$$

Where current assets is the sum of stock, debtors and cash; and current liabilities is the sum of creditors, overdrafts and any other short-term loans.

It is clear that liquidity is closely related to working capital since

Working capital = current assets − current liabilities

In the accounts for Quickeats, the first year's picture on the balance sheet shows current assets at £23 100 and current liabilities at £6690. Therefore, the current ratio for Quickeats is

$$\text{Current ratio} = \frac{23\,100}{6690} = 3.4$$

This shows current liabilities to be covered 3.4 times, and the ratio is usually expressed in the form 3.4:1. In the second year, this has come down to 2.2:1. The first year's ratio represents a business which is more able to meet its current liabilities. On the other hand, it is achieving this by having more working capital in the business and this in turn will reduce the return on capital employed (ROCE). Therefore, as with nearly everything in business, there is a tricky balance to be struck between risk (the ability to meet you financial obligations) and reward (your ROCE).

For this reason, the general rule about the current ratio is that it should be as close to 1:1 as the safe conduct of the business will allow. This will not be the same for every type of business. A shop buying in finished goods on credit and selling them for cash could run safely at 1.3:1. A manufacturer, with raw material to store and customers to finance, may need over 2:1. This is because the period between paying cash out for raw materials and receiving cash in from customers is longer in a manufacturing business than in a retail business.

Quick ratio (or acid test)

The quick ratio (or acid test) is really a 'belt and braces' ratio. In this ratio, only assets that can be realized quickly, such as debtors and cash in hand, are related to current liabilities.

$$\text{Quick ratio} = \frac{\text{debtors + cash}}{\text{current liabilities}}$$

In the Quickeats example, in year 1, we would exclude the £10 000 stock because, before it can be realized, we would need to find customers to sell to and collect in the cash. All this might take several months. So, the quick ratio for Quickeats in year 1 would be

$$\text{Quick ratio} = \frac{13\,100}{6690} = 1.9$$

If anything, this quick ratio of 1.9:1 is, perhaps, too respectable since, once again, it indicates that the business is tying up working capital in debtors and cash. This might indicate that Quickeats could be collecting payment from their customers more quickly or that the cash could be being used to invest in further growth.

Once again, general rules are very difficult to make, but a ratio of 0.8:1 would be acceptable for most types of business.

Measuring working capital

As we have seen, liquidity is closely related to working capital where

Working capital = current assets − current liabilities

The larger the difference between current assets and current liabilities the higher the current ratio − but also the higher the level of working capital. And, the higher the level of working capital, the higher the overall amount of capital that is being used. That in turn means that profits have to be that much higher to make the same (or better) return on capital employed (ROCE). The converse is also clearly true, i.e. if you can make the same profit with a lower level of working capital, then you will be achieving better ROCE.

So, tight control of working capital is a good way of improving the profitability of the business and generating funds for growth (see also Chapter 13). So, let's consider some of the key measures of how you are managing your working capital.

Average collection period (or debtor days)

Most businesses whose customers are other businesses give their customers credit (i.e. allow them to pay at some later date). This means that you create debtors (people who owe you money) from whom you need to collect cash. Since you will probably have already paid for the items which you have needed to buy in order to deliver to the customers, one of the effects is that you will be spending money before it comes back in. As a result, and as any growing business selling on credit knows, cash flow can quickly become a problem.

Surprisingly enough, bad debts (those which are never paid) are rarely as serious a problem as slow payers. Many companies think nothing of taking three months' credit, and it is important to remember that even if your terms are 30 days it will be nearer 45 days on average before you are paid. To some extent, this depends on how frequently invoices are sent out. Assuming they do not go out each day, and perhaps more importantly, that your customer batches bills for payment monthly, then that is how things will work out. This is particularly true if the customers are big companies, and that is despite the wave of legislation in many countries to encourage prompt payment.

There are several techniques for monitoring debtors, the most well used of which is the average collection period, also known as debtor days. This ratio is calculated by expressing debtors as a proportion of credit sales, and then relating that to the days in the period in question.

$$\text{Average collection period} = \frac{\text{debtors}}{\text{sales in period}} \times \text{number of days in period}$$

In our example, let's suppose that all Quickeats' sales are on credit and the periods in question are both 365-day years (i.e. no leap years). Then in year 1 the average collection period is

$$\text{Average collection period} = \frac{13\,000}{100\,000} \times 365$$

$$= 47 \text{ days}$$

And, in year 2, the average collection period is 36 days.

So, in year 2, Quickeats management are collecting their cash from debtors 11 days sooner than in year 1. This is obviously a better position to be in, making their relative amount of debtors lower than in year 1.

It is not making the absolute amount of debtors lower, and this illustrates another great strength of using ratios to monitor performance. Quickeats sales have grown by 30 per cent from £100 000 to £130 000, and their debtors have remained at £13 000. At first glance then, their debtors are the same, neither better nor worse. But, when you relate those debtors to the increased levels of sales, as this ratio does, then you can see that the position has improved.

This is a good control ratio, which has the great merit of being quickly translatable into a figure any businessperson can understand, showing how much it is costing to give credit. If, for example, Quickeats is paying 10 per cent per annum for an overdraft, then giving £13 000 credit for 36 days will cost £128.22 ((10 per cent x £13 000 x 36) ÷ 365).

Average payment period (or creditor days)

Of course, the credit world is not all one-sided. Once you have established your business, you too will be taking credit. You can usually rely on your suppliers to keep you informed on your indebtedness, but only on an individual basis.

Therefore, it is prudent to calculate how many days' credit, on average, you are taking from suppliers, i.e. the average payment period or creditor days. This is a very similar calculation to average collection period. The ratio is as follows:

$$\text{Average payment period} = \frac{\text{creditors}}{\text{purchases in period}} \times \text{number of days in period}$$

In our example, in year 1, the average payment period is:

$$\text{Average payment period} = \frac{1690}{30\,000} \times 365$$

$$= 21 \text{ days}$$

And, in year 2, the average payment period is 47 days.

The difference in these ratios probably reflects greater creditworthiness in year 2. Generally speaking, the longer the credit period you can take from your suppliers the better, provided that you still meet their terms of trade.

It's also quite useful simply to relate days' credit given to days' credit taken. If they balance out then you are about even in the credit game. In year 1, Quickeats gave 47 days' credit to their customers and took only 21 days from their suppliers, so they were a loser. In the second year, they got ahead, giving only 36 days while taking 47.

Stock (inventory) control

Any manufacturing, sub-contracting or assembling business will have to buy in raw materials and work on them to produce finished goods. They will have to keep track of three sorts of stock (or inventory): raw materials, work in progress and finished goods. By comparison, a retailing business will probably only be concerned with finished goods, and a service business may have no stock at all.

Clearly, the more stock you have, the more money (working capital) you are using simply to finance that stock. A common failing of businesses of any size is to plan production levels to get the most out of the plant and equipment without taking account of the costs involved in holding stock. There will be a direct cost in terms of borrowings while obsolete items may have to be sold at a discount, and possibly even at below cost. Equally, in periods when demand falls, be wary of attempting to keep the workforce and the plant busy. If you go on building up stock, you will face a bigger cash drain.

So, good control of your stock levels is a key element of managing your working capital.

The most commonly used ratio for measuring stock is stock days. This is the average number of days worth of stock that you are holding and can be calculated for each of raw materials, work in progress and finished goods. The calculation for finished goods is as follows

$$\text{Finished goods stock days} = \frac{\text{finished goods stock}}{\text{cost of sales in period}} \times \text{number of days}$$

Cost of sales is used because it accurately reflects the amount of stock. The overall sales figure includes other items such as profit margin and, therefore, is less accurate. Nevertheless, if you are looking at a business from the outside, it is probable that the only figure available will be that for sales and so you may have to use it as an approximation.

The same basic equation can be applied to both raw materials and work in progress stock. In the case of raw materials, you should substitute raw materials consumed for cost of sales.

If we assume that all of Quickeats's stock is in finished goods, then

$$\text{Finished goods stock days} = \frac{10\,000}{50\,000} \times 365$$

$$= 73 \text{ days}$$

In year 2, the ratio is 64 days.

It is impossible to make any general rules about stock levels. Obviously, a business has to carry enough stock to meet demand, and a retail business must have it on display or to hand. However, if Quickeats's suppliers can always deliver within say 14 days it would be unnecessary to carry 73 days' stock.

Once again, the strength of this ratio is that a business can quickly calculate how much it is costing to carry a given level of stock, in just the same way as customer credit costs are calculated.

Another way to look at stock control is to see how many times your stock is turned over each year. This ratio is almost the inverse of stock days and is calculated as follows

$$\text{Stock turn} = \frac{\text{cost of sales}}{\text{stock}}$$

So, for Quickeats this is 50 000/10 000, or 5 times a year.

Circulation of working capital

Whilst the current ratio gives an overall feel for a business's ability to pay its creditors, the manager of a business is usually more concerned with how efficiently the working capital is being used to generate sales. The most useful ratio for this is working capital circulation calculated as follows

$$\text{Working capital circulation} = \frac{\text{sales}}{\text{working capital}}$$

Remembering that working capital is equal to net current assets on the balance sheet, we can see that, for Quickeats, working capital has shrunk from £16 410 in year 1 to £14 000 in year 2. Not too dramatic. But let's now look at these figures in relation to the level of business activity (sales) in each year.

In year 1

$$\text{Working capital circulation} = \frac{100\,000}{16\,410} = 6 \text{ times}$$

and in year 2

$$\text{Working capital circulation} = \frac{130\,000}{14\,000} = 9 \text{ times}$$

We can see that not only has Quickeats got less money tied up in working capital in the second year, but it has also used it more efficiently. In other words, it has circulated it faster. Each pound of working capital produces £9 of sales in year 2, as opposed to only £6 in year 1. And as each pound of sales makes profit, the faster the working capital is turned around the higher the profit.

Measuring solvency

Just as liquidity is concerned with the short-term position, *solvency* is the term used to describe a business's long-term financial position. Trading whilst insolvent is a serious matter, and one that could strip away the protection of limited liability. The key indicators of the long-term financial position are the proportion of a business's funds that are borrowed as opposed to being put up by the shareholders, known as gearing, and how well the business is able to meet any interest costs associated with such borrowing, known as interest cover.

Gearing

The more borrowed money a business uses, as opposed to that put in by the shareholders (either through initial capital or by leaving profits in the business), the more highly geared the business is. High gearing may seem attractive in the sense that it is preferable to use someone else's money. However, borrowed money does of course need to be paid back with interest. So, highly geared businesses can be vulnerable when either sales dip sharply, as in a recession, or when interest rates rise rapidly.

Gearing is calculated as a percentage as follows

$$\text{Gearing} = \frac{\text{debt (long-term borrowings)}}{\text{debt} + \text{shareholders' funds}} \times 100$$

So, in our example, in year 1

$$\text{Gearing} = \frac{10\,000}{10\,000 + 18\,910} \times 100$$
$$= 35\%$$

Indicating that 35 per cent of the money employed in the business was borrowed. In year 2, the corresponding figure is 24 per cent.

Gearing levels for smaller businesses range on average from 60 per cent down to 30 per cent. But, many businesses entering the first stages of growth are seriously over geared leaving them exposed.

Interest cover

Whilst gearing is important, it is equally important to look at you business's ability to service the interest on the borrowing.

If you were fortunate enough to inherit £0.5 million, you could borrow another £0.5 million and buy a substantial house for £1 million and still only be 50 per cent geared. What you may find a little difficult is to find the money to pay the interest on the loan each month. Similarly, a business must be able to meet the interest on its long-term borrowings out of profit. This is known as interest cover and is calculated as follows

$$\text{Interest cover} = \frac{\text{operating profit}}{\text{interest on long-term debt}}$$

So, in our example, the interest cover in year 1 was 8 times (17 000/2150), and in year 2 it increased to nearly 12 times (24 000/2050).

Anything upwards of 4 times interest cover would be viewed as respectable, below 3 might be worrying.

Chapter summary

Before you embark on the challenges of growth, you should develop a deep understanding of the financial health of your business. A thorough analysis of the financial performance of your business, or 'financial position audit', is the best way to achieve this.

In this chapter, we have described, and given worked examples of, each of the main financial performance ratios for measuring growth, profitability, liquidity, working capital and solvency.

The calculation of these ratios for your business should point to a range of questions to be asked and areas to be further investigated. In turn, this should help you identify:

- 'quick wins' where some immediate action can result in significant gains
- whether there are specific areas of the business in which you need to take action
- how you are performing compared to the past and compared to your competitors
- the key levers that you need to pull in order to deliver growth
- the main areas of financial risk
- whether there are untapped sources of internal funds to help finance the growth (see Chapter 13 for more on this).

Assignments

1. Undertake a complete financial position audit for your business by calculating all the ratios described above for each of the last three years.
2. Are there any areas where you should take immediate action either to obtain a benefit or to reduce a risk?
3. What trends can you see? What does this tell you about what is happening in your business and its environment? What do you need to do as a result?
4. Obtain as much financial information as you can about your top three competitors and calculate the same ratios for each of them. How do your ratios compare with theirs?
5. Where competitors appear to perform better, try to find out how they are achieving this better performance.

Profit and loss account year to:	31/3 yr1 £	%	31/3 yr2 £	%
Sales	**100 000**	**100**	**130 000**	**100**
Cost of Sales				
Materials	30 000	30	43 000	33
Labour	20 000	20	25 000	19
Cost of Goods Sold	**50 000**		**68 000**	
Gross Profit	**50 000**	**50**	**62 000**	**48**
Expenses				
Rent, Rates etc	18 000		20 000	
Wages	12 000		13 000	
Advertising	3 000		3 000	
Depreciation	–		2 000	
Total Expenses	**33 000**		**38 000**	
Operating or Trading Profit	**17 000**	**17**	**24 000**	**18.5**
Deduct Interest on:				
Borrowings	**2 150**		**2 050**	
Net Profit Before Tax	**14 850**	**14.8**	**21 950**	**16.8**
Tax Paid at 20%	2 970		4 390	
Net Profit After Tax	**11 880**	**11.88**	**17 560**	**13.51**
Number of employees	**2**		**4**	

Balance sheet	at 31/3 yr1 £	at 31/3 yr2 £
NET ASSETS EMPLOYED		
Fixed Assets		
Furniture and Fixtures	12 500	30 110
Less Depreciation		2 000
Book value		28 110
Current Assets		
Stock	10 000	12 000
Debtors	13 000	13 000
Cash	100	500
Total Current Assets	**23 100**	**25 500**

Balance sheet	at 31/3 yr1 £	at 31/3 yr 2 £
Less **Current Liabilities**		
Overdraft	5 000	6 000
Creditors	1 690	5 500
Total Current Liabilities	**6 690**	**11 500**
Net Current Assets	**16 410**	**14 000**
Total Assets	**28 910**	**42 110**
less creditors over 1 year		
Long-term bank loan	10 000	10 000
Net total assets	18 910	32 110
FINANCED BY		
Owner's Capital	10 000	18 940
Profit Retained (Reserves)	8 910	13 170
Total Owner's capital	**18 910**	**32 110**

Table 2.7.2

(continued)

8 Do you know how you win business?

Introduction and objectives

Having successfully got into business, you are obviously winning some orders from some customers. And, we use the word 'winning' here very deliberately – you are always competing for customers' business since they always have the choice of spending their money elsewhere or not at all. So, one of the key questions you need to address is 'What are the factors which enable you to win those orders?'

In every market, there are typically a limited number of factors that are the keys to competing successfully. How well any one firm performs in terms of each factor ultimately determines whether it has a sustainable business. 'Sustainable' is, of course, a relative term: over the long run, say, 50 years, 90 per cent of firms may go out of business. But, a lifespan of 20 years is a perfectly attainable target, and long enough for most company founders to realize some of the value they have created.

The key factors for success are those things which matter to customers (or your customers' customers) and for which they are willing to pay. When starting a business, the management team will have a view on what it is that customers really want, usually supported by market research. That view may, however, alter once the business is trading, and the feedback from customers comes in. As the business grows, the relationship with some of these early customers will also mature. As a result, what you need to do to ensure that these customers remain loyal to you, may also change.

By the end of this chapter, you should have a good understanding of the following key topics:

- Key factors for success in winning business.

- Benchmarking yourself against the competition.

- The performance indicators you need to use to track how well you are doing.

- The customer life cycle and the actions you can take to enhance your customers' loyalty to you.

- How to keep track of competitors as they change too.

Case Study

When Angus Thirlwell and Peter Harris set up their own direct delivery gift business, Choc-Express*, they were keen to retain control over the supply chain. They partnered with Thornton's, the UK's leading independent manufacturer and retailer of chocolate, who already supplied the company with bulk chocolate. Thornton's customers who wanted to send chocolates as a gift could pick up a ChocExpress leaflet at any Thornton's shop. ChocExpress would then handle all aspects of processing and fulfilling the order.

For Thornton's, the partnership allowed them to offer an additional service to their customers without major investment. For ChocExpress, the partnership provided national marketing and distribution reach that leveraged Thornton's brand and market presence. ChocExpress were entering a market for delivered gifts estimated at £500 million annually, and dominated by Interflora. Having a large partner was likely to prove an important competitive asset.

Angus and Peter believed that their existing business had two key strengths which would translate into success in the market:

- excellent marketing, which presented and sold the chocolates in a compelling way
- an ability to innovate and constantly surprise their customers with appealing new products.

Within a short time of being in the market, however, it became clear that there was another factor which was key to success: delivery to the right person, at the right time, of an undamaged product. No matter how good the chocolates, if they went to the wrong address, or arrived damaged or a day late, the recipient's gift was ruined. If the recipient's gift was ruined, the sender's day was also spoiled, creating not just one, but two unhappy customers! Suddenly 'the last mile' looked like it could be the most important success factor of all in this business.

*renamed Hotel Chocolat

Key success factors (KSF) and benchmarking against the competition

As the business grows and the number of customers and products offered increases management needs to check that the 'key success factors' (KSF) which helped establish the business are still the most important from the customers' point of view.

One way to do this is shown in Table 2.8.1. You can list the main success factors in your market and rank their importance as shown in the example. Then attempt to do the same for two or three nearest competitors. What customers require should then be translated into the internal tasks necessary for the company to satisfy these requirements and to monitor how well you are doing.

There are several important points to bear in mind when using this approach:

1. Most small(er) businesses start by making a subjective assessment: that is, they complete the table using the opinion of the management team. That is no bad thing, since this tool can be used to make explicit the assumptions about competitors held by different people in the business.

Table 2.8.1			Your business	Competitor A	Competitor B	Competitor C
Using key success factors to rank your business and your competitors: an example	Key success factors (KSF)	Rank importance of KSF	(Score out of 10: yourself and your main competitors)			
	KSF1 An affordable price	50%	9	9	5	5
	KSF2 Rapid response	25%	7	6	7	8
	KSF3 Broad product range	15%	7	6	6	7
	KSF4 Innovation in the market	10%	5	7	7	6
	TOTAL (weighted average, % × score)[1]	100%	7.8	7.6	5.9	6.2

Note: The factors, ranking and scores are examples only and are used simply to demonstrate how this technique works. In order to use this technique on your business you will have to identify the factors that are key in your market, their relative importance to customers and how you rate against the competition.
[1]To calculate weighted average multiply each score by KSF per cent, e.g.:

Your business KSF1 is 50% × 9 = 4.50
Your business KSF2 is 25% × 7 = 1.75
Your business KSF3 is 15% × 7 = 1.05
Your business KSF4 is 10% × 5 = 0.5

Weighted average = 7.80

(You must choose the weighting. In most markets there is usually one dominant success factor which accounts for 50 per cent or more of the buying decision.)

When using this on management development programmes, we have often found that managers in the same company have very different perceptions about a) who their competitors are and b) the strengths and weaknesses of different competitors. The resulting discussion usually sharpens the focus on competitors dramatically.

2. If it is possible to feed into this exercise the perceptions of customers (because you have, for example, the results of a recent customer survey), then do so: you will have a much more robust set of conclusions. If you have no such data, a good proxy is usually the opinion of either your salesforce, if they sell direct, or any intermediaries who sell through to the end users. These are, after all, the people who are closest to the customer. You will need, however, to conduct some kind of customer survey to have real confidence in the conclusions (or to modify them if your customers challenge your assumptions).

3. If you have a business which competes in different markets or different market segments, where the buying criteria are clearly not the same, you are best to do this exercise separately for each market or segment. Trying to do something at too general level will not produce useful conclusions and you won't be able to turn these conclusions into action.

4. Beware the inevitable temptation to flatter yourself about how good your business is versus the competition. In surveys of car drivers, most respondents consistently rate themselves as above average drivers (although women are less inclined to do so than men!). This is another reason why your conclusions should be confirmed by what the market thinks.

To revert to the example in Table 2.8.1, what might you conclude from this analysis, and how might that be usefully turned into action?

In general terms, this market is price- and time-sensitive. New product development and a wide assortment of products to choose from are not particularly important, possibly because there is a lack of demand for these things or perhaps because suppliers have not focused much on innovation in the past.

In competitive terms, it looks like our business comes head to head with competitor A: the total scores are very close, and the two firms lead the market in terms of price. Competitors B and C compete on other factors, and may well serve less-price-sensitive customers who will pay more for response or for product innovation.

To take each key success factor (KSF) in turn, and the possible implications for this hypothetical business:

1. *KSF1*: We are clearly very competitive on price. Trying to lower price further would most likely reduce profitability and could precipitate a price war. Would we be sure of winning it? On the other hand, to remain a price leader, we need to monitor our unit costs very carefully. We need to check our intelligence on competitor A to see that they are not driving their cost base significantly below ours (through automation or outsourcing, for example). If they do, we need to find strategies to match them.

2. *KSF2*: We outperform A on this factor, but C are better still. What could we learn from their operation that we could incorporate into ours? Is there some extra value in improved response times for which a section of our market would be prepared to pay, if the offer is carefully packaged? Alternatively, we should look at targeting C's customer base to see whether we could offer them a similar level of service but at a significantly better price. Looking at the price comparison between us and them, we should have the scope to undercut them and make money.

3. *KSF3*: We seem to meet the market's needs on this factor. However, no supplier seems to do this very well at the moment. Are we too complacent? A new entrant might identify this as the weak spot and choose to enter with a significantly wider offer. Perhaps we should look carefully at other national markets to see whether there are any players capable of doing this. One strategy to pre-empt this might be to license their products for sale in our market.

4. *KSF4*: This KSF links closely with the last KSF. Improved product coverage usually results from innovation, and we are notably poor at new product development. This looks like the point of greatest vulnerability. Just because the market currently doesn't place much value

on innovation, doesn't mean it won't react favourably to significantly better technology in the future. Our business is a follower, not a leader in this area. We should investigate ways to improve this. If the company culture is such that we will never become a leader in new product development, then we need to look at alternatives such as licensing, or co-development with a partner.

Key performance indicators

Monitoring the achievement of the company on key success factors is, we believe, one of the key requirements for the growing company. Monthly financial accounts are an essential indicator of the overall health of the company, but they do not pinpoint in the same way the areas where remedial action should be taken. Key success factors can frequently be measured and monitored through *key performance indicators*. These vary from one industry to another. Retailers, for example, traditionally measure their performance by stock turnover, sales per square metre and profit per square metre. Big operators will monitor these figures store by store and weekly, if not daily. Airlines measure their load factor (filled passenger capacity per flight) and yield (income per head per flight), hotels their occupancy rates. There are also 'softer' performance indicators, such as staff perceptions or customer satisfaction scores, which may be no less important in measuring how your business is performing over time. Your choice of key performance indicators will depend on the following:

- What are the norms in your industry?
- What are the key success factors (typically closely related to the norms)?
- What else is important for you to measure, in that it tracks the ways that you are different from or better than the competition?
- What can be measured and what will yield useful information at an affordable cost?

Large companies are notorious for collecting huge amounts of data which are filed and forgotten. The growing business cannot afford this luxury. Information is only worth collecting if it can be gathered (relatively) cheaply, efficiently and can be turned into action that will benefit the business.

Case Study

In the fast food business there are a number of key performance indicators which firms use to monitor and measure their performance. Two of the most important are:

- average transaction value
- average customer waiting time.

Average transaction value is key to profitability. Even if the gross margin is high – and in fast food operations it could be 70 per cent or more – if the average transaction value is too low the business will never sell enough to cover its fixed costs. That is why fast food operators are constantly offering their customers 'meal

▶

deals', carefully packaged food and drink offerings which encourage people to raise their spending from, say, £3.95 to £4.95 per transaction. Meal deals allow the operator to 'flex' the offering depending on the time of day, the different gross margins of the different menu items, and the type of purchase (for adults, for children, for groups and so forth).

Average customer waiting time is also critical. Fast food is, after all, supposed to be fast! All the big franchise chains, such as McDonald's, set strict boundaries on what is the maximum time a customer can be expected to wait (in fact franchisees who consistently fail inspection on this parameter can forfeit their franchises in some businesses). Customers who find themselves at the end of a long or slow-moving queue will soon drift off elsewhere.

In his first few months of operation at Real Burger World, Naz Choudhury paid constant attention to these two performance indicators, and regularly adjusted both the menu offering and the staffing rotas as he learned more. These measures still get his full attention, day in, day out.

Welcome complaints!

It may sound strange, but you should welcome complaints with open arms. In Tom Peters' classic *In Search of Excellence*, the highly regarded New England retailer Stu Leonard says: 'The customer who complains is our best friend'. Why? Because the customer complaint is the 'last chance for you to complete the sale', to put things right. As far back as the early 1990s, McKinsey research showed that companies lose two-thirds of their customers, not because of product quality or unsatisfactory price but simply through indifference to customer complaints. Well over 80 per cent of customers would re-purchase if their complaints were quickly resolved. More to the point, disappointed customers tell their friends. The customer may not always be right, but you need to hear what they have to say if they are unhappy.

The systems that you create for monitoring and responding to complaints will reflect your management style. Whether you prefer to do this formally or informally, you as the top management will need to explain to your staff that complaints are to be seen primarily as a way to improve the business, not as a device to punish them. If your staff see every complainant as a nuisance or, worse, a threat, then they will have good reason to make sure that you never learn from them.

The customer life cycle

Put a frog in a saucepan of tepid water, raise the temperature slowly and continuously, and eventually the frog will boil to death. Incremental changes in the heat of the water do not cause the frog to react by leaping out: its body adapts. Pointing out that customers and competitors change over time may seem like a statement of the obvious – but we have seen too many firms go out of business because they left it too late to react to changes in their environment.

A firm's relationship with individual customers changes over time. Consider Table 2.8.2.

| Table 2.8.2 | Customer life cycle |

	Courtship	Engagement	Honeymoon	Wedlock	Either deadlock	Or re-kindled relationship
Customer attitude	Suspicious	Moderately suspicious	Trusting	Boring	Disenchanted	Newly interested
Supplier objective	Get first order	Get repeat order	Increase sales volume	Maintain sales	Sell in new products	Rebuild commitment

Source: Adapted from Alan Melkman (2001) *Strategic Customer Planning*

The relationship with someone who becomes a significant customer is in some respects like a marriage. At first, a potential customer's attitude to your company is likely to be cautious, if not suspicious (think back to the McGraw-Hill corporate advertisement described earlier in Chapter 4). If you convince the customer to place a first order, that caution or suspicion will reduce. It is unlikely to change immediately to an attitude of complete trust until you have successfully satisfied a number of repeat orders. There then follows a period of 'honeymoon', when the relationship works well for both parties. If problems occur at this stage they are quickly resolved, with goodwill on both sides. Unfortunately, that state of contentment cannot be taken for granted. Over time the relationship can slip into boredom or disenchantment, just as couples who cannot make their marriage work fall out of love.

If you think this analogy is a bit fanciful, stop for a moment and reflect on your own behaviour as a consumer. How many brands of goods and services do you remain consistently loyal to over a long period of time? If you are a typical consumer, the answer is precious few. Most of us like a balance in our lives between the familiar and the new, and the attachment to what we already know can often be supplanted by what we see as a better or more interesting alternative.

The most likely causes of commercial disenchantment are failure to communicate – through visits, newsletters, telephone calls and so forth – or inadequate improvements to products and services as they age. The British motorcycle industry of the 1960s saw its business melt away as consumers turned instead to Japanese and continental imports. British producers 'knew' that 'real' motorbikes were big, noisy and oily, and that's what they carried on making. Most British motorbike consumers knew that they wanted a quiet, clean, reliable mode of transport. American car manufacturers suffered a similar shock in the 1980s. America, after all, invented mass automobile production, and the big car US companies had always taken their domestic market for granted. But brand loyalty fast disappeared when consumers were presented with the alternative of cheap, efficient, Japanese models that better fitted their lifestyle.

For your business, it may be a stimulus to action to categorize your major customers broadly by these stages. The quickest way to re-kindle sales may be through re-launching the relationship, by researching and re-analysing customer needs in the wedlock and deadlock stages – before you lose the business to competitive suppliers. When too many people in your firm begin to think primarily of your established customers as 'debtors', rather than the reason why you are in business, take this as a warning sign. In *How to Handle Major Customers Profitably* Alan Melkman has several positive suggestions to make as to how to 'revive' the relationship (and sales!). These include:

- finding reasons to re-visit
- sharing market information
- developing joint promotional activities with key customers
- initiating or strengthening electronic buy/sell link.

All of the above are aimed at building barriers to customers seeking alternative suppliers.

Competitors change too!

Equally, your competitors do not stand still. They will also be seeking to improve their products and services and the ways in which they win business. As a result, you will need to repeat the KSF analysis outlined above on a regular basis to take account of these changes.

In addition, the competitors themselves may change over time, as new entrants or substitute products or services appear in your market. Some of the more tried and tested methods for keeping track of competitors are:

- buy and analyse their products and services
- visit trade exhibitions
- ask customers what they think about your competitors
- work with them, in trade associations, in pursuit of higher trade standards! This might, at least, not only serve the customer needs better, but by raising standards, build barriers to entry to new competitors in your market.

Stu Leonard, who we mentioned before, organizes staff visits, by specially ordered buses, to major competitor store openings.

Chapter summary

Thoroughly understanding how you win business with your customers, compared to other alternative ways in which they could meet their needs, is fundamental to successful growth. In this chapter, we have looked at key success factors (i.e. the limited number of factors which are the keys to winning business). Identifying these factors from your customers' point of view, and using them as a means of outperforming your competitors, will unlock potential for growth in your business.

We've also looked at how to develop key performance indicators from the success factors so that you track your performance and turn knowledge rapidly into action.

And, just like your business, your customers and competitors do not stand still. Relationships mature and people move on. On the other hand, retaining customers tends to lead to greater profits than constantly seeking to acquire new customers. The customer relationship life cycle should help you understand the changing relationship with your customers and what you can do to increase customer loyalty.

Assignments

Key success factors and performance indicators

1. From your customers' point of view, list the three or four main reasons they buy from your company.
2. Calculate your company's KSF score compared with your main competitors.
3. List the two or three main key performance indicators (KPIs), coming from your KSF analysis, which you should check regularly to ensure the health of your company.

Customer life cycle

4. How do you research, or keep in touch, with your major customers and their changing needs?
5. Name and classify your major customers under the following categories: *courtship, engagement, honeymoon, wedlock, deadlock.*
6. What market segments are still open for you to exploit?

Competitors

7. How do your major competitors' products and services satisfy customers' needs?
8. What do you see as your major competitors' principal weaknesses?
9. What changes have your major competitors made in the last 12 months in their competitive approaches?
10. How are you regularly tracking major competitors' activities?

Suggested further reading

Melkman, Alan (2001) *Strategic Customer Planning*, London, Thorogood.
Peters, Thomas and Robert Waterman (1988) *In Search of Excellence*, New York: Warner Books.
Porter, Michael E (1998) *On Competition*, Boston: Harvard Business School Press.

9 How can you further develop your distinctiveness?

Introduction and objectives

In the previous chapter, we considered *how* you win, that is, why your customers choose to spend their money with you rather than with someone else or not at all. As we have seen, this will be because, in some way, your product or service matches their needs in a distinctive way which is better than the alternatives. In this chapter, we will concentrate on exploring how successful firms further develop their distinctiveness and customer focus.

Focusing on your customer, and delivering distinctive value for them, is the very essence of marketing and marketing planning. And yet, a survey conducted in 1997 by Cranfield School of Management and Kellock Factoring ('Putting the case for SME financing: a survey of smaller companies' views and wishes') highlighted the fact that fewer than half of companies with turnover under £5 million (approximately €7 million) employ formal marketing planning.

By the end of this chapter, you should have a clear understanding of the following key topics in developing distinctiveness and customer focus:

- Developing customer segments and product/service quality.

- Optimizing price and margins.

- Promotional activities.

- Distinctive distribution.

- Improving the effectiveness of the sales team.

Of course, not all of these components applies equally to every business. There is no single formula for achieving competitive advantage. It is the role of top management (in the small growing business, that usually means you, the entrepreneur) to decide where are the opportunities for the business, and how these should be integrated into the marketing and sales targets set out in the marketing plan.

Developing customer segments and product/service quality

Through continuing analysis and segmentation of your customers, you will be best placed to identify new product/service offerings which will grow your business – but do not compromise your points of difference in the market. It is even possible to turn what look like threats to your business into opportunities.

Case Study

Cobra Beer is a remarkable success story. Its founder, Karan Bilimoria, is an Indian national with no formal training in brewing who chose to launch a beer brand in the most competitive beer market in the world: the UK. No wonder that the company's motto is 'to aspire and achieve – against all odds.'

The original idea for the business came from the fact that Karan was frustrated by not being able to find the right sort of beer to drink while eating curry. All the hundreds of different beers on the market were too 'gassy'. Karan decided to make his own beer and believed that there would be many other consumes who would want to drink it too. He also decided that his beer would be distinctively 'Indian' – extra-smooth and less gassy.

India has a well-established brewing heritage and Karan ended up by importing a beer brewed to his exact requirements. He decided to trademark the name 'Cobra' because of its distinctly Indian connotations. He was also obliged to use a 660 ml glass bottle, not a standard size for the British trade, because that was the only readily available format suitable for export from India. This worked to his advantage, as things turned out, since the large Cobra bottles were highly visible on restaurant tables and their distinctly Indian shape and colour lent authenticity to the product.

The business focused on selling to the Indian restaurant trade. Through hard work and sheer determination the numbers of customers steadily rose. By 1997, Cobra was brewed under licence in the UK, and was available in both draft and bottled form, allowing the brand to penetrate an estimated 80 per cent of Britain's 8000 Indian restaurants. Big supermarket buyers were also starting to show an interest in stocking the Cobra brand.

In 2000, the Cobra management team felt that they needed to take some strategic decisions about the company's portfolio if the rate of growth was to be maintained. Although ten years old, Cobra was still exclusively a beer business. The restaurant customers loved the brand, because it allowed their customers both to drink and eat greater quantities, and a growing number of consumers had adopted it as their first choice of beverage to drink with curry.

However, analysis of the market showed that long-term trends were against them. Beer sales in the UK were in gradual decline. Sales of wine, however, had been steadily rising over the decade. In Karan's experience, the basic choice that diners made was between drinking beer and drinking wine. It was clear that the balance was being tipped more and more towards wine. The strategic choice for Cobra was this: do we fight the wine challenge or do we turn this into a business opportunity? The answer was to create their own range of red and white wines. Research told them that the choice of wines in many Indian restaurants was poor. Cobra would offer a range of good value table wines, on which the restaurant owners could make good margins, and which the restaurants could effectively present as their

▶

own house wines. The wines were branded 'General Bilimoria', and dedicated to Karan's father, Lt. General F. N. Bilimoria, PVSM, ADC.

Launched during late 2000, the wines proved a huge success. In the words of Karan Bilimoria: 'The Cobra beer brand has not suffered at all – in fact it's stronger than ever. What we are now is a broadly based beverages business, with even better potential to grow'. In 2003, the company had sales of over £50 million at retail price and offices in the UK, the US, India and South Africa. Many entrepreneurs would feel that they had come a long way at this point: Karan reckons he has only just begun. By 2010, the company target is $1 billion sales worldwide!

Quality challenges

For any business, quality is not merely a 'nice to have'. Accustomed to continual improvements in every area of consumption, today's customers have very little tolerance of poor quality. Just because you're a smaller growing business, don't expect that your customers will see your offering any differently from that of larger competitors. Sticking with the beer market, mark the words of James Koch of the Boston Beer Company. He observed that the biggest problem for the new and growing company was in creating in customers' minds an image of quality. 'You can't sell a product you don't believe in and in cold calling the only thing standing between you and the customer's scorn is the integrity of your product'.

Nevertheless, delivering superior quality entails an endless battle or trade-off against cost and service levels. In this battle you have to seek improvements along two, or even all three, dimensions simultaneously.

In the words of Real Burger World co-founder Naz Choudhury, 'to succeed in our market, we had to look and feel like a big brand from day one'. This would demand significant investment. Real Burger World's desired target positioning is in the low cost, high differentiation segment, as shown in Figure 2.9.1.

High costs with low differentiation is clearly the box to avoid!

Differentiation is also the fundamental rationale behind building strong brands, whether these are products or services (such as Cobra Beer), or the company itself. Brands build reputation and trust, for which customers are prepared to pay extra.

The quality of your offering is not, of course, just what you do, but also *how you do it*. Jan Carlson of Scandinavian Airways (SAS) pioneered the concept of

	DIFFERENTIATION	
	Low	High
Low	OK *e.g. kebab van*	Superb *RBW target positioning*
COSTS		
High	Awful *e.g. unbranded hamburger outlet*	OK *e.g. Pizza Express*

Figure 2.9.1

Differentiation in the fast food market

'moments of truth', when a customer experiences the reality of who you are and what you do. This is illustrated in Table 2.9.1.

At the moment of truth there is no hiding place. This is especially the case in the airline industry, where typically 80 per cent of staff have direct and regular contact with customers. There is no substitute for spending time and resources (chiefly, but not exclusively, money) on instilling a culture of quality within a business. In the early days, this tends to be absorbed informally by employees, through observing and copying the behaviour of the boss. As the business grows and the number of employees increases informality has to give away to formal processes, like employee induction and training programmes, as new recruits are told 'how we do things around here'.

Case Study

David Courteen and Steve Taylor founded Fitness Express in 1987, and spent the next 13 years building the business. Both graduates in sports science, they focused on a particular niche in the health and leisure industry. Their market was independent hotels who wished to offer their clients health and fitness centres, but who did not have the expertise to manage them. David and Steve would staff and run each centre under contract, rewarded through a mixture of fee and profit share.

As the business grew, so a clear formula started to evolve. Firstly, each centre was carefully tailored to appeal to a clearly defined market segment. This might be predominantly a family membership, or older people in retirement who felt intimidated by the atmosphere in a typical fitness centre. Secondly, good systems and procedures were essential to ensuring that every member had a positive and high-quality experience every time he or she came. Happy members translated into renewed subscriptions, which translated into profitable business. Thirdly, Fitness Express's continuing

success depended crucially on high-quality staff: on recruiting, training and retaining the right people.

In particular, Fitness Express employed the UK government backed Investors in People (see www.investorsinpeople.com) method to formalize staff management. The training in health and safety, swimming pool supervision, and so on led their staff to obtain formal qualifications and to improve their career prospects in sports management. As a result, Fitness Express's staff retention rate, at 67 per cent per annum, was twice the industry average.

In 2001, David and Steve sold their business to Crown Sports plc, a large, diversified sports group, which was fast building a network of health and fitness clubs. The value placed on the business, approximately £4 million, was considerably greater than the value of the contracts under management. The difference reflected the quality of the systems, procedures, people and ways of managing staff which David and Steve had put in place – and which Crown wanted to see in the rest of their clubs.

Customer retention and adding value

Both academic studies and our personal experience of working with literally hundreds of smaller businesses tell us the same thing: in almost every case, it costs less, much less, to retain your existing customers than it does to acquire new ones. This is especially so in business-to-business markets. Yet, we are constantly

Customer contact point	Customer expectation	
Sales	Reliability	
Invoices	Responsiveness	What does the customer think of you at each contact point, at each 'moment of truth?'
Telephone	Competence	
Reception	Courtesy	
Packaging	Credibility	
Delivery	Security, tangibles	

Table 2.9.1

Jan Carlson's 'moments of truth'

surprised by how little time, effort and money many firms devote to keeping the customers they already have. It is now over ten years since a McKinsey study demonstrated convincingly that the biggest reason why industrial customers defect is because they feel neglected by their existing suppliers. Yet, many people still don't seem to have got the message.

Ask yourself this: would you rather spend £100 on creating a really good offer for a valued existing customer, or £1000 to recruit a new customer to replace the valued customer you just lost? The arithmetic speaks for itself. Below are some simple but effective guidelines to help you think about keeping the customers you value, and adding value to your product/service offering.

1. Stop asking the question 'How can our customers make money for us?' – which is how most companies look at the issue most of the time – and start asking the question 'How can we make money for our customers?'. (If you are selling direct to consumers, you might re-frame that question as 'How can we improve the quality or lower the cost?'.) To revert to the Cobra Beer example cited above: when Karan Bilimoria decided to add wines to his portfolio, he was also creating an opportunity for several thousand restaurateurs to offer a profitable new range of beverages to their customers. Unsurprisingly, they were happy to stock the products.

2. Early on, in Section 1 of this book, we pointed out that a powerful way of identifying opportunities at the start of a business idea is through asking 'Where is the pain?' That is, where are the real irritants, big or small, that you can help your customers deal with? If you are not constantly re-addressing that question, you should be. The only way you will find out is by being out there in the marketplace, constantly talking to your customers.

3. By focusing on identifying and creating value for the customer, you will find new reasons to talk to – and sell to – your customers. That value does not necessarily have to be a radical enhancement of what you are already offering. The UK kitchenware retailer, Lakeland Ltd, has built a very successful €140 million-plus business through offering its customers a continuing range of innovative products sourced from around the world. Very few involve breakthrough new technology, but incrementally they make household management easier and more pleasant. As a result,

Lakeland mails customers seven or eight times a year with new catalogues, as opposed to the single catalogue of twenty years before.

Challenges for services

One advantage which product-based businesses like Cobra have over service-based businesses is that they can easily make their differences tangible and visible. Service businesses such as Fitness Express are inherently more difficult to differentiate. Because they are intangible, services are often seen as a commodity. One insurance policy document, for example, looks fundamentally the same as the next one. Services are usually difficult to test or assess in advance and customers even play a role in determining the quality and delivery of a service: the quality of the service you receive from an advertising agency, for instance, is usually closely related to the quality of the briefing. To build differentiation in a service business, therefore, requires strong, consistent branding. The company name is frequently the brand and everything which the customer sees – the product literature, the company offices, any tangible 'evidence' of the uniqueness of that offering – has to work to strengthen the image of the brand. It is no accident that banks generally occupy big impressive offices: the subliminal message to the depositor is that this is a solid, enduring institution where your money will be safe. If you are able to make the company name synonymous with good quality, you will make the 'service' more tangible. After all, at the end of the day, your company name and reputation may be the only difference between you and your competitors.

Price and margin optimization

We have seen how you can further develop your distinctiveness by careful focus on the needs of different target groups of customers, and through attention to quality. In the minds of most customers, quality is closely linked to price. Intuitively, we make judgements about the quality of a product or service based on the price relative to other offers in the marketplace. Charge too much for the quality, and your offer is not competitive. But, charge too little, and there is an equal danger that your offer is perceived to be of low quality.

A business which has been trading for some time usually has a good idea of where to pitch its prices in the market. If that business is also trading profitably, then normally it has high enough gross margins to support its overheads and to allow for necessary re-investment.

Beware, however, the danger of 'price leakage'. In many companies, sales force bonuses depend on sales volume, rather than profitable accounts. Discounts for order size, discounts for early payment, 'loss leaders', can all chip away at the margin. Be ruthless in examining your firm's discount policies and determining whether they can really be justified.

Margin enhancement by focusing on the most profitable customers

It is not just across the board pricing and discounting that affect profitability. Even quite mature businesses are frequently unaware of other profit opportunities that they are missing. All customers are not necessarily created equal, certainly as far as margins are concerned. In many businesses the 80:20 rule applies: 80 per cent of the profit is produced by 20 per cent of the customers (and this is often true of the product range as well). But, how many businesses actually know who their most profitable customers are, and which areas of business they should concentrate on?

Case Study

Many businesses simply don't realize that they already have the information they need to improve their profit performance.

Giles Latchford established Hidden Resource (www.hiddenresource.co.uk) in 2003. It is a consultancy that specializes in the analysis of data which client companies can use to improve their profitability. He discovered this business opportunity through a project undertaken during his MBA programme at Cranfield. What follows is his account of what he found.

The client for the MBA project designed jewellery and marketed a range of 150-plus products to the UK public via press advertising (one-page, product-specific, magazine adverts) and direct mail.

It had been trading since 1999 and in that time accumulated over 45 000 transactions with 5000 separate customers, through 150 separate adverts and numerous mail shots. So there was plenty of data to work with! The primary issue was that the company wanted to improve the return on its magazine campaigns. It also wanted to increase the number of campaigns per year that it was engaging in. This meant raising funds from a VC (*venture capital*) firm to increase working capital. However, there was a sense that the process was not working that well, and that, if they could improve the bottom line, they would be better placed to raise the additional money.

We were commissioned to identify: first, who their most important customers were; and second, which publications they should focus on for their future advertising.

The analysis immediately highlighted a previously unidentified regional demand for their products in the UK. Sales in this area were 23 per cent more profitable than the national average. On the other hand, the client was unaware that any customers were loss making. We were able to demonstrate that actual contribution per customer (profit before overheads) ranged from a loss of £100 to a profit of £200. Half the total profit came from the 20 per cent most profitable customers, and only accounted for 21 per cent of total acquisition costs. On the 25 per cent least profitable customers the company only broke even – but these accounted for 30 per cent of total acquisition costs.

Our analysis proved that there was no historical relationship between acquisition cost and profitability. This had a profound impact on the client's approach to advertising! We were then able to illustrate a hierarchy of profit-generating publications, and this in turn enabled our client to become far more specific with their marketing campaigns.

The analysis took less than one month to perform and the client implemented the recommendations with immediate effect. The cost of the analysis represented a small fraction of the increased profit gained from the results. The company was then in a position to decide which products should be targeted to which customers and through which publications. The bottom line impact has resulted in a substantial increase in shareholder's return on equity. Crucially, this process enabled the company to present a much more attractive proposition to potential VC partners.

Promotional activities

Word-of-mouth marketing

Many owner-managers of growing businesses rely on a small range of promotional activities. By far the most popular is 'word-of-mouth' i.e. one of your existing customers (or suppliers, etc.) recommending you to someone else. While this approach to promotion may appear to run contrary to some of the more formalized approaches advocated by marketing professionals who work with large businesses, for the owner-managed growing business, there is much to be said for it.

Firstly, it appears to work! Many surveys have consistently shown that the number one source of new customers for smaller business is recommendations from existing customers, suppliers and other referrers.

Secondly, word-of-mouth marketing also seems to fit more closely with the characteristics of many owner-managers who have strong preferences for personal contact and direct interchange with customers rather than impersonal mass promotions. This leads to strong conversational relationships with customers in which owner-managers can listen, and respond, to the real voice of the customer. This closeness to the customers also tends to lead to real understanding of the customers' needs. And such understanding of the customers' needs is at the very heart of successful marketing. For many owner-managed businesses, this personal contact between the owner and the customer can represent a unique selling point of the business – in other words, it is the very reason that the customers buy.

Thirdly, word-of-mouth marketing tends to lead to a slow build up of new business and, hence a slower pace of growth. This means that the business is in a better position to manage the resources required to meet the new and increased demand.

Finally, and perhaps most importantly for the growing business, word-of-mouth marketing costs very little. Referrals incur, few, if any, additional direct costs.

On the other hand, word-of-mouth marketing also has disadvantages:

- It is self-limiting. This is the flip-side of the fact that word-of-mouth leads to a slow build up. If a growing business is dependent on recommendations for new customers, then its growth will almost certainly be limited to those markets and segments in which the sources of recommendations operate.
- It is difficult to plan and control. You can try to influence what other people say about you and your business, but you can't control what they say, when they say it, or to whom they say it.

Nevertheless, the ambitious owner-manager will employ a range of pro-active and planned methods to encourage referrals and recommendations such as:

- explicitly asking for referrals from existing customers (e.g. 'Do you know anyone else who might be interested in what we do?')
- 'refer a friend' schemes where referrers are rewarded for introducing a new customer

- asking for citations and recommendations which you can use on sales literature
- offering merchandise carrying your brand (for example pens, mugs) which your customer uses, thus exposing the brand to others
- building a favourable image of your business in the marketplace in order to encourage positive word-of-mouth messages about you. The most important thing you can do here is to ensure that you always deliver on your promises to customers at the quality required. In addition, there may be ways in which your business can participate in local community events, trade events, charity events, etc. all of which contribute to the image of your business.

More formal marketing approaches

As a result of this preference for word-of-mouth marketing and personal contact, owner-managers of growing businesses tend to spend significant amounts of their time in direct contact with customers. However, as the business grows, other more formal marketing approaches may also be valuable.

For historical reasons, marketing budgets are often split between advertising, referred to as 'above the line' activities, and promotional, or 'below the line' activities. As a general rule, advertising campaigns are aimed at building long-term customers, while sales promotions are typically short-term activities designed to achieve quick results. Determining the most effective ways of spending your money is equally important in each case.

Below the line marketing activities

Most growing businesses will spend more on sales promotion techniques than on advertising. Some typical aims of sales promotions are to speed up stock movement, encourage repeat purchases, get bills paid on time and induce trial purchase. The target customers for such schemes vary. For example, your target customers may be trade buyers but also your own employees and you may be offering money (prizes, bonuses), goods (gifts, vouchers) or even services (free training, free services). However, for the growing business, promotional opportunities that stimulate interest and awareness among new and existing purchasers, at lowest cost, are the most important. While discounting to move discontinued or slow moving lines may be necessary from time to time, the main positive promotional activities would include:

1. ensuring all your company 'small items' are co-ordinated and convey the same image and message, from business cards to Christmas cards
2. participating in exhibitions, with specially-designed leaflets and brochures
3. experimenting with direct mail and/or email, using lists generated from data-bases, and tele-marketing
4. having a website which is aligned with your overall business image and attracts enquiries.

Most smaller, growing businesses do not have thousands of customers. For this reason, in such businesses, the most appropriate use of marketing money is usually direct marketing, to a market segment you can clearly identify. Before you start, the most important thing is to be absolutely clear about the action you are hoping to encourage the customer to take. If you want the customer to make a purchase based on the direct marketing, make sure that there are minimal obstacles to their actually buying – and plenty of reasons why they should. If the purpose is to generate enquiries, make sure that there is an efficient mechanism in place to handle and follow up the calls and emails.

Your company's website

Even if yours is not an internet-based business, such as Moonpig or InternetCamerasDirect, your website will be an increasingly important promotional tool. Indeed, many of the smallest of start-up businesses often now have a website right from the start. On the other hand, it is not absolutely necessary for every business to have a website. Nevertheless, given the all-pervasive nature of the world wide web and the internet, in many industries and sectors, it has become a minimum expectation that a business will have a website. It is also increasingly the case that customers, suppliers and potential new staff members will look at your website as part of their deciding whether to work with you. In effect, websites have become one of Jan Carlson's 'moments of truth'. So, having a site which is attractive, welcoming and easy to use can be an advantage in the initial skirmishes of 'the battle for the customer' and 'the battle to recruit talented people'.

In addition, websites are one of the few places in which smaller growing businesses can compete on a 'level playing field' with bigger businesses since, on the internet, no one knows how big (or small) you are. The flip-side of this is that there is nowhere to hide. Unlike most other marketing and promotional tools, your website is accessible to anyone and everyone who has internet access.

It is now relatively easy, and not very costly, to develop a basic website either yourself or by making use of the services of a web designer. However, the key decisions are not technical ones, neither are they artistic/design ones.

The key to successful exploitation of websites and the internet is to see them simply as one more element of your overall promotional, sales and distribution activities. The way you use your website should be integrated with other business activities and closely linked to the way in which you seek to distinguish your business. A survey by the international accountancy firm PriceWaterhouseCoopers in 2001 found that businesses with an internet plan integrated with overall business strategy grew faster than those that didn't. In other words, as in nearly all other areas of your business, the key decisions are *business decisions* which *you* need to make.

The first step is to ensure that, at the very least, you meet the minimum expectation for businesses in your industry. This will vary hugely by industry. In some industries, all the serious competitors will have sites and they may be very sophisticated. To be considered as a serious player in the industry, you will need a site which meets this minimum expectation. In other industries, very few competitors may have well-developed sites and there may be an advantage to you if you did. So, take a look at what the competition is doing – they can't hide either – and see if you can do better.

After this, here are some simple rules to follow in developing a basic website to be used for promoting your business

1. Don't confuse people:

   - Keep it simple.

   - Make sure it's easy to use.

   - Get your main messages across on the front page if possible. This should particularly include what you do and what you want visitors to the site to do.

   - Avoid effects (e.g. graphics) which require the user to have special technology. Many won't have it and will be put off.

   - Ensure your web presence is consistent with your overall business, your strategy and your offline presence. Remember, the people who speak to you on the phone and deal with you face-to-face will also sometimes use your website. They are the same people and they want to see a consistent message in whatever way they deal with you. This applies to the 'look and feel' of the site, the content and the functionality.

Case Study

On a recent Cranfield Business Growth Programme, two of the participating entrepreneurs ran separate graphic design businesses. As one would expect in their industry, both had sophisticated websites. However, the two sites looked totally different to one another and had some different functionality which perfectly reflected their different offline positions and strategies.

One of the graphics businesses focused on serving customers who were themselves fairly traditional businesses. The colour scheme, layout and functionality of their site were conservative and conventional conveying the impression of solidity and trust that their customers looked for.

The other graphics business dealt primarily with youth-orientated sports brands. The design of their website was funky with more brash colours and language which reflected a younger target group. This site also included some 'off the wall' interactive games which again suited the target marketplace.

Any customer, supplier or potential staff member accessing either of these two sites would very quickly form a view about what sort of business they were, which would be wholly consistent with what they would find in the real world.

---

2. Welcome all your visitors:

   - Identify all the potential types of visitors to your site (customers, suppliers, potential new staff, people looking to buy your business, people from different countries who may not speak your language). If possible, give a clear message to them all. In some cases (for example, someone looking to buy from you in a country to which you do not deliver) this message may have to be a polite 'go away'.

- Identify which type of visitors you really want. Make it very obvious to them which parts of the site are aimed at them.

3. Watch what happens:

   - It's relatively easy to capture information about who visits your site and what they look at. This information could be very useful in helping to improve the site and, more importantly, in helping you to understand your customers even better and to segment them more accurately.

   - Make sure that you provide a mechanism for users to make enquiries from the site. By so doing, you can ask them to provide you with their email addresses and other basic data.

4. Benchmark against other sites:

   - We have already suggested that you can benchmark your site against your competition in order to meet the minimum expectations. Preferably, of course, you should have a better site than theirs.

   - For ideas to add distinctive value to your customers which none of the competition is offering, it's useful to look at other sites outside your industry. These might be customers' sites, suppliers' sites or sites that you use yourself.

5. Be good to your existing customers:

   - Continuing to satisfy your existing customers is at the core of growth and profitability for many smaller companies. At a very minimum, your website creates an additional channel through which they can communicate with you and you with them. Do you know what they think of the site? Have you asked them for feedback and comments on it?

   - Consider how you can deliver even more value to your existing customers through your site. For example, you could produce an online newsletter, you could have discussion areas for existing customers, and you could provide answers to commonly asked questions and guidance about how to use your product/service. You may even be able to allow your customers to obtain quotations, place orders, track deliveries and view their accounts online.

6. Watch out for different expectations:

   - People may behave very differently and have different expectations when dealing online. For example, most of us are quite used to the idea of queuing at the supermarket checkout. And yet, when buying online, many purchasers will abandon the sale if the processing of the payment takes more than 15 seconds. Table 2.9.2 illustrates a number of other differences in behaviour when people deal with you online.

Above the line marketing activity (advertising)

In 1985 the great economist, J. K. Galbraith, observed that consumption was being driven primarily by advertising. The merits of a product or service were less important than how it was promoted.

Physical world	Online world	Table 2.9.2
'Oh look, the new Hotel Chocolat brochure has arrived'	'Don't email me without my permission'	Traditional buying and buying online: a comparison
'No, I don't mind waiting'	'If something doesn't happen in 7 seconds, I'm clicking on to another site'	
'Thanks, that information was very helpful'	'Let me see what other customers have said'	
'Now that I'm here, it's not worth the effort of finding an alternative'	'The competition is only a click away'	
'I'll pay now'	'I won't buy unless it's easy'	
'Can I pay by credit card?'	'I don't trust you with my credit card details'	

Good advertising is a powerful way to differentiate products and services. But, advertising is expensive – and it must be carefully controlled. Advertising guru Tim Bell, formerly CEO of Saatchi & Saatchi, advises:

- set specific campaign objectives (building sales or market share)
- decide strategy (budget, choice of media, geographic profile)
- target audience (market segment, demographic profile)
- decide advertising content (highlight specific product/service benefits)
- be sure about execution and style (humour or hard sell?). For instance, ask yourself, if your product/service was a car or a newspaper, which kind of car (a Rolls-Royce, say, or a Mini), or which kind of newspaper (the *Sun*, perhaps or *The Times*) do you want to be seen as? In these examples, both car brands are owned by BMW and both newspapers by News International. The individual brands, however, appeal to very different markets!

Case Study

In 1997, Karan Bilimoria decided that the time was ripe for Cobra Beer's first ever advertising campaign. At this point, Cobra was available in restaurants throughout the UK, and there was an exciting opportunity to raise mass awareness and to reinforce the loyalty of existing Cobra consumers.

Working with the agency Team Saatchi, Cobra's Marketing department created the character of 'Curryholic Dave' a curry addict who would become the new spokesman for the brand. The campaign was launched in February 1998. 'Dave' offered help and advice

– such as a restaurant 'hotline' for vindaloo addicts – to other curry fans. 'Dave' never actually appeared, but the advertisements were hugely successful, winning major creative awards.

'Curryholics' was discontinued in 2000, when Karan felt that the campaign had achieved its aim of raising Cobra brand awareness. New campaigns followed, retaining a humorous edge, but more subtle in tone. In 2003, the 'Ingenious' campaign was launched, with the aim of reinforcing Cobra's brand identity. The Cobra team had been aware for

▶

some time that aspects of Indian culture, especially the Bollywood film genre, were making big inroads into mainstream British culture. The Ingenious campaign was designed to exploit this. Cobra's Indian pedigree was celebrated and linked to surreal examples of Indian ingenuity, such as a car-wash operated by elephants. This campaign also looks set to garner awards.

Of course, advertising embraces a very wide range of different media, such as TV, radio, newspapers, magazines, the internet, billboards, handbills and so on. As an extra dimension, many of these media will have 'channels' which are aimed at different markets. Taking newspapers and magazines as an example, it is easy to recognize that there are national newspapers, local press, publications aimed at a particular demographic segment (such as women's magazines) and trade press aimed at people who work in a particular industry.

Typically, the criteria which drive the cost of advertising are the size of the audience, the difficulty of reaching that audience through other means, and the spending power of that audience. So, national TV advertising is usually the most expensive form of advertising. But, for the vast majority of growing businesses, the most cost effective form of advertising is usually something more focused using local and/or trade specific channels.

It is not always necessary to take professional advice from, for example, an advertising agency. On the other hand, such professionals will be able to help you determine the most suitable advertising mix for your business. They are particularly valuable if you plan a large-scale campaign involving significant expense. One key point that Cobra learned about working with advertising agencies is to set very clear goals for each campaigns. It's a great deal easier, for both parties, if the mechanism is in place to judge the results.

Distribution

Distribution is all too often the poor relation in the marketing mix, unlike advertising and promotion which traditionally are seen as glamorous and exciting. The consequence of this is that companies who think carefully about their distribution strategy often see opportunities that others overlook. Take the issue of market share, for example. When marketing professionals are set the challenge of growing market share, they typically approach it from two ends:

- increasing product range, through launching new products
- and taking share from competitors.

Sometimes it may be smarter to look at distribution opportunities. Take the situation illustrated in Figure 2.9.2.

The (simplified) model describes an industry where this business covers 50 per cent of the market with its products. These products are present in 25 per cent of the channels through which end users are reached, and four out of ten customers in these channels buy these products rather than those of competitors. The end result is a market share of 5 per cent ($100\% \times 50\% \times 25\% \times 40\%$).

Products supplied   Presence (distribution)   Customer hit rate   Market share

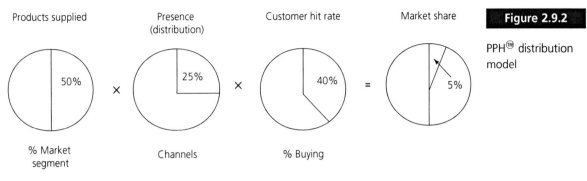

Figure 2.9.2

PPH™ distribution model

% Market segment   Channels   % Buying

Source: Frank Lynn Associates

Let's assume the aim is to increase market share, from 5 per cent to 7.5 per cent, that is to raise it by half as much again. One approach is to launch new products that address the 50 per cent of the market which the business does not currently serve. Holding the other key variables – presence and customer hit rate – constant, this could be achieved by launching new products that attack half of the market not already addressed. This would increase market coverage from 50 per cent to 75 per cent. The arithmetic then looks like this: 75% × 25% × 40% = 7.5% market share.

It *could* be that this is an untapped opportunity, but consider the following:

- in many, if not most, markets, new product failure rates are alarmingly high, certainly well over 50 per cent of all products launched
- the business has no expertise in this area
- sales of the new products might (depending on the circumstances) cannibalise existing products.

Alternatively, we can go to the other end of the process and look at raising the customer 'hit rate'. Assume the goal is still to raise market share from 5 per cent to 7.5 per cent. That implies increasing the hit rate from four to six customers (100 × 50% × 25% × 60%). Four out of ten customers is already a high hit rate. How much will have to be invested in dealer discounts, special promotions, advertising campaigns and so on to gain those extra two customers?

Consider, instead, a strategy of improving channel distribution. Currently, in our example, that is only 25 per cent. To hit our market share target of 7.5 per cent, we need to achieve channel distribution of 37.5 per cent (100 × 50% × 37.5% × 40%). That means broadening our channel distribution by 50 per cent – *and we would still be covering fewer than half of the channels to the end user.* In many markets this is a much more achievable target than either launching new products or increasing the customer hit rate – but it is surprising how often it is ignored by companies seeking to grow. All too often pricing is the factor identified by management as the key variable to address to improve market share, when in fact better distribution may provide the answer.

In some circumstances, it makes sense for a growing business to discontinue supplying a market segment because the right distribution channels are not available. These are usually situations where a business has different product lines and it does not have the resources to grow in all directions.

Case Study

Light Emotions was founded in 2000 by two electronics engineers, Christophe Mermaz and Dominique Pecquet. Christophe's natural flair was for sales and marketing: Dominique's talents lay in research and development.

In his own time, Dominique had developed a prototype of a plastic champagne flute that lit up when liquid was poured in. The glass gave off an attractive glow, especially effective in candlelight or outside at night. When the glass was emptied, the light was switched off. People to whom they showed the product loved it. On the strength of these reactions, and driven by a desire to build their own business, the two partners quit their jobs and founded Light Emotions.

Each partner's role was clear: Dominique would continue to improve the existing concept and develop new ones while Christophe would handle the sales and marketing. Initially, the champagne flutes were sold to anyone and everyone who was interested, through Christophe's personal selling efforts and his network of contacts. Dominique, meanwhile, was busy perfecting their next product, the light stick. Shaped like a baton, this had a metal cap at the end. When the cap was tapped, the stick lit up, when tapped again on the other side, it switched off. Other products already in the market could achieve similar effects, but were based on a chemical reaction. Once switched on, they could not be switched off and had a typical life of two to three hours. The Light Emotions stick lasted the same time, but the power could be conserved by switching it off.

In the first four months of 2001 the business sold 15 000 items in total, in the UK, France and Switzerland. The light sticks were a spectacular success at night-time events in ski resorts. The partners were very encouraged by this.

Christophe had clear views on the overall strategy of the business. They should aim to build a high-value, premium brand. As a result, he turned down approaches from bigger organizations who wanted to license the technology for their own product lines, which didn't fit the Light Emotions' image and which would not use the Light Emotions' branding. During 2001, he focused a lot of energy in targeting the growing sector of party shops in the UK, which he felt was the natural outlet for the glasses. Because of the margins available, he would need to sell direct rather than through a wholesaler. After several months of making small volumes of sales to individual outlets, Christophe concluded he needed to accelerate the operation. To make contact with the wider market, he packed some samples and attended a trade fair in Birmingham, where some 500 party firms were present. It rapidly became apparent that he faced some major obstacles:

- The shops loved the product, but wanted a wider range.

- The minimum order size that Christophe needed to sell was too large for most retailers; they just wanted to buy a small quantity and to re-order in small quantities.

- Their business was built on constant innovation, and so Light Emotion would have to introduce regular new product lines, much more frequently than Christophe or Dominique had envisaged.

This was not what he wanted to hear! At the start of 2002, with money tight and feeling under increasing pressure, the two partners sat down to thrash out their segmentation and distribution strategy. Potentially there were four market segments for Light Emotions to address:

1. Private corporate events, for example trade fairs at which drinks manufacturers would launch new products. Light Emotions had developed some promising business with champagne houses.

2. Marine Safety. This was a market with huge possibilities for the night stick product. Existing competitors used the chemical technology and Light Emotions' product superiority was self-evident. It was also a market that could be reached efficiently through deals with wholesalers

3. Marketing Promotions. This segment was similar to private corporate events, except it was the venue – such as a high-profile nightclub – rather than a manufacturer who was the target customer.

4. The party shops segment.

The partners were agreed that the business was spreading itself too thinly, and that the key to success lay in focus. After some debate, it was decided that they would discontinue distribution to the party shops sector. What had seemed such a promising, and obvious, target market was actually proving a distraction from the real business opportunities. Moreover, by attempting to meet the needs of this segment they felt they would be cheapening the quality image of the brand.

In summary, the distribution strategy has to match the other elements of the marketing mix, to maintain the differentiation and focus sought by the company.

Improving the effectiveness of the sales effort

In earlier chapters, we referred to the authoritative study of new business creation, The *Origin and Evolution of New Businesses* by Amar Bhidé. Based on his research, Bhidé makes a strong case that successful new ventures start with the founders doing most, if not all of the selling personally. As the business grows, however, the sales task will devolve to other people. Some of these may be trained professionals, others may acquire selling skills on the job.

Personal selling is the vital link in the communication process between company and customer, but as one noted authority has put it:

> Among European sales forces, there is an alarming lack of planning and professionalism. Sales people frequently have little idea of which products and which groups of customers to concentrate on, have too little knowledge about competitive activity, do not plan presentations well, rarely talk to customers in terms of benefits, make too little effort to close the sale and make many calls without any clear objective. Even worse, marketing management is rarely aware that this important and expensive element of the marketing mix is not being managed effectively.

> (McDonald 2002: 346)

Studies have shown that if the average salesperson's salary is, say, €50 000 pa, the real cost to the company after travel, expenses and benefits, is frequently double that. Add sales administration support and the real total cost is three times the salary. At the same time, less than a third of the typical salesperson's working day is spent in front of the customer. Hence, the need for responsible sales management able to:

- set and monitor sales target achievement

- motivate, train and support the sales staff
- recruit and organize competent staff.

Setting and monitoring sales targets

At the simplest level, setting sales targets may consist of ensuring enough sales to recover the salesperson's costs. To take our example of the salesperson costing €50 000: the salesperson's 'true' cost could well be €150 000. If the gross margin on the products sold is 50 per cent, then our salesman needs to achieve a target of €300 000 just to cover the associated costs. One obvious conclusion that follows is that it pays to maximize the amount of time the salesforce spend selling – yet in many businesses, as mentioned earlier, it could be as little as one-third of their salaried time, or even less. Expensive sales staff should not be spending their time in chasing unqualified leads or carrying out routine administration!

A common model adopted by many successful organizations to help their sales staff achieve their targets is to divide the selling effort into 'hunters' and 'farmers'. The hunters' role is to secure and nurture new business. The farmers' role is to take over from the hunter the management of the account, once the relationship with the customer is sufficiently established. The names indicate the different qualities required for each role: hunters are individuals who relish the challenge of being in the marketplace, are naturally competitive (and often aggressive) and can take rejection. Farmers, by contrast, are less motivated by doing deals, prefer a steady-state working routine, and are happy to relieve the hunters of the routine administration that comes with selling. This kind of organization plays to people's natural preferences and helps to create effective teams who support each other. It also means that targets can be set and monitored partly on the basis of individual performance, and partly by team performance – which helps to build a sense of shared commitment and responsibility.

Sales forecasting and control

The best sales plans are developed from the ground up. However, your marketing analysis, and the sales and marketing plans that flow from it, tend to start at the macro level, that is to work top down. So, you will be working with:

- known industry or market segment growth rates
- estimated market shares for yourself and your competitors
- your own initiatives to maintain, grow or disengage from various market segments.

The task of the salesforce is to turn what is a statement of intent into a detailed plan of action – and that is best built from the ground up, by looking at:

- sales by month
- sales by individual customer account or group of customers
- estimates of new business sales, again allocated to specific customers
- resource needed to achieve this: people, budget, sales literature and so forth
- and any other relevant metrics.

Sales forecasts targets that are arbitrarily imposed from the top are much less likely to be 'bought into' than sales forecasts that are built from the ground up, based on a frank exchange with the salesforce. If you expect them to achieve last year's sales plus an extra 10 per cent, *where exactly* are the extra sales going to come from? Where are the opportunities? Where should they be focusing their efforts? And, if sales are not going to plan, is there an early warning system in place to address the problem?

Case Study

Harry Clarke co-founded Cobalt Telephone Technologies in October 1997 with £20000. The first eight months were spent trading from a Portakabin located in the car park of another company. Formerly an Army officer, Harry had been trained to extract the maximum possible leverage from the scantiest of available resources. Cobalt would be an opportunity to test this principle in the commercial world.

Whilst taking the initiative to bring efficiencies to his then employer, Harry had researched the emerging area of automated telephone call handling. Most businesses offering such services, appeared, he believed, to do it badly. His own company, he resolved, would do it better. Five extremely tough years later, he was managing a business with a turnover of £750000 and a staff of six.

In that time Harry had become the business's chief salesman. Apart from a year at business school, he had no formal training, just his degree in engineering and his time as a soldier.

Still, he found that running a growing business that was constantly short of cash was not that dissimilar from clearing pathways through minefields in Iraq!

Keeping an eye on cash flow is always critical for a small business, but even more so when the funding is organic and the ability to borrow limited. Bitter experience had taught Harry that sales forecasting by its very nature tends to be over-optimistic. Over time, therefore, he developed the *Cobalt cash flow estimator* as his primary forecasting tool for new business. The spreadsheet asks three key questions when considering the new business pipeline:

1. What is the probability that this customer is going to buy anything (*likelihood to buy*)?
2. What is the probability that this customer will buy from Cobalt (... *from Cobalt*)?
3. If they do buy, when will they pay (*When*)?

An example of the spreadsheet is shown in Table 2.9.3.

| Table 2.9.3 | Example of the Cobalt cash flow estimator spreadsheet |

Project	Value £k	likelihood to buy	...from Cobalt	When? Aug.	Sep.	Oct.	Nov.	?	Total	Discount factor	Forecast actuals
Port of Felixstowe	£16	0.3	0.8			1			0.73	0.1752	£2 803.20
Cendant	£40	0.2	0.1				1		0.66	0.0132	£528.00
Screwfix	£80	0.6	0.2		1				0.81	0.0972	£7 776.00
NRC Phase 3	£6	1.0	1.0	1					0.9	0.9	£5 400.00
British Benzol	£20	0.1	0.3					1	0.5	0.015	£300.00
									0	0	£0.00
	£162			0.90	0.81	0.73	0.66	0.50			£16 807.00

▶

In each step, a discount factor is applied, to reflect the likelihood of the outcome. The actual timing of the payment is discounted to express the difference in value to the business of cash now, as opposed to cash in the future, even if it only a week away. The value is only free of discount factors once it is actually in the form of cleared funds. It's a simple system, and Harry saw two major benefits from it:

- It forced everyone to be realistic and rigorous about their assumption (note the forecast actuals only produce a tenth of the apparent pipeline value).

- It proved uncannily accurate, not at the level of the individual project but when all the new business was taken together.

- The estimating accuracy improved with time.

Even today, when the business is strapped for cash, Harry continues to use this tool as a vital cash management discipline.

A company will also modify its sales forecasting in response to:

- known industry production and distribution capacity, with the effect of planned additions or deletions
- the impact of seasonality and the effect of economic trends
- the timing of any tactical promotional expenditure.

Chapter summary

In most cases, growth does not occur by accident, but through careful planning and focus on key business issues. For the typical ambitious smaller business the best way to grow is through continuing differentiation and improvements that translate into better customer service. Focusing on your customer, and delivering distinctive value for them, is the very essence of marketing and marketing planning.

In this chapter, we have considered the various elements of the marketing mix, all of which can enable greater distinctiveness and even more customer focus

1. developing customer segments and product/service quality
2. optimizing price and margins
3. promotional activities
4. distinctive distribution
5. improving the effectiveness of the sales team.

In your business, there may be opportunities in some, or all, of these areas. Whatever is the case, they need to be addressed coherently and consistently if the business is to go forward.

Assignments

Products/service

1. Is your business still dependent on one product or service for over 80 per cent of profits?

Customers

2. Do your top five customers still account for more than 50 per cent of your sales?
3. How do you measure customer satisfaction with the quality of your products and services?

Prices

4. When did you last increase your prices and by what percentage?
5. How do your prices compare with your major competitors?

Advertising and promotion

6. What is the most cost-effective advertising/promotions media for your business and why?
7. How much do you budget for advertising and how much for promotion activity?
8. When did you last have a press release and with what effect?

Distribution

9. Describe the distribution chain between you and the customer?
10. Do your customers and target market segments have easy access to your goods and services? How do you monitor this?

Sales force effectiveness

11. What targets are set for each salesperson and what incentive is there to achieve targets?
12. What was your achievement against sales forecast last year?

Suggested further reading

Bhidé, Amar V. (2000) *The Origin and Evolution of New Businesses*, New York: Oxford University Press.

McDonald, Malcolm (2002) *Marketing Plans: How to Prepare Them, How to Use Them*, 5th edition, Oxford: Butterworth-Heinemann.

10 What is changing in your business environment?

Introduction and objectives

When you started your business, your primary concern in scanning the business environment was to prove that there was a market opportunity for your idea. Subsequently, as the business grows, customer research is the major tool used to ensure that products and services are in tune with the requirements of new and existing customers. Markets and customers change, however, and today the rate of change in most markets is faster than ever. It follows that businesses which do not, or cannot, change to meet new demands will not thrive in the long term. Customer research, as we have already discussed in earlier chapters, has an important part to play in enabling you to meet changing needs. However, periodically you also need to undertake a comprehensive review of the environment so that customer needs are seen in the context of wider developments in the marketplace. That review, or scanning process, is the subject of this chapter by the end of which you should have a clear understanding of:

- Whether you should be thinking about incremental or radical change, as you plan 'a new business for a new tomorrow'.

- How to use environmental scanning tools, to identify factors of importance likely to impact on your business.

- How to translate those conclusions into action planning.

- Revisiting your strategy and your mission statement.

Incremental or radical change?

As far back as the 1960s, the great management guru, Peter Drucker, observed that top management had three basic tasks to perform:

- to run today's business

- to improve today's business
- and to create 'a new business for a new tomorrow'.

Improving today's business is generally a matter of making incremental changes: of de-listing old products, for example, or upgrading information systems to enhance employee productivity. In well-managed businesses, incremental changes take place all the time. Some are driven by senior management; other changes arise because employees see an opportunity to make improvements, and have the discretion to do so.

On the other hand, creating 'a new business for a new tomorrow' implies deeper and far-reaching changes. In some cases, the changes are the result of careful planning over a sustained period. Thus, a conventional retail business might decide to develop both a direct sales catalogue and a website as new channels to market. Both the catalogue and the website will require the business to introduce new systems and processes, as well as requiring significant investment in sales, marketing, logistics and technology management. The business will need to acquire and embed not just 'hard' assets – warehousing, say, or computing power – but also the knowledge and skills to build new capabilities.

Radical change can also come about not because it has been planned, but because the business faces a crisis: the emergence of an unforeseen substitute technology or an unexpected new player in the market, or the business failure of a key supplier.

Whether radical changes are planned or not, they always take place within the broader business environment. As a business grows and matures, so it becomes increasingly important to build regular environmental scanning into the planning process, so that you can create a new business for a new tomorrow.

Environmental scanning

The purpose of environment analysis for the growing business is, therefore, to determine what elements are changing in the marketplace which helped give birth to the company in the first place, and what the implications of these changes are for the future growth and direction of the company. As a business moves out of the start-up phase and into the growth phase, regular environmental scanning should become part of the planning process.

PESTEL analysis

One useful format for such scanning, to ensure consistency in approach, and in order that no stone is left unturned, is to consider trends under each of the following headings:

Political: factors affecting the business and/or its market which are due to political changes or trends (e.g. changes of government policy, creation of regional bodies).

Economic: factors affecting the business and/or its market which are driven by the economy (e.g. whether the national economy is growing, flat or in recession, likely changes in the price of key commodities).

Social: factors affecting the business and/or its market which are driven by social changes (e.g. major demographic changes or changes in consumers' lifestyles).

Technological: factors affecting the business and/or its market which are due to technological developments. These are likely to be very specific to a particular market and are typically dependent on the rate of innovation within that market (e.g. new technologies to enable more oil to be extracted from wells).

Ecological: factors affecting the business and/or its market arising from environmental changes (e.g. global warming) or ecological concerns (e.g. the need to conserve fish stocks).

Legal: factors affecting the business and/or its market arising from new or planned legislation (e.g. tighter data protection laws in many countries).

The first four of these factors form a PEST analysis which has been a standard tool in strategic planning for many years. Recently, the latter two factors have been added to create the more comprehensive PESTEL analysis.

For the typical growing business, it is a straightforward process to identify and list environmental factors using this framework. Here are some guidelines on how to go about this:

1. This is an exercise that should be done by the senior management team, not just the boss in isolation, to ensure a broad spread of views. It may also be useful to feed into the process contributions from any advisers whose opinions you respect.

2. It is more important to identify a significant environmental factor than to spend time debating whether it is, say, a political or an economic factor.

3. Do not worry if you cannot identify a significant factor under a particular heading. It could just be the case that there is no planned legislation, or change in consumer lifestyle, which is going to impact on your business.

4. At the end of the listing, determine which are the key factors (probably no more than six) that are really going to affect your business. Make sure that these are clear in everyone's mind, and that they are taken account of in the planning process.

5. Do not spend too much time over this exercise (you will risk losing focus on what is important). A small to medium-sized business can comfortably complete the task in less than half a day.

Much of the macro-economic and market data that you will need in order to complete a PESTEL analysis is publicly available. Therefore, the information with regard to desk research set out in Chapter 3 is equally relevant here.

SWOT analysis

PESTEL analysis of this type can be usefully combined with an analysis of the business's strengths, weaknesses, opportunities and threats – commonly known as SWOT analysis. The opportunities and threats detected in the external environment are combined with an internal analysis of the company's own strengths and weaknesses.

The opportunities and threats parts of a SWOT link closely to the PESTEL framework, because opportunities and threats are future possibilities, outside what the firm is currently doing, and governed by the external environment. For this reason, it makes sense to review these carefully in the light of your conclusions from the PESTEL analysis. The identification of opportunities and threats will also benefit hugely from a contribution from those people who have a daily involvement with the customers and the wider market, such as sales and marketing staff. They should have a good sense of where opportunities lie, and also where there are threats, especially from the competition.

Strengths and weaknesses describe the current state of the business. It is not, as a rule, difficult to identify these. They are the issues which, when managers stand back from day-to-day activities, are the important, longer-term aspects of the business which give it its profile in the market. The strengths and weaknesses part of a SWOT is, so to speak, a kind of non-financial balance sheet, in which 'assets', such as reputation, are contrasted with 'liabilities', such as an average revenue level per client which is too low. Unlike a balance sheet, there is no resultant numerical conclusion, such as the business's net asset value. On the other hand, it is like a balance sheet in that it attempts to paint a picture of the current position, highlighting the key factors of importance.

This exercise should be conducted in a similar way to the PESTEL exercise – indeed, businesses often combine work on both frameworks as part of a strategy or planning day. The whole senior management team should be involved, supplemented by relevant outside expertise, if appropriate. It is important to focus on the important issues and to discuss and agree their implications, and not get distracted into debates over secondary matters. Aware of this danger, many businesses purposely appoint an outside facilitator who is skilled in helping managers work through this process. The following case study shows the process at work, in a business facing the need to make radical changes.

Case Study

On 16 March 2001, a new management team, headed up by Christopher Young, took control of the Impact Group. Prior to agreeing the deal, Christopher had undertaken the standard process of due diligence, assisted by legal and accountancy advisers. Part of that due diligence process was to identify all of the liabilities and commercial risks related to the existing business, and to ensure that these were provided for in the new company structure. A further part of that process was environmental scanning.

The environmental scanning revealed that the Impact Group's most significant challenge was a failure to think through the implications of the world wide web, and thus not having appropriate policies and products to offer the client base. All of Impact's customers had to respond to this emerging technology, and, as a networking organization for Chief Information Officers (CIOs), Impact should have been on their shortlist of key partners to help them. The reason for Impact's lack of a suitable offering was also clear to see: in its recent past, Impact had been very focused on the Y2K issue. Developing strategies for the millennium bug had proved very profitable. Unfortunately, the

▶

year 2000 had come and gone and with it Impact's main source of business. No real thought had been given to what Impact should do next! Meanwhile, the dot com revolution had taken off.

When the new owners arrived, the business had seven employees – including two feuding senior managers – and contracts with 20 individual consultants, located across the UK, who worked on a commission basis. The employees focused on administration: running the office, organizing events, maintaining records and so forth. The selling activity was largely contracted out to consultants. Nominally, Impact had over 230 members from 85 different organizations, nearly all of which were in the FTSE Top 1000 UK companies list. However, when Christopher investigated further, he found that many of these members were no longer an active part of the network, and that many of the companies had not renewed their subscriptions. Moreover, there was no consistency in the way in which the client relationship was managed. The main reason for this was that most of the client contact was in the hands of the consultants, who followed no defined processes. When Christopher looked at the numbers more closely, it emerged that the average annual revenue per client company was no more than £13 000 – out of an IT budget which typically ran into millions of pounds!

A SWOT analysis helped bring the issues into focus as illustrated in Figure 2.10.1.

Figure 2.10.1	**Strengths**	**Weaknesses**
Impact Group: SWOT analysis	A recognized brand name A great blue-chip client list Acknowledged expertise in the IT field	Internal management disagreement No 'ownership' of clients Revenue per client too low Heavily loss-making Product portfolio needs restructuring
	Opportunities	**Threats**
	Strengthen relationships with clients Leverage current clients to gain new ones Develop new products around the internet	Clients defect if Impact cannot add value Competitors will take Impact's position in the market, unless Impact acts quickly If Impact cannot develop a compelling proposition, it has no future . . .

Action planning

Like any other managerial tool, this process of environmental scanning is only meaningful if it leads to an agenda for action. That means a prioritized list of actions, which, by definition, cannot be too long. A large multinational cannot manage and implement 20 priorities, so it is pretty unlikely that a business employing 50 people or fewer can do so! Yet, we have found over and over again that a major obstacle to the growth ambitions of smaller businesses is a lack of focus – either because priorities have not been defined, or because there are too many of them, and the energy of management is dissipated in too many directions.

Case Study

It was clear to Christopher and the new management team of the Impact Group that the immediate priority was to safeguard and strengthen the client base. In the past, only clients at a certain level of expenditure had been allocated a dedicated account manager, who was a retired IT professional acting as a consultant. To a large extent, their earnings from Impact were based on client review meetings, not from selling. The old management had attempted to change this by bringing account management in house, but had not really succeeded. Christopher swiftly allocated all clients an account manager, brought the entire function in house (and strengthened it), and introduced a plan which incentivised account managers by sales targets.

A second urgent priority was to sort out the product portfolio, update it to include better internet or e-strategy content, and to position it in line with the needs of the different types of member, as shown in Table 2.10.1.

Table 2.10.1	Impact: managerial planning exercise		
Decision maker	**Customer**	**Need**	**Example services**
Company Boards	CIO	Independent evaluation of the risks embedded within IT systems.	IT Health Review
CEO	CEO	To understand whether best value is being achieved from the IT expenditure.	IT Effectiveness Review Project Benefits Review Executive Team Review
CEO/CIO	CIO & Team	Forum for the large team to examine business changes and external best practice.	Bespoke Executive Programme
CIO	CIO	Enhancing performance by learning from others.	Executive Programme IT Effectiveness Review Executive Team Review EMU Scope & Scale
IT Directors	IT Director	Enhancing their value contribution to the business. Getting into the inner circle of the board.	Executive Programme IT Effectiveness Review Executive Team Review EMU Scope & Scale
CIO/IT Director	IT Management Team	Ensuring that the IT management team is maximizing their potential. Developing individuals to assist in succession planning.	IS Leaders' Network IS Leaders' Academy
Senior IT Manager	Senior IT Manager	Developing themselves to allow them to become an IT director.	IS Leaders' Academy IS Leaders' Network
HR Directors	IT Management Team	Recognizing that IT has its own specific requirements, IT needs to ensure that it develops and keeps its key people to enhance the value contributed by each individual.	In-house Programmes

▶

A third priority was to focus on the target market that would deliver the kind of revenue growth required to make Impact a viable business. Christopher identified a 'hit list' of UK organizations that were 'IT intensive', defined as having an annual IT budget of over £25 million, or a spend per employee of over £3500. Table 2.10.2 below shows the sector data that allowed him to start this search process.

The fourth priority was to address the weak cash position. Firstly, costs were drastically reduced, especially those relating to the outside consultants. Secondly, two plans were prepared:

- a plan for growing the business which assumed that more outside investment could be found
- and an alternative plan, based on funding growth through retained earnings.

By May 2002, fourteen months after Christopher and his team had taken over, the results were showing through. After some very tough months, the business was now generating cash. New FTSE 100 clients were being added at the rate of one a month. Costs were down by 30 per cent. Average client revenue per annum had reached £17 000, up from the £13 000 which the new team had inherited. Renewal rates of membership were also increasing, from 70 per cent to 90 per cent.

Table 2.10.2	Sector	IT spend per employee (£)
IT spend per employee by sector	Computer services	16 485
	Banking & finance	13 835
	Energy & water supply industries	12 847
	Insurance	10 796
	Central government	4 281
	Metal goods, engineering, vehicles manufacturing	3 654
	Metals, minerals, chemicals manufacture	3 654

Revisit strategy and mission statement

Having completed these environmental analyses, you should be well placed to answer what strategist Cliff Bowman of Cranfield School of Management has termed 'the five essential questions which determine whether you have a competitive strategy', that is, do you know:

1. Where you should compete (market segment)?
2. How you can gain sustainable competitive advantage?
3. What competencies, and what kind of organization, do you require to deliver the strategy?
4. What do you look like now?
5. How can you move from 4 to 3?

In other words, if you know which market segment you are competing in, and could define a clear competitive advantage, you could then define your organization to deliver the strategy. Clearly, the most important of these from a strategy point of view is number 2; are the factors and the strategy still in place that enabled your company to grow?

Case Study

By mid 2002, Nigel Apperley had been in business for three years. During that time, he had remained a dedicated internet retailer specializing in selling digital cameras, accessories and related services over the web. The early days of the dot com frenzy were over, and Nigel had proven that he, for one, had a sustainable business model.

Over that time the readiness of consumers to make transactions over the internet had greatly increased, thanks in large part to more secure payment systems. The growing popularity of mass consumer websites like the auction house, e-bay, and the expansion in low-cost airlines like Easyjet and Ryanair, most of whose customers booked on the web, also helped. Nigel felt the time was right to expand out of digital cameras into other areas where he could exploit the competitive assets of the business. These were:

- unrivalled market knowledge
- excellent buying relationships with key suppliers
- a streamlined supply chain
- in-house warehousing, with unexploited extra capacity
- a growing database of customers that could be sold to directly.

Accordingly, by the end of 2002 the business had moved into CCTV cameras, and during 2003 into digital recorders and flat-screen TV sets.

The mission statement

Back in Chapter 3 we discussed the value of a vision or mission statement in defining the distinctive purpose of the business, and describing why it should exist. These days well-constructed mission or vision statements tend to be accompanied by 'guiding principles' or 'value statements', all of which aim to demonstrate how the competitive advantage of the company can be built. For example, management consultants McKinsey's mission reads:

To help our clients make positive, lasting and substantial improvements in their performance and to build a great firm that is able to attract, develop, excite and retain excellent people.

Attached guiding principles include:

1. *Serving clients*: adhere to professional standards and follow the top management approach.
2. *Building the firm*: show a genuine concern for our people, foster an open and non-hierarchical working atmosphere.

McKinsey is thus still able to recruit the cream of MBA students, focus on major companies and grow as a worldwide firm. Mission and vision statements are not, however, the preserve of big businesses or just those with a commercial focus. One of the newer and fastest-growing English housing associations (New Progress HA) has produced and proceeded to justify, both a mission statement and a set of guiding values as shown below.

We are committed to providing high quality, innovative and affordable housing and related services for all in the community

Core values
- Delivering promises
- We keep our word
- We believe only the best is good enough

Staff
- Every member of staff is important
- We are committed to keeping our staff informed
- We are committed to ongoing training

Customer care
- Every customer is important
- We listen and react to our customers and seek to keep them informed

Tenant empowerment
- Tenants are represented on the board
- We will provide tenants with a flexible range of options for participation

Quality homes and services
- All services are delivered to the highest standards
- We build high-quality homes

Equality of opportunity
- We believe all people have a right to a good home
- All people should have equal opportunity in their job application and staff development.

Periodically, a business may need to revisit its mission statement and associated values, to modify them in response to a change in strategy, or a re-positioning in the market. Up to 2001, the Impact Group had never had a meaningful mission statement. This meant that there was a lack of clarity within the organization, as well as in the market, about what Impact stood for. As a result, there was nothing on which to focus when the business got into trouble. As part of turning the business around, Christopher Young introduced a new mission statement and set of guiding values:

The IMPACT Programme will become the UK's premier personal development network for leading CIOs. It will demonstrably assist those CIOs it is working with to transform their effectiveness and that of their teams and function as a whole.

The IMPACT Programme helps its members to develop their roles and personal performance through:

> Personal, leadership and team development through training, networking and mentoring.

> Benchmarking, to model excellence and improve performance to the standard of the best.

> Research, investigating the new practices that IT executives need to understand and implement.

IMPACT works in alliances with leading academic institutions around the world and draws its members from the FTSE 250 and the UK's major public sector bodies. The business sees itself as a membership organization and not as a consultancy.

Renewed mission statements, reaffirming the existence of the firm, need then to be accompanied by specific and measurable objectives and most importantly the people, marketing and financial strategies that will make them achievable, as we will examine in the following chapters.

Chapter summary

As your business grows and changes, so the markets in which you operate and the customers you serve are also inevitably going to change. In this chapter, we have considered a number of ways of reviewing your external environment so that you are aware of what is happening around you and can respond accordingly.

We began by reviewing the differences between incremental and radical changes in a business, as you think about planning a new business to meet the challenges of tomorrow. Environmental scanning, in the form of PESTEL and SWOT frameworks, will help you to do this in a systematic way. It is important, however, that these conclusions are translated into a realistic set of priorities which are the subject of a clear plan of action.

As a result of this consideration of the external environment, you may well wish to revisit your thinking about your strategy and to review whether your mission statement is still as relevant to the business as it was when you started.

Assignments

1. Complete a PESTEL analysis for your company's business sector. What are the key factors you need to monitor regularly?
2. Complete a SWOT analysis for your company. What are your key action priorities?
3. In which market sector(s) are you competing?
4. In what way does your company have sustainable competitive advantage in these sectors?

5. Do you have the right competencies to deliver your strategy? What are you lacking and how do these feed into your priorities?

6. Revisit your original mission statement. Should it be rewritten to reflect your current market strategy and, if so, how?

Suggested further reading

Bowman, Cliff with D. Faulkner (1994) 'Measuring product advantage using competitive benchmarking and customer perception', *Long Range Planning*, 27, (1), 119–32.

11 What is your growth strategy?

Introduction and objectives

In previous chapters you considered how you currently win business, how you can further develop your distinctiveness, and what is changing in your external environment. Now you will need to make some decisions about how you actually achieve growth, assuming that is your aim.

Many of the firms we have worked with over the years have experienced, after a while, a kind of 'glass ceiling': they seem to have reached a plateau in their sales and/or profit, and cannot go beyond it, yet management still has aspirations to take the business further.

In this chapter, we will review a number of options for growth strategies which have been successful in helping firms break through this 'glass ceiling'. These options are not necessarily mutually exclusive – in theory, at least, it is possible to pursue more than one at the same time. However, our experience, from having worked with hundreds of growing businesses, indicates that *focus* is probably the single most important characteristic of a successful growth strategy.

At the highest level, we suggest that you consider two broad options for your growth strategy:

1. Can you improve productivity?

2. Can you increase sales volume?

Each of these can be further broken down as shown in the framework in Figure 2.11.1.

In this chapter, we will review each of these options in turn.

Improving productivity

Improving productivity should be a constant requirement for the growth-orientated business. It is, after all, a fundamental part of the constant search to be better than your competitors and different from them. Many, however, see this as an activity just for periods of economic recession. If this is your management

Figure 2.11.1 Optimizing product/service returns

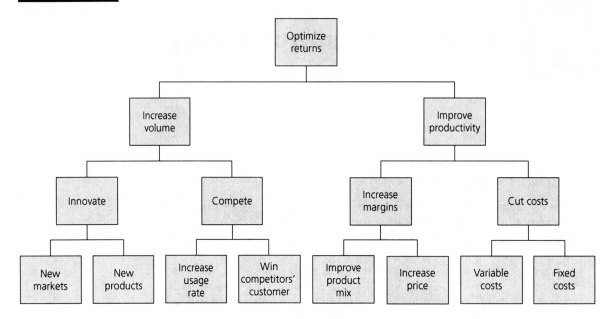

philosophy, then there is a real danger that the business will swing from complacency (and inefficiency) when times are good, to frantic and unrealistic cost-cutting when times are bad: with an attendant high risk of unhappy employees and dissatisfied customers.

Cutting costs

In any business, costs need to be controlled and balanced constantly against the needs for quality and service. The starting point for reducing costs is always to separate your *variable* and your *fixed* costs. Earlier in the book we contrasted the 'lean and mean' with the 'capital-intensive' organization, suggesting that at start-up you focus on keeping your fixed costs as low as possible. The implication of this strategy, of course, is that your *variable costs* are higher:

Case Study

In the business plan for his first Real Burger World outlet, Naz Choudhury was keenly aware of the need to keep fixed cost investment as low as possible. He, therefore, planned to invest only in the essentials and to buy everything else on a variable cost basis. For example, the outlet needed a drinks fountain to dispense soft drinks. In the long run, the cheapest alternative would have been to purchase the equipment and buy the drinks syrup direct from the manufacturers. Instead, Naz chose to enter a contract with a supplier who could provide the fountain and the syrups, and maintain the equipment, a service package for which Real Burger World paid on a per usage basis. Naz adopted a similar approach with freshly-squeezed juice. The alternative of having their own juicer was too labour-intensive, when the priority was for the restaurant staff to focus on the core product range.

However, he was not prepared to compromise the philosophy of the business, which was freshly made, quality food. For his potatoes he could have gone to a supplier of frozen foods or purchased vacuum-packed chips. But, Real Burger chips are all prepared from fresh, whole sacks of potatoes, to ensure the taste and quality are what their customers expect.

In the case of both the juices and the soft drinks, Naz was well aware that this was not the most cost-efficient way to run the business. But, in the early days, this approach would reduce the need for fixed or semi-fixed (i.e. staff) investment, and allow the management to focus on getting the business formula right. As the business grew, he would review these and other activities, to see where he could reduce costs.

As businesses thrive and grow, so the reverse holds good: *fixed costs* often start to increase, as the business has the funds to invest in doing things more cheaply in-house. Purchasing is a good example of this. At some point, many businesses choose to consolidate their purchasing activities within a single department, and recruit an experienced purchasing manager and support staff to take control of this activity across the enterprise. These staff will all need office space and IT equipment, but the benefits of investing in co-ordinated purchasing (typically, lower prices and better terms from suppliers) should outweigh the costs. And, the same will hold for other support functions, such as information systems, personnel, and so forth.

Businesses, of course, move in cycles, and there will come a point when you should start to question whether the emerging fixed cost structure is really necessary to run the business effectively and efficiently. Are there activities which would be better outsourced or bought in only as and when required? Could certain operations be subcontracted to specialists?

Case Study

At Hotel Chocolat (formerly ChocExpress), Angus Thirlwell and Peter Harris keep their fixed costs under constant review: 'We are all too well aware how easy it is to let the costs run up,' says Peter, a qualified accountant. 'In our case, the supply chain accounts for most of the costs. With each stage of business growth, we ask ourselves: do we need to do this or that activity, or would we be better out-sourcing it to someone else?'

Here are some general guidelines on reviewing your cost structure:

1. Focus on the big items. As with most business issues, the 80:20 rule applies. Better to focus your energies on attacking areas where the gains will be significant, rather than those where improvements will make a marginal difference.

2. There are no sacred cows or 'no-go' areas. Just because something has always been done in a particular way, does not mean it should be done like that forever.

3. Look for 'easy wins'. In many product-based businesses, for example, there is a tendency for the product portfolio to grow: the rate at which innovations are introduced exceeds the rate at which old products are discontinued. However, in any business with a wide portfolio, there is a strong chance that a handful of products are really profitable, there is a second group which is marginally profitable or trades at break even, and the rest are losing money.

4. Be ruthless!

That said, you should not throw out the baby with the bath water! Reducing fixed costs should not, on the whole, mean discontinuing investment in technology that brings not only economies, but also flexibility for the future. Similarly, it is not as a rule wise to outsource a 'core competence' – a set of processes, say, or technical know-how – that is part of what makes you stand out from the competition.

Increasing margins

Increasing margins may be the result of actions to improve variable costs. It can also result from finding ways to *enhance your sales product mix* or, even, from *increased prices*.

Case Study

The ruthless competition in the fast food business ensures that companies are always looking for ways both to cut costs and raise margins. As Naz Choudhury built the Real Burger World business, so he found new ways to cut costs and raise margins.

He particularly focused on increasing average customer spend per visit. A special 'meal deal', comprising a burger, chips and a milk shake made with fresh fruit for just over £5, proved popular. By such means, the average customer spend quickly increased from £3.76 to £4.23.

Improving product mix

If you have a number of different products/services, then it is almost certainly the case that you earn different gross margins on each different product/service. Clearly, if you can sell more of the higher margin products, then you will increase overall profitability.

Analysis of the product mix, of course, depends critically on knowing the accurate *gross margins* for each product/service line (*net margin* is often far more difficult to identify accurately, since the exact allocation of indirect costs is as much an art as a science).

Increasing prices

In mathematical terms, *increasing your prices* is probably the easiest way to improve margins. But, it's also nearly always difficult to convince your customers. You know instinctively what to do when cutting prices to stimulate demand: you make a lot of noise and publicity. Some people argue that increasing price should be the opposite, being silently passed through to suppliers and customers alike. In some markets, this strategy seems to work: newspapers and magazines heavily publicize reductions to their cover prices, but make no reference to increases. If your business has been in existence for a number of years, you will know what the industry practice tends to be. That said, a price increase *with no added value* is rarely the way to generate long-term loyalty. On the other hand, if the perceived added value is significantly greater, then customers will be prepared to spend considerably more.

Case Study

Steve Jolliffe has a simple philosophy on business: 'Find something that frustrates you, improve it and start a business on the back of it.' He had already founded, grown and sold out a successful 'mystery shopper' market research business when he hit upon the idea for his next venture.

Out on the golf course with a friend one day, Steve applied his philosophy to the golf driving range. To Steve's mind, the driving range was a classic case of the need for improvement through added value. Driving ranges are places where golfers go to practise and improve. In Steve's experience, this meant hitting a sub-standard ball from an old mat into a muddy field. It certainly didn't capture the imagination or reflect the challenge of the game. Certainly, no-one who wasn't already a golfer was likely to invest in a full set of clubs based on their experience of a driving range.

The discussion produced a train of thought and, by the end of the day, the two men had come up with a new idea: 'to bring ten-pin bowling to the golf driving range'. Players would hit balls towards a range of targets and be awarded points based on the accuracy of their shots. The targets would reflect the challenges of the game and good shots would acquire extra points. The score would be relayed automatically to a TV screen in the golfer's bay and a group of friends could compete with each other for the biggest total.

The idea was brilliantly simple, but the technical challenges were immense. To make it work, they needed a golf ball with a microchip inside it. This would enable each ball to be traced and the exact point where it landed to be located. The ball and embedded chip also needed to be capable of withstanding both the manufacturing process and being struck by a golf club dozens of times. And, of course, it needed to behave just like a normal golf ball. After two years, and an investment of £500 000, Steve and his team finally produced their ball. To demonstrate to potential commercial partners that this was a viable business, Steve raised £3.6 million from private investors to purchase an existing driving range near Watford, north of London. The range he acquired was four years old and turning over just under £400 000 per annum.

For over a year, Steve had a team of 30 people working on the design and operation of the site. He negotiated partnership deals with big-name suppliers to ensure that, from the day it opened, the first TopGolf centre felt like a slick, established business. Compaq led the development of the information systems;

▶

catering was subcontracted to Europe's biggest catering specialist; Dunlop Maxfli supplied the balls; American Golf Discount opened a shop in the entrance; and the world-leading David Leadbetter Academy was on hand to offer tuition to TopGolf customers.

Under the previous management, the driving range received a few hundred customers a week, with an average expenditure of less than £5 per head. Within a year of opening, the TopGolf centre was receiving on average 500 customers per day, seven days a week, spending on average £18 on the game, equipment, tuition and food and drink. Turnover had increased almost nine times, to £3.3 million, and the business was in profit.

Increasing sales volume

So far we have looked at strategies for growth through increasing productivity, by reducing costs or improving margins. Alternatively, you can seek growth through increased volume, in other words, selling more. Increased volume consists of:

- competing more strongly: winning market share from your competitors
- innovation: growing through new products or new markets.

These different strategies have different risks attached to them. Many years ago, in his seminal work *Corporate Strategy*, the US business strategist, Igor Ansoff, highlighted these in a simple two-by-two matrix as shown in Figure 2.11.2.

In the Ansoff matrix the strategy of maximum risk is identified in the box called 'diversification': selling new products to new customers (or, as one of our colleagues describes it with brutal frankness, 'selling things you don't understand, to people you've never met'). Conversely, the strategy of minimum risk is to focus on the box labelled 'market penetration': selling more of what you

Figure 2.11.2

Growth matrix

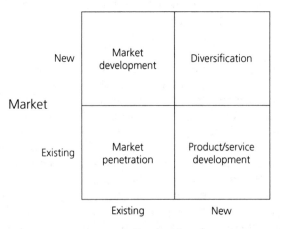

Source: Adapted from Igor Ansoff (1965) *Corporate Strategy*

already sell to existing customers (or ones very similar to them). Selling new products to your existing market and existing products to new markets – the other two boxes in the matrix – are strategies of intermediate risk.

There is much research to show that the most successful growth strategy for the owner-managed firm is market penetration: selling your existing products/ services to your existing customers and others just like them. Our own research at Cranfield makes the case convincingly. Across our sample population of growing businesses, 50 per cent focused on a low-risk market penetration strategy, while 10 per cent pursued the high-risk strategy of diversification. However, nine out of ten of the high-performing firms, showing consistently profitable growth, focused on selling existing products and services to the market they already knew.

There are exceptions to these general rules. Businesses, for example, which are in terminally declining markets must either diversify or die. For these the strategy of greatest risk is to continue with what they are currently doing. However, if you are a growth-orientated entrepreneur, you are very unlikely to have set up a business in a 'sunset' industry, and the implications of the Ansoff matrix will almost certainly apply.

Competing more strongly

In our experience, some of the hardest people to convince of the merits of this strategy can be the business's own sales force! Competing more strongly, with existing products, within existing markets, appears to be a more pedestrian, less exciting option than launching new products into new markets. For the smaller growing business, however, improving competitiveness usually ensures better returns. Putting this into practice is normally a two-stage process. First, you sell more to existing customers, increasing their usage rate. Then, you look to capture customers from your competitors.

A simple, but powerful way to think of increasing customer's usage rate *and* capturing new customers is to think in terms of 'squeezing the lemon'. When they cook, most people take an (understandably) relaxed attitude to squeezing a lemon for its juice. They slice the lemon, squeeze one half, discard it, and may or may not retain the other half. Mostly, however, they fail to extract the maximum juice possible from the lemon. Many businesses take the same approach with their customers. There is no plan for developing the sales relationship with larger customers, no plan to encourage smaller customers to become larger ones, and no plan for leveraging existing customers to help find new ones!

Here are some tried and tested approaches to changing this situation:

- In Chapter 8 we introduced the idea that, in many markets, the relationship between supplier and customer often follows the same path as a marriage. In the early days, a kind of courtship takes place, when the customer and supplier get to know each other. If both like what they see, a relationship develops and, if things go well, a 'honeymoon period' takes place, in which each party values and respects the other. However, just like a marriage, if the 'partners' start to take each other too much for granted, the 'magic' disappears and, in the worst case, divorce is the end result. It is a valuable exercise to group customers by the stage of their relationship with you and to ensure that they get the right sort of care and attention. Identify those who are at risk of defecting to competitors – because they have been neglected – and those who have defected and could be won back. Then, create a plan for addressing the situation. Remember, it invariably costs far more to acquire a new customer than to retain an existing one.

If you think the wedding analogy is a fanciful one, a McKinsey study in the early 1990s found that most industrial customers who defected from their existing suppliers did so because these suppliers showed little or no interest in them.

- Customers who value you are your best ambassadors. Many smaller growing businesses have customers who are many times larger than themselves. The people who buy from you may well be happy to recommend you to others in their organization – and, in particular, people you don't already know – but they have to be asked. More to the point, frequently a customer who buys one thing from you doesn't know, or has forgotten, that you have other things to sell. It is up to you to remind them. You can also ask your existing customers for referrals along the lines of 'Do you know anyone else who would value our product/service?'

- Big company buyers are inherently risk-averse. Becoming an approved supplier may take you years. Big companies are, however, intensely competitive. Often, a competitor to an existing customer of yours will be prepared to see you just on the off-chance that, by using your services, their rival has obtained some competitive advantage, however slight. (Also, if you supply a competitor who operates similar policies to theirs, you must have good credentials to have made it on to their approved list.) Again, exploit this to your advantage.

- Think carefully about the different ways in which you 'touch' different audiences. Are there untapped opportunities? Hotel Chocolat (formerly ChocExpress), for example, has always viewed each order as having two customers: the person who requests and pays for a delivery of chocolates, and the person who receives them. The buyer is an *actual* customer; the recipient is a *potential* one. Hotel Chocolat makes sure, therefore, that the recipient knows exactly who supplies the chocolates, and encourages that person to become a customer in turn. For the company, a transaction is only successful if both the giver and the receiver are happy!

Innovation

Innovation, or investing in new products and new markets, is clearly a higher-risk strategy than competing more effectively. However, there are also ways in which you can manage the risks involved in innovation to a level which is acceptable.

The least risky innovation is likely to be the new product or service actively requested by existing customers. When this happens, you often have an opportunity to develop the innovation in close collaboration with one customer, or a select few. This is common practice in many technology-based industries, such as bio-science, information systems and defence procurement. The advantage with this approach, of course, is that, if successful, you have a guaranteed sale and, in many cases, help with cashflow. The disadvantage is the danger that the product or service is so customized for a limited group of customers that it cannot be sold to a wider target.

The term innovation often suggests something radically new. In fact, new products can equally mean simple line extensions to the existing core business. Measured by market value, the Coca-Cola Company is the world's biggest food and drink business. Even today, however, more than a century after its foundation, the company derives most of its revenues from its core Coke portfolio, of Coca-Cola and a handful of variants such as Diet Coke or Vanilla Coke. In the 1980s, when the management attempted to ditch the old flavour and substitute a replacement, loyal customers revolted and forced the company to back down. Since then, Coca-Cola has focused its innovation strategy on a small number of line extensions, carefully researched and tested before they are taken to market. Outside its core cola portfolio, the company prefers to acquire or license new products, which have been successfully developed by other people. The Austrian company Red Bull has built a significant global beverages business around one product and a handful of variants.

On the same theme, what *appears* to an outsider to be radically new or different may in fact be a clever new combination of existing features and technologies. Many businesses have built strong positions not through innovating a particular technology, but in re-presenting existing technology in an attractive way to the customer. It has been argued that Japanese industrial strategy of the 1970s and 1980s was largely based on this idea, certainly in the field of consumer electronics, and underpinned the success of companies such as Sony, Matsushita and Hitachi. Companies at the leading edge of technological development are sometimes prone to focus on the features, as opposed to the benefits to the customer: but in the commercial world there are no guaranteed prizes for originality.

Case Study

The TopGolf concept is clearly a major innovation in the field of golf. But, Steve Jolliffe freely admits that much of the success comes from taking ideas from elsewhere and configuring them for TopGolf. 'Going ten-pin bowling is not just about the game. It's an evening out with friends and family. Cracking the microchip problem was absolutely essential to getting TopGolf started. But, getting people to come to a driving range as a destination visit, seeing it as entertainment, that's about creating a complete environment with all the right ingredients: food, drink, a comfortable atmosphere, a sense of excitement and so on. We've learned from other leisure retailers.'

Chapter summary

In order to grow, you will need to make some key decisions about how you actually achieve that growth – how you sell more and how you make more profit. In this chapter, we have looked at a range of strategies for growth which have proved to be successful in many of the businesses with which we have worked. These strategies break down as follows:

- Improve productivity.
  - reduce costs
  - improve product/service mix
  - increase prices.
- Increase sales volume:
  - increase your existing customers' usage rate
  - win customers from your competitors
  - introduce new products/services and/or enter new markets.

In theory, several of these options can be pursued at the same time. However, when considering these options, you need to recognize and manage the inherent risks of departing too far from serving your core market with your core product and service offering. Our experience, from having worked with hundreds of growing businesses, indicates that *focus* is vitally important and that most successful businesses concentrate on 'selling more of what you already sell to your existing customers and customers just like them'.

Assignments

1. What opportunities are there for you to improve productivity in your business:
   a) Through cutting costs?
   b) Through improving product/service mix?
   c) Through increasing prices?
2. How can you increase sales volume in your business:
   a) By increasing existing customers' usage rate?
   b) By winning customers from the competition?
   c) By introducing new products/services?
   d) By entering new markets?
3. What will be the focus of your growth strategy?

Suggested further reading

Ansoff, Igor (1965) *Corporate Strategy*, London: Penguin.
McDonald, Malcolm (2002) *Marketing Plans: How to Prepare Them, How to Use Them*, 5th edition, Oxford: Butterworth-Heinemann.

12 Can you develop a balanced management team?

Introduction and objectives

In recent years, many a large organization has trumpeted the phrase 'our people are our greatest asset', only for their staff to be the first casualty when times get tough. Not surprisingly this has led to much cynicism among employees. Nevertheless, it remains true that you'll never have a great business without great people. So, managing your people, ensuring that they are well-motivated in their work and work well together as a team, is one of the most important aspects of your growth strategy. Even if you have a unique proposition, a clever strategy and the most carefully thought through plan, without great people, in the right jobs, you have very little chance of achieving your growth aims. In addition, the quality of your people, particularly the management team, can add significant value to your business and is one of the key factors which influence investors and purchasers.

We'll look at the issues involved in building a great team under the following headings:

- Finding the people in the first place, namely, recruitment and selection.

- Keeping them happy once you've found them, namely, motivation and retention.

- Helping them grow with the business, namely, training and development.

- Helping them work together to achieve your aims, namely, leadership and teams.

- Removing people if you have to.

Case Study

Dave Courteen received a lot of encouragement to go into the business from his parents, who owned and managed a sub post office in Islington, London. Sport, however, was his real love, particularly football and cricket. An important early influence on Dave came from a visit to Lowestoft to a holiday camp, as a teenager. He enjoyed it so much that he applied for a summer job there, returning for seven seasons. The experience that he gained, looking after people and ensuring that they had a good time, was to prove key for his subsequent enterprise. His observations on how the privately owned holiday camp retained and developed quality staff were important in shaping his own managerial style.

The quality of the staff, and their ability to communicate with the guests in the holiday camp, was fundamental to the overall experience and would often be the most important factor in deciding whether or not a guest would return the following year. As such, staff were more likely to be hired on the basis of their personality than on their fitness. Any future business run by Dave would pay great attention to the recruitment, retention and training of the staff.

Later in life, Dave met fellow sports science graduate and kindred spirit Steve Taylor, and in 1987 they founded Fitness Express together. They focused early on a niche in the health and leisure industry. Their market was independent hotels who wished to offer their clients health and fitness centres, but who did not have the expertise to manage them. Fitness Express would staff and run each centre under contract, rewarded through a mixture of fee and profit share.

As the business grew, so a clear formula started to evolve. Firstly, each centre was carefully tailored to appeal to a clearly defined market segment. This might be predominantly a family membership, or older people in retirement who felt intimidated by the atmosphere in a typical fitness centre. Secondly, good systems and procedures were essential to ensuring that every member had a positive experience every time he or she came. Happy members translated into renewed subscriptions, which translated into profitable business. Thirdly, Fitness Express's continuing success depended crucially on their staff: on recruiting, training and retaining the right people.

In the early days, staff management was informal. Clear direction was given, Dave and Steve were easily accessible to any of their staff and any problems were resolved over a drink in the pub. But, as the company grew the two founders could not devote the time needed to all their staff. So, they employed the UK government backed 'Investors In People' (see www.investorsinpeople.com) method to formalize staff management. Training in health and safety, swimming pool supervision, and so on enabled the staff to obtain formal qualifications, and to improve their career prospects in sports management. As a result, Fitness Express's staff retention rate, at 67 per cent per annum, was twice the industry average.

After 13 years, Dave and Steve sold Fitness Express to Crown Sports for more than £10 million. A key part of the value was the quality of the staff and the thoroughness of the staff management systems which Dave and Steve had put in place.

Recruitment and selection

If you're going to build a team, then you're going to need some more people – which gets you into recruitment. In the very early stages of the business, most entrepreneurs have a very small team, primarily made up of people that they already know. As you set out on the path to growth, you will need to think more carefully about where you find the best people for your business and how you select them.

Through our work with many growing businesses, we have found that recruiting the right people for key roles is one of the biggest headaches of all for owner-managers. It can be a major constraint on development plans. Getting the right people is a difficult, time-consuming and costly business. Getting it wrong is even more expensive and can be extremely painful. Few growing businesses can claim not to have had some bad experiences with recruitment. Perhaps this is because so many owner-managers seem to leave recruitment until it is too late and then do it in a rush.

There will always be circumstances where recruitment needs to be undertaken at short notice (e.g. someone leaves unexpectedly). Nevertheless, wherever possible, the recruitment of key staff should be a planned activity, based on the requirements of the growth strategy, rather than something that is left until the point at which current staff are so overloaded with work that you simply must recruit. Your growth strategy and business plan should enable you to identify the key staff and skills you are going to need, and the time at which you will need them.

Based on this staff plan, you can then provisionally plan when you need to start recruiting. Don't underestimate the length of time it takes to recruit someone. You will need time to think about your requirements, to consider where to find the people, to advertise the position(s) if appropriate, to receive and review applications, to interview and select. And, of course, the person you offer the job to may well already be working for someone else, in which case they may have to work out their notice before joining you. Taking all this into account, for key management positions, it is prudent to allow up to six months from the point at which you start the recruitment process to the point at which the new person joins.

Before starting the actual recruitment for any job, you should develop a written job description for the role. Don't just give the job a name, such as 'sales manager', and expect that every potential applicant will know what you mean. You may have a very different interpretation of such a role than in other businesses. The job description should include the job title and purpose, responsibilities, reporting lines, limits of accountability and main tasks.

In addition to the job description, it is also good practice to have a person specification. This sets out the characteristics of the sort of person who you believe will be successful in the role. Once again, it is advisable to write this down rather than believe that you will 'know the person when you see them'. The person specification could include items such as experience, skills, personality, attainments, general intelligence, education, special aptitudes, interests, physical make-up, disposition and circumstances, etc. It may also be beneficial to identify a minimum level and a preferred level for each of these areas. For instance, under experience, it may be a minimum requirement for the applicant to have worked in a similar role in another business, while the ideal would be for the person to have worked in a similar role in the same industry. The more specific you can be about these requirements, the better, since you can use them in any advertising for the jobs, which will help to reduce inappropriate applications, and you can also use them as part of your screening of the applications.

In seeking potential applicants, most growing businesses use a limited range of sources and tend to use the same sources for all types of jobs. The most common ones are existing contacts (including in competitor businesses), recruitment agencies and local press advertising. To find the right person, you may need to be a little more thoughtful and creative. Firstly, consider the job and the person specification you have put together: How difficult are these sort of people to find? Where are you likely to find them? What publications do they read and/or media do they use? What are they likely to be doing now? Where are they likely to look for new jobs and career opportunities and whose advice are they likely to seek? Are there institutions such as schools and universities from which such people may be graduating? Is the role for which you are recruiting such that the right person would relocate, and therefore, it is worthwhile extended your search outside you immediate locality?

Having considered these questions, identify a range of different ways of attracting potential candidates. This may well include the usual approaches mentioned above but could also include activities such as:

- speaking at schools, universities and/or business networks such as Chambers of Commerce and in so doing let your audience know that you are recruiting
- hosting work experience and student projects within your business
- having an open invitation and/or specific job opportunities on your website
- pro-actively letting all you business contacts, including people like your accountants and lawyers who come into contact with many other businesses, know that you are recruiting
- asking existing members of staff to recommend people they know
- considering specific key contacts in other businesses with which you deal and, if appropriate, making informal approaches to selected individuals
- hosting open days/evenings either at your business premises or at local hotels, etc.

If you do advertise for the role, try to ensure that the wording is as specific as possible so that you are not inundated with inappropriate applications.

Once you receive the applications, the next step is to select a shortlist for consideration. The job description and person specification should be the primary screening mechanisms. Nevertheless, there is bound to be a certain degree of subjective judgement. Therefore, it's a good idea to have more than one person read the applications independently and then compare opinions.

The next step is usually to interview the shortlisted candidates. But, beware: 45 seconds, it is claimed, is the time a typical manager takes between meeting an applicant and deciding whether or not they are the right person for the job. True or false, fears that the interview can be very subjective, and thus a biased way of selecting staff, are promoting the trend for companies to use additional methods such as aptitude and personality tests (called psychometric tests). Once the preserve of big businesses, these techniques are being used increasingly by smaller businesses to help improve the selection of new employees and those in line for promotion, and for self-development by owner-managers themselves.

It is reasonably self-evident that being a successful sales person calls for a different type of person than a successful librarian. They may be equally intelligent, but their abilities, aptitudes and personalities will probably be poles apart. Fortunately, that is exactly what aptitude and personality tests set out to measure.

There are aptitude tests for most types of role from secretary to sales manager. There are also hundreds of different types of psychometric tests which test for different things. Some are based on many years of rigorous research while others are less reliable and robust. Unfortunately, there is no policing body for psychometric testing at present. Most of the more reliable tests should be used only by a qualified or accredited person and we would recommend that you involve such a person if you intend to use one of these tests.

You can find more about psychometric tests, and locate appropriate tests for your business, through the British Psychological Society (`www.bps.org.uk`) or the Chartered Institute of Personnel and Development (`www.cipd.co.uk`)

Other useful techniques to add objectivity to the interview process include:

- Inviting the applicant to undertake a short piece of work which is directly relevant to the job for which they are applying.

- Describing tricky scenarios which would typically happen in the job and asking the applicant to describe how they would deal with that scenario, preferably based on their own previous experience.

- Allowing the applicants time to meet other members of the team with whom they would be working. This could be arranged by way of a 'tour' of the business in which the applicant spends a little time with a number of key members of staff. The opinions of these staff members can then be sought and taken into account in the final selection.

- For key management roles, involve more than one person in the interviewing, including perhaps someone who knows your business but does not actually work in it, and have more than one interview with each candidate.

One final word on interviewing: don't forget that you may have to sell the job to your preferred candidate – after all, if they're that good, they may well have other offers!

Having selected your preferred candidate, make sure that you check their references and their claims about past employment and qualifications. This sounds like such a straightforward and commonsense thing to do, and yet, many growing businesses still don't do it – and in some circumstances live to regret it. In one extreme case, a business with which we were working (we shall not name them) recruited a business development manager who proceeded to forge orders from customers and commit the business to buying equipment to fulfil these orders. This deception, and the negative cash flow that it created, very nearly caused the business to go bust. The individual in question was, of course, dismissed and it was only at this point that the owner-manager contacted the referee at the individual's previous employer. To both parties' great surprise, the individual concerned was still employed by his 'previous' employer and had been on long-term sick leave for stress. The whole sorry episode could have been avoided simply by taking up this reference at the beginning.

So, here's a quick summarized checklist which should help increase the odds of successfully recruiting the right people for the right jobs:

- Based on your growth strategy and business plan, decide on the *numbers of people* and *skills mix* you are going to need over the next one to three years.
- Prepare written *job descriptions* for each different type of job.
- Prepare a written *person specification* outlining the sort of person you think is likely to be effective in the job.
- Think carefully about the most likely ways to find potential applicants and use a range of sources.
- Weed out application forms or CVs of those who don't fit the job description and person specification and identify a shortlist.
- Select the most appropriate person from the shortlist using a range of techniques – not just one short interview.
- Check their references.

Motivation and retention

As you are probably already aware, recruiting great people is no easy task. So, once you've got them, the key challenge is to keep them – and, of course, for them to be motivated to perform to optimum levels. Indeed, in most service based businesses in particular, all you have is your people – and demotivated people will walk. If morale and levels of job satisfaction are low, then performance will suffer, the business results will not be as good as they should be and, ultimately, people (usually the ones you really want to keep) will leave. Hotel Chocolat is as much a service business as it is a fine chocolates business, and Angus Thirlwell, its managing director, says 'Keeping people and good morale is crucial to our business'.

Money talks – or does it?

One of the biggest mistakes that many owner-managers make is to assume that money alone is the way to motivate and retain staff. In fact, the motivating effect of a salary increase by itself is minor, shortlived and dependent on expectation rather than the actual amount. So, if you expected a salary increase of 5 per cent and this is what you got, then the effect is zero. If you expected 5 per cent and only received 3 per cent, then you will be demotivated. And, if you expected 5 per cent but received 7.5 per cent, then your job satisfaction and motivation will increase. But, unfortunately, this warm glow soon wears off.

Professor Frederick Hertzberg, an American professor of psychology, discovered that distinctly separate factors were the cause of job satisfaction and job dissatisfaction. His study of 200 engineers and accountants showed that five factors stood out as strong determinants of job satisfaction: achievement, recognition, responsibility, advancement and, of course, the attractiveness of the work itself.

When the reasons for dissatisfaction were analysed they were found to be concerned with a different range of factors: company policy, supervision, administration, salary, working conditions and interpersonal relations. Hertzberg called these cause of dissatisfaction 'hygiene factors', reasoning that the lack of hygiene will cause disease, but the presence of hygienic conditions will not, of itself, produce health.

So, lack of adequate 'job hygiene' will cause dissatisfaction, but its presence will not itself cause satisfaction. It is the 'motivators', such as recognition, responsibility, achievement, etc., which cause satisfaction. Both hygiene and motivator factors must be considered if you are to be successful at the art of effective management.

So, some of the non-monetary ways in which you can motivate your staff include:

- ensuring that everyone understands where the business is now, where it is heading and how they can contribute
- providing clear individual and team roles and responsibilities
- providing lots of feedback for people (this can be as simple as saying 'thank you')
- creating a good working environment for all staff
- offering people autonomy and new challenges
- ensuring that people feel that they are contributing and making a difference (for example by listening to their ideas about what should be done and how things could be improved)
- having clear development plans and career paths for each member of staff
- having training and development activities which support these plans
- offering the opportunity to experience other areas of the business and other roles
- having excellent communication mechanisms (which can include 'state of the nation' talks when you get everyone together to discuss the realities of the business and its performance, monthly management meetings, and, if appropriate, regular briefings and internal newsletters)
- informal, social meetings (e.g. weekly visits to the pub, sporting activities, etc.) and celebrations.

Measuring motivation and morale

Although good motivation and morale are often observable in the way people behave at work, it is good practice to have some more objective measures such as staff turnover rates, attitude survey and exit interviews.

Attitude surveys

If, every year or two, you carry out a simple internal survey of staff attitudes you will be able to pinpoint problem areas in the parts of your business which you can't reach. In much the same way as you might survey customers to find out how happy they are with your products and services, employees are surveyed to find out what they feel about their employment conditions. Attitude surveys provide an objective measure to counterbalance the more descriptive view obtained from discussions and gossip. They also provide a useful way to see if morale is getting better or worse over time.

You may decide to introduce attitude surveys because of a particular event, such as a number of key staff leaving at the same time, or some other obvious problem. But, once started, it makes sense to keep the practice up. At the very least, it demonstrates your concern, and at the best, it will give valuable pointers to raising morale, output and profits.

A word of warning. There is a danger that your attitude survey will reveal two basic facts that every attitude survey reveals. Namely that everyone believes himself or herself to be underpaid; and that communication is bad.

Most people believe they are underpaid both by market standards and in relation to the effort they put in. They also believe that the differentials are wrong and that the gap between levels is too great. This belief exists irrespective of how much people are actually paid, or indeed how hard they work. If you ask them why they don't leave, they will tell you about loyalty to the business, or, perhaps more flatteringly, loyalty to you.

Nearly all employees also believe their boss knows a secret that directly affects them that he or she is not willing to divulge. It may be about restructuring, moving, merging or outsourcing. This phenomenon happens at all levels. The 'shop floor' believes supervisors have secrets; supervisors believe managers withhold crucial information on plans that involve them; while those remaining managers know the directors are planning their future in secret. So, they become convinced there is a communication problem in the organization, because no one will tell them what is 'really' going on.

Both these feelings are fairly normal and you can at least draw comfort from that. But, more importantly, you have to take all the information from your employees into consideration when sizing up the situation, and not just the results of one attitude survey.

Examples of attitude surveys can be found in many places on the web, for instance, www.zoomerang.com.

Exit interviews

Of course, it is inevitable that some people will leave. Sometimes, these will be people that you would rather keep; on other occasions, you may be relieved to see them go. At such times, it is useful to undertake an exit interview.

The exit interview is a means of arranging for anyone leaving the company to be questioned by an impartial person who can establish the reason why. For example, is that person leaving for more money, because of a better opportunity or because they feel frustrated? Most people in these circumstances are quite happy to talk freely and you can learn a great deal which should help you improve things for other staff.

Appraisal

Appraisal lies at the heart of assessing, improving and developing people's performance for the future of the business. However, to be an effective tool, appraisal needs to be approached seriously and professionally by all involved.

Case Study

Innovex, which provides marketing services to the pharmaceutical industry, had at one stage, a fairly half-hearted appraisal system. Not all managers carried out appraisals, some interviews only took half an hour or so, assessment of areas for improvement was distinctly lacking, there were no clear objectives, people were assessed against personality characteristics (such as 'common sense') rather than results. Yet, the great issue for Innovex was the lack of depth of management resource. This could have easily become a limitation on its phenomenal growth rate. There were no obvious successors and managers were already 100 per cent stretched in their current jobs. The requirement was 'to grow people to run businesses in the UK and Europe'. There were some significant gaps between the management 'animal' at the time and the one Innovex would need for the future. As Barrie Haigh, Innovex's founder said at the time, 'The key is to look hard at our people, look hard and develop'. The mechanism for doing this is appraisal.

Innovex put all its managers and secretaries through appraisal interview training and took a good look at its appraisal system and revamped it along the lines listed below. Now at Innovex, appraisal is viewed as:

- a 'talk between people who work together'
- an open two-way discussion with both appraiser and the person being appraised preparing for the interview in advance
- a results-orientated rather than personality-orientated exercise (the interview starts with a review against objectives and finishes by setting objectives for the year to come)
- a narrative, rather than tick-box and ratings format, that covers achievements, areas for improvement, overall performance, training and development and career expectations
- an interview lasting for one and a half hours on average
- an annual event supplemented with quarterly reviews.
- an opportunity to identify training needs and act on them.

Rewards and recognition

As we have already noted, for many key staff in growing businesses, money is not their primary motivation. If it were, they would most probably be working in larger companies, which usually pay better. Provided the money is adequate, these people place great value on job satisfaction and the opportunity to make progress and develop their careers. It is in these two areas that the smaller growing business may well have an advantage over bigger, more bureaucratic organizations. In other words, you have to pay enough to keep your people but, if you've done the types of things mentioned above to help them feel valued and motivated, then you shouldn't have to pay over the odds.

So, rather than considering financial reward as the primary way to spur people on to greater performance, you should perhaps think of it as part of an overall rewards and recognition system which may include some or all of the following:

- Pay at least the going rate for the job/skill in your market and geographic area.
- Ensure that your pay system distinguishes good performers from poor performers.

- Use cash bonuses including 'instant' ones – little, immediate and frequent rewards are preferable to large, one-off bonuses.
- Make performance awards visible, e.g. by putting people's pictures on notice boards and internal publications or using badges.
- Have open and frequent celebrations of exceptional achievements including excellence awards.
- Use rewards such as tickets for the theatre or sporting events, gift vouchers, extra holidays, etc.
- Recognize good performers in front of their peers. This could be as simple as saying 'Well done!' when other people are listening.
- Recognize that employees have a life outside work. For example, when a person works late it is not just that individual who is making a sacrifice but also the individual's family. A small gift to acknowledge this can make a big difference to how that individual and their family view the company.
- Have team-based rewards as well as individual ones.
- Consider allocating shares in the business, or options to buy shares, to key individuals.

It is also crucially important to recognize that different stages of growth demand different reward packages, from the hands-on commission-based sales linked rewards of an infant business, through the cost and budget management of an adolescent into the challenges of giving the whole management team a share of the future which comes as a business matures.

As the business grows, it is likely that the recognition and reward package will need to be slanted more towards:

- encouraging genuine 'ownership' of and commitment to the business (e.g. share options)
- providing some element of reward for team performance as well as individual success
- demonstrating a direct relationship to performance.

Suggestion schemes

Staff suggestion schemes can be used to improve the performance of the business and, equally importantly, to encourage employee involvement and to provide a base on which to recognize people's contribution.

Once regarded as only being appropriate in large manufacturing companies, suggestion schemes have increasingly found favour in growing businesses.

Case Study

Richer Sounds, a small specialist hi-fi chain, gets most of its best ideas from its own staff. A discount scheme which boosted sales of cassette tapes tenfold; a bell at waist height

▶

to allow disabled customers to ring for attention; a policy of telephoning customers to check that they were satisfied with its repair service. All were proposals made by employees through the company suggestion scheme.

To encourage staff to come up with the ideas, Julian Richer, founder of the £12 million a year turnover company, funds a monthly brainstorming session in local pubs for the teams of employees from each of his stores. As an additional incentive, the number of suggestions also counts towards a monthly competition for the most highly rated store.

Richer spends one week in two at his Yorkshire mansion headquarters. On his regular train journey north, Richer scrutinizes the 80 or so suggestion cards that come in each fortnight and scribbles a comment on each one. 'The suggestions have to be seen by someone that staff will want to impress, not by a committee. You have to reply to them quickly – I do it within 14 days – and the good suggestions have to be used. I hit the department involved with the suggestion and make it happen.'

Richer also takes the view that all suggestions must be rewarded, although many companies only pay for suggestions which are adopted. The simpler suggestions made by Richer's staff win between £5 and £25, while the people who make the best two suggestions each quarter win a gold badge (another part of the company's incentive scheme) and a trip on the Orient Express.

Follow these five rules to make your suggestion scheme successful:

1. New suggestion schemes must be carefully planned and provided with the resources and management backing to sustain them over the long term. There are a lot of dead schemes around – they die very quickly if they are not properly run.

2. Suggestion schemes require constant promotion.

3. They should be fun. Schemes can be enlivened with short-term campaigns aimed at encouraging suggestions in areas such as energy-saving, the environment or customer care. League tables, a lucky dip from a tub of accumulated suggestions or a chairman's prize for the best of the year, can all sustain interest.

4. Suggestions must be handled quickly and efficiently. 'If the guys on the shop floor have an idea and get excited they should not be kept waiting more than 24 hours for an acknowledgement', advises Jim Byers of Ingersoll Engineers, a manufacturing consultancy. 'The company should come up with a response to the suggestion within a week.' If the suggestion is turned down, employees should be encouraged to submit new ones. Describing ideas it turns down as 'not adopted' rather than 'rejected' may prove more motivational.

5. Suggestions should be rewarded – though opinions differ on the scale of payment. One school of thought believes the rewards should be significant. Businessmen like Richer, however, believe in giving 'a little and often'. On average, schemes payout 18 per cent of savings made.

Training and development

Training people, on a regular basis, in all aspects of their jobs, is a sure-fire way to improve performance by reducing mistakes, getting costs down and increasing customer satisfaction. Training can also play an important part in retaining and motivating your staff since it demonstrates your commitment to invest in them. Some short-sighted employers ask 'Why train them when they stay for such a short time?' Answer: it costs 2 per cent of salary to train them, which is less than 10 per cent of the costs of their mistakes. And once trained, who knows, they may even get enough job satisfaction to want to stay – just think how much you'll save if that happens.

In addition, training can be one of the fastest payback routes to cost reduction. One study carried out by a major American corporation concluded that its productivity was improved by between 5 per cent and 20 per cent simply by explaining to people why their jobs matter. This single action saved it a net $9 million, after training costs, over the past three years.

Smaller businesses are notoriously bad at investing in training of any type.

- Over 40 per cent of small businesses devote only one day or less to staff training each year
- Only 13 per cent invest five days or more in training.

Amateur football teams spend more time in training than the average growing business! So, it is hardly surprising that few teams in these businesses ever realize their true potential, or come anywhere near becoming 'professionals'. And yet all the evidence is that training pays a handsome and quick return.

In the study 'Taking people seriously: do SMEs treat HR management as a vital part of their competitive strategy?' (Cranfield Working Paper) undertaken by Colin Barrow, Lesley Mayne and Chris Brewster in 1997, smaller businesses were clustered into four categories according to the rates of sales and profit growth. *Businesses in decline* were those where sales and profits were both dropping; *unprofitable growers* were those where sales were growing but profits were not; *profit enhancers* were those whose profits were growing on static sales figures; and the final group called *champions*, were those where sales and profits were both growing. The study compared businesses which invested significantly in people and training with those which did not. Virtually no businesses in the former category were in decline and the majority were either *champions* or *profit enhancers*. Those businesses which did not invest in people, by contrast, were most likely to be in *decline* or *unprofitable growers*. The message from the study was clear: *champions and profit enhancers invest in their people.*

If owner-managers are reluctant to invest in training in general, then they are even less likely to invest in training and developing *themselves*. And yet, investment in the development of the owner-manager is perhaps the quickest way of obtaining a return from training. In a different study, we compared businesses where the owner-manager has taken part in the Business Growth and Development Programme which we run at Cranfield with a sample drawn from over 30 000 independent businesses, mostly with a turnover of between £1 million and £7 million. The results are striking. Over the two years which were studied, the businesses which participated in the Business Growth and Development Programme:

- grew sales by 54 per cent (compared with the average of the sample which grew by just under 12 per cent)
- almost doubled their profitability (measured in terms of return on shareholders' funds) while the average business made only a marginal improvement.

Case Study

ACE/Chem-Resist, which employs 36 people and produces a range of industrial process plant in plastics, found that it was the victim of its own success. The order book had grown substantially and the current workforce was fully stretched. Meanwhile, the market, both in the UK and elsewhere in Europe, was becoming very complex.

Recruitment difficulties were looming and the management realized that its internal communications needed to improve. It was recognized that the company needed to develop a complete range of training and management systems to cope with the challenges ahead.

The business plan included some tough targets in terms of improvements in turnover and in gross margins. Central to the achievement of the business plan objectives was the development of management skills at the senior level. With the help of a consultant, the MD identified a suite of training needs covering the mainstream management skills including leadership and delegation, time management, staff appraisal, negotiating skills and recruitment. Training sessions were then developed and delivered during 30 training days spread over a period of one year and timed so that all members of the management team could participate.

All the goals set in the business plan were substantially achieved (and in most cases exceeded). There was a 44 per cent increase in fabrication turnover; the gross margin on material sales went up by 50 per cent; and there was a 47.8 per cent increase in technical sales. As a result senior managers now feel confident of being able to cope with the increasing demands being made upon them and they now have a keen appetite for learning and further self-development.

Frank Baines Saddlery was started with the aim of producing high quality saddles mainly for the export market. Success was achieved at an early stage with 90 per cent of output going to Sweden. But, as demand from Scandinavia grew, it became necessary to recruit more people in order to cope with demand. It was decided, in conjunction with the principal customer in Sweden, to develop a three-year training programme for young people.

The trainees were recruited through the local Chamber of Commerce and the training was delivered partly on the job through working alongside experienced saddle and bridle makers and partly in conjunction with a training college which specialized in the leather goods industry. National skill assessment and qualification awards were available and assessments were devised in conjunction with the leading saddlery trade bodies. Secondments were arranged for the trainees with leather factories in both Sweden and Germany.

The firm has doubled its original staff of five and output has trebled within three years. At the same time, the quality of the saddles and bridles has been maintained. Exports continue to grow and the firm has won commendations and recommendations from both Europe and North America.

▶

◀

J.V. Murcott and Sons Ltd is a family-run, 60 year-old business employing 140 people in Birmingham. They specialize in the manufacture of aluminium pressure diecastings. Continuous growth has increased the calls on management and supervisors and as the demands intensified the need for training became apparent.

Managers and supervisors were given the responsibility for creating and implementing departmental training so that their teams could meet the goals and objectives laid down in the company's recently issued business plan. Before the company could tackle departmental and organizational issues, however, it was necessary to resolve individual weaknesses. Personalized training plans were drawn up for managers, supervisors and chargehands. It was recognized that there were problems over poor commu-

nications and a lack of trust, and programmes were drawn up specifically to deal with this. For individual supervisors a course leading to a nationally recognized qualification was devised, while for departmental and team training there were outdoor programmes. Departmental training was developed to improve quality assurance, and to enhance the product and the overall skill base. Training was also implemented for a variety of technical departments using national standards.

Turnover has gone up by 46 per cent in the last two years while gross margins are up by 7 per cent. There has been a reduction both in finished stock and work in progress as well as in customer arrears. There is now much greater all-round commitment to the future of the company.

The training plan

Unfortunately, when asked what training they need, most people find it difficult to answer. It is, therefore, essential to find time to identify the training needs of your team, for each key individual and also yourself. Training needs are the gap between performance now and the performance you would like in the future. The appraisal interview provides a good opportunity for identifying training needs, another approach is to carry out a training needs analysis. Interviewing members of staff to determine key issues such as their background, role, skills needed in the job, strengths and weaknesses, career aspirations. A good survey will also include a discussion of changing business requirements, and the gap between these demands and present capabilities (see Table 2.12.1).

The choices you have for the delivery of training include:

- *On the job coaching*: This is where people learn how a job should be done from someone more experienced. The advantages are that it is free and involves no time away from work. It should also be directly related to an individual's training needs. However it is only as good as the coach and, if they are untrained, you could end up simply replicating poor working standards.

- *In-house classroom training*: This is the most traditional and familiar form of training. Some, or all, of your employees gather in a 'classroom' either on your premises or in a local hotel. You hire in a trainer or use one of your own experienced staff. This method provides plenty of opportunity for group interaction and the instructor can motivate the class and pay some attention to individual needs. The disadvantage, particularly if it is held away from your premises, are that you incur large costs that are more to do

Table 2.12.1

Technical/job related	Accounting or sales skills	Example of a training menu
	Negotiating skills	
	Computer skills	
Management skills (existing and potential managers)	Leadership and motivation	
	Team building	
	Appraising, counselling and disciplinary interviews	
	Managing change	
	Recruitment and selection	
	Training and developing staff	
Business	Basic finance	
	Principles of marketing	
	Putting together the business plan	
	Understanding strategy	

with hospitality than training, and it is time consuming and difficult to release a number of employees at the same time.

- *Public courses*: These are less expensive than running a training programme in a hotel. You can also select different courses for different employees and so tailor the training more precisely to their needs. Most public courses are generic and the other attendees are more likely to come from big business or even the public sector. So much of what is covered may be of little direct relevance to your business.

- *Interactive distance learning*: This kind of training can be delivered by a combination of traditional training materials, teleconferencing, and the internet and email discussions. You miss out on the personal contact, but the costs are much lower than traditional training. Most of the learning programmes are aimed at larger businesses, so some material may not be so relevant. e-Learning Portals, where you can find out more about e-learning include, Click2Learn.com (www.click2learn.com), HeadLight.com, (www.headlight.com.), Hungry Minds (www.hungryminds.com) and Learndirect (www.learndirect.co.uk)

- *Off-the-shelf training programmes*: These come in packaged kits, which may consist of a training manual, video or a CD Rom. Once again, the cost is lower than for face-to-face training, but you miss out on a professional trainer's input.

- *Colleges*: Many universities and business schools now offer programmes tailored for the needs of growing businesses. They are usually delivered by professional instructors who understand the needs of growing businesses. They are relatively expensive but can often be very effective.

Government initiatives

Governments have an interest in encouraging training in smaller businesses. As well as providing information on where their training schemes are being run, governments often provide training grants to help with the costs. The agency in your country responsible for advising and helping new and growing businesses should be able to suggest routes to both finance and training resources. In the UK, the Department of Trade and Industry and in the US the Small Business Administration (SBA) are the relevant agencies.

Leadership and teams

The essence of leadership is the activity of orchestrating the resources of others towards solving problems, not in being the hero oneself. The Chinese philosopher, Lao-Tzu said: 'When the best leader's work is done the people say we did it ourselves.' The idea of leader as hero has been replaced by the concept of leader as conductor of an orchestra of players.

Unfortunately, many entrepreneurial chief executives learn this lesson the hard way. They like to keep on being the hero. That is one reason why successful CEOs often have to leave at a certain point. They have to leave because there is a dependency on them which they can't shift, and they can't let go. Most entrepreneurs will have to learn the transition from the 'meddler' to 'strategist' if they are to avoid being a constraint on the growth of their own organization. The essence of visionary leadership lies in two aspects: firstly in articulating the vision or direction of the business and secondly in mobilizing the energies of all the employees towards the vision.

Leadership can be best described not as a quality, nor as a combination of technical skills demanded by particular situations, but as an activity. This is why John Adair's 'action-centred leadership' model has proved so successful, both in training the officers of Sandhurst and in many walks of business life.

Action-centred leadership

We do not all have the same potential for getting results through people, nor do all organizations require the same sort of leadership behaviour. However, when we are concerned with developing the competence to lead we might more appropriately ask 'What does a good leader do?' rather than what qualities does he or she have.

The essence of the functional approach is that the leader must satisfy three distinct but interrelated sets of needs:

- the needs of the *task*
- the needs of the *team*
- the needs of the *individual*.

Task needs

The difference between a team and a random crowd is that the team has some common purpose or goal. Without this common objective, it would not stick together as a group. If a work team does not achieve the required result or output, it will become frustrated. Organizations have a task: to provide a service, to cover costs or even to survive. So anyone who manages others has to achieve these results.

Team needs

To achieve these objectives, the group must be held together. People need to work in a co-ordinated fashion in the same direction; teamwork will ensure that the team contribution is greater than the sum of its parts. Conflict within the team must be used effectively, arguments can lead to ideas, or to tension and lack of co-operation.

Individual needs

Within working groups, individuals also have their own set of motivational needs. They need to know what their responsibilities are, how they will be judged, how well they are doing. They need an opportunity to show their potential, take on responsibilities and receive recognition for good work.

The leader's job must be to satisfy all three areas of need by achieving the task, building the team and satisfying individual needs. If leaders only concentrate on tasks, for example, in going all out for achieving output whilst neglecting the training and motivation of their people, they may do very well in the short term. Eventually, however, those people will give less than they know they are capable of. Similarly, neglecting the task will not get the maximum contribution from employees. They will lack the real sense of achievement which comes from accomplishing the task. Examples of task, team and individual behaviours are:

1. Task-orientated behaviour:

    agree objectives
    plan and allocate resources
    make decisions
    control progress
    review and evaluate.

2. Team orientated behaviour:

    select the right people
    communicate with them
    encourage
    harmonize
    co-ordinate.

3. Individual orientated behaviour:

    trust and respect
    listen
    identify training needs
    appraise

delegate
develop
motivate
recognize and praise.

Teams

One perspective on organizations such as businesses is that they are nothing more than groups of individuals brought together to achieve a particular purpose. And, since well co-ordinated teams are generally more effective than groups of disparate individuals, teams are becoming ever more important in nearly all organizations.

In the early stages of a growing, entrepreneurial business the people tend to be highly motivated, small teams who spend a lot of time together at work and socially. As the business grows in numbers, sheer size will start to crack the foundations of this camaraderie. The introduction of new people without the original motivation will change the flavour of relationships. It is at this point you will find yourself consciously having to introduce ways and means of getting the team together and keep them facing the right way. Involving your team in preparation and presentation of the business plan can, in itself, be a good way of providing co-ordination to a growing business.

It is amazing how many business people expect a team to work as a team without any practice. After all, it doesn't work this way for sports teams. The way to build a team is to find many formal and informal ways of bringing them together: cascade briefings, state of the nation addresses, lunches, social events, special project teams, happy hours (fun is actually quite compatible with profit). The importance of informal contact between people, as a way of building productive networks, cannot be over-emphasized, but again it will not happen without the mechanism to make it happen.

It is absolutely clear that the more you are trying to grow and change the business, the more you will have to communicate. Briefing groups are an excellent discipline for downward communication but there is a lot more to it than that. You need processes to ensure upward communication, and especially to co-ordinate across the barriers which your organization will establish as it grows. There are plenty of examples to help here and plenty of ways of building your team, for example, outward bound programmes, internal team-building events.

The Belbin team role profiles (see Table 2.12.2) are a particularly useful way of identifying individuals' preferred team roles. Differences are essential for effective team-working and for learning to live with each other. Belbin suggests a successful team needs a mix of eight roles.

Removing people

Unfortunately, there will inevitably come a time when you have to remove someone from the team. This may be because they are no longer capable of doing the job you need them to do, perhaps because the business has changed and they are unable to change with it, or because you no longer have a need for that

Table 2.12.2

Co-ordinator (or Chairperson)

Stable, dominant, extrovert

Concentrates on objectives

Does not originate ideas

Focuses people on what they do best

Plant

Dominant, high IQ, introvert

A 'scatterer of seeds', originates ideas

Misses out on detail

Thrusting but easily offended

Resource investigator

Stable, dominant, extrovert sociable

Contacts with outside world

Salesperson/diplomat/liaison officer

Not original thinker

Shaper

Anxious, dominant, extrovert

Emotional, impulsive

Quick to challenge and respond to challenge

Unites ideas, objectives and possibilities

Competitive

Intolerant of woolliness and vagueness

Implementer

Stable, controlled

Practical organizer

Can be flexible but likely to adapt to
    established systems

Not an innovator

Monitor, evaluator

High IQ, stable, introvert

Measured analysis not innovation

Unambitious and lacking enthusiasm

Solid, dependable

Team builder

Stable, extrovert, low dominance

Concerned with individuals' needs

Builds on others' ideas

Cools things down

Completer, finisher

Anxious, introvert

Worries over what will go wrong

Permanent sense of urgency

Preoccupied with order

Concerned with 'following through'

Belbin's team role
profiles

---

particular role, or because they have done something unforgivable. Whatever the reasons, you will face this uncomfortable situation at some time and it is important to grasp the nettle.

Unfortunately, growing businesses tend to hang on to people long after they should have been fired. No one pretends firing is easy or fun – but sometimes it is essential. If people who don't perform are seen to get the same job security and rewards as those who do, you will be sending the wrong signals to everyone.

It is a most painful experience, reaching the decision that one of your team is going to have to leave, and then dismissing either him or her. Especially so, if the member is, as so often happens, one of your founding team. You may have to reach this decision very suddenly – discovering, for instance, that the person has done something quite unacceptable. Or more likely, it has gradually become clear over time, for one reason or another.

There may be a temptation to fire someone on the spot, in the heat of the moment. Conversely, the fear of the legal consequences, and of facing a claim for unfair dismissal, may make managers nervous about taking any action at all. Your own reasons for deciding that you want to dismiss someone will probably fall into one of the following categories:

- the employee is unable to do the job properly
- there is no longer any need for the business to continue to employ someone in that particular role
- he or she has done something unforgivable or even criminal.

Whatever the reason in your own mind, pause for thought, and plan your line of action carefully.

- *Unable to do the job*: This can include such reasons as certain kinds of permanent disabling illness or simply being insufficiently skilled to carry out the tasks that you need the person to do. A key rule here is to satisfy yourself absolutely that you are right to conclude that the person is unable to do the job. For instance, you cannot safely assume an illness will be long-lasting and disabling unless you have asked the employee for permission to talk to their doctor, and the doctor confirms this.

  If, on the other hand, it is a question of level of performance, you need to track and record output if you can, and to offer the employee time and opportunity to improve in the specified areas – by providing special training if appropriate.

- *Not needed*: If someone's job is being abolished, then technically this is called redundancy. Separate rules and regulations then apply, of course. But often things are not so clear cut. For example, a firm may grow and find that it now needs a proper finance director, and so wish to replace the current accountant's role with someone of higher calibre, doing a much bigger job. This is probably defensible as redundancy following reorganization, provided a new accountant is not then appointed in a similar role to the old one. And, provided the current person is offered any relevant suitable vacancy – such as a new post being created underneath the new finance director. And provided you have reasonable proof that your present accountant is not up to assuming the role of finance director.

- *Misconduct*: The contract of employment, drawn up when the employee began working for you should cover this area to some extent. To take some examples, a violent and unprovoked physical attack on a colleague at work is a reason for dismissal unlikely to be challenged in law, provided there are good witnesses. You will want to be certain of the event's real character – that it hasn't been exaggerated in the telling. Likewise, if you find that someone is stealing from the till – provided that you are absolutely certain you have proof of who the culprit is, and do not jump to conclusions without first asking for explanations.

But misbehaviour at work leading to dismissal can take many much less grave forms, right down to repeatedly wearing the wrong clothes if, for instance, it has clearly been a condition of employment, from the start, that employees should wear a uniform.

Procedure

How you go about dismissing someone is almost as important in law as your reasons for doing so. By now, most employers know that it is safest to meet formally with the person concerned, to explain fully, to give the employee the fullest possible chance to state his or her case, to keep agreed notes of the meetings, and to give at least two written warnings with full reasons. Do give the proper period of formal notice when it finally comes to terminating the employment.

Classic mistakes

To keep the threat of industrial tribunals at bay, whatever you do:

- Don't dismiss anybody on the basis of information you have had by hearsay from a third party.
- Don't dismiss anybody just because they have got married or become pregnant.
- Don't dismiss someone in the heat of the moment, however personally provoked you may be, as can sometimes happen in small teams working at close quarters.
- Don't dismiss someone for something which you have never even mentioned to them before.
- Make sure you investigate causes and possible remedies, and involve them in the process.

Handling the termination

No matter what the circumstances, all employees are entitled to a high level of consideration and compassion, and the benefit to the company of treating dismissed employees well maintains morale and your image as a caring employer. It avoids making unnecessary enemies and causing avoidable stress and pain to departing employees. Termination planned and carried out in a professional way helps to ensure this.

Plan the interview in advance

Decide the best time and place. Don't fire on a Friday – the dismissed employee needs time to adjust before facing his or her family. If possible choose neutral ground for the task – a private place, quiet and free from interruptions. Rehearse the interview if necessary, and decide in advance how to direct the individual after termination.

These are the 20 questions and comments most commonly heard from the employee being dismissed. Make sure you have your responses ready.

- Why me?
- Are the terms negotiable?
- Do I have the right to appeal?
- I intend to take the matter further!

- What about my car?
- What about my life cover and health care?
- What about my pension?
- Why wasn't I given prior warning?
- What help will you give me to find a new job?
- Are there any alternative jobs I could do even at a lower grade?
- Can I apply for, or will you consider me for any future vacancies?
- Can I work my notice?
- Who's going to do my job?
- I think this is totally unfair especially given my service and ability!
- Am I the only one affected?
- Can I return to my office?
- What have my colleagues been told?
- Can I tell my staff?
- Who will supply me with a reference?
- When does this come into effect?

Don't procrastinate

Once the decision to let someone go has been made, get on with it, otherwise word of impending action might reach the employee's colleagues causing them to shun him/her. Procrastination is not only the thief of time but also of the individual's self-confidence and future job prospects.

Tell them the truth

Explain the clear, specific and precise reason for the dismissal, without being brutal, preferably backed up by documentary evidence. Many employees cannot believe that they are being fired and will look for any sign of uncertainty as an indication that the job is still negotiable. If the reasons are held back it may cause unnecessary worry and loss of self-esteem.

Don't be emotional

The emotional manager will either plunge in too quickly, without sensitivity, trying to get the whole thing over and done with or hedge about, failing to make the point and leaving the employee unsure about the situation. Diffusing an emotional situation is one of the most immediate goals of a termination from the company's point of view, and one of the main reasons terminations go disastrously wrong is the emotional state of the manager as well as of the employee.

Don't prolong the agony

The initial interview should last no longer than 15 minutes. There is no point in going into a great deal of detail at this stage – the person may be in a state of shock and unable to take in much of the conversation. Give them a chance to respond, though, and make a subsequent appointment to discuss details of severance pay, and perhaps references.

Chapter summary

You'll never have a great business without great people. The successful achievement of your growth aims will be as much dependent on having the right people, in the right jobs and performing well, as it is on your strategy or product/service.

In this chapter, we've looked at how to get the right people in the first place through thorough recruitment and selection approaches. We've considered how to retain them and keep them motivated once you've got them. We've looked at the impact that training and development of your staff, and perhaps most importantly yourself, can have on the success of the business. We've explored different leadership styles and the different roles and capabilities required in truly effective teams. And, we've also considered what to do when you make mistakes with people.

In order to grow your business to any significant size, you will need to work through, and with, other people. Mastery of this demands both an understanding of the ideas presented in this chapter and an instinctive understanding for other people, their drivers, motivators and needs. For many entrepreneurs, this area is often the most challenging part of their business. Of course, seeing other people grow and develop as a result of your leadership can also be one of the most personally satisfying things that you do. In addition, the quality of your people, particularly the management team, can add significant value to your business and is one of the key factors which influence investors and purchasers.

Assignments

Recruitment and selection

1. Identify the key roles and skills that you will need to implement your strategy.
2. Draw up a job description, person specification and recruitment plan for the first two key appointments that you expect to have to make.

Retention and motivation

3. What is your staff turnover rate and how does it compare to your competitors?
4. Carry out a staff attitude survey to discover how people feel about working in your business.
5. Review your approaches to rewarding, recognising and motivating people. What can you do to make your business an even better place to work?

Training and development

6. Develop a training plan for key individuals (including yourself!) and roles, and identify ways of delivering these needs.

Leadership and teams

7. What major task, team and individual needs have to be satisfied to ensure your business can succeed?

8. Ask each member of your management team to complete a Belbin team role questionnaire. In discussion with the team, consider each individual's profile against the role that they do. Is there a good fit? If not, how can you help that individual develop and/or accommodate in other ways. Looking at the profiles of the team as a whole, are there any particular areas of weakness or areas where there is too much concentration (i.e. you're all trying to do the same role and getting in each other's way)? If so, how will you allow for this?

Removing people

9. Is there anyone on your staff who you believe should be removed for whatever reason? If so, plan carefully and then do it!

Suggested further reading

Adair, John and Neil Thomas (2004) *The John Adair Handbook of Management and Leadership*, London, Hawksmere.

Barrow, Colin (2003), *E-Training and Development*, Oxford: Capstone Reference.

Belbin, Meredith (1984) *Management Teams: Why They Succeed and Fail*, Oxford: Butterworth-Heinemann.

West, Michael and Lynn Marciewicz (2003) *Building Team Based Working*, Oxford: Blackwell.

13   How do you fund growth?

Introduction and objectives

Whatever strategic direction you propose to pursue in order to grow your business, it is almost certain to require money. By now, you will have discovered that a healthy business has an equally healthy appetite for cash. For the first years of a business's life, its strategic choices are invariably limited by the availability of funds. Once it gathers momentum and begins to plan its strategic direction, the 'corset elastic' is usually the limited availability of good opportunities and the management to exploit them successfully.

The constant search for funds is not in itself a cause for concern. Businesses, after all, exist in part at least to turn money into goods and services, which can be sold on for a profit. It usually takes a while for the business cycle to move from strategic ideas to profit and so, as long as you are growing, more money will be needed.

What should concern you, however, is where that money comes from. There are two main sources of money: internal and external, with a number of sub-divisions of each sector. Getting the right balance of funds from these different sources is one of the keys to profitable growth – and perhaps even to survival itself.

By the end of the chapter you should have a clear understanding of the following key topics:

- Internal sources of funds including squeezing working capital and ways of making more profit.

- External sources of funds, in particular debt (or borrowing) and equity, and the different expectations of the providers of these types of funding.

- Other ways to fund growth including franchising and corporate venturing.

Internal sources of funds

Surprisingly enough, many businesses have much of the money they need to finance growth already tied up in the firm. It may require a little imagination and some analysis to uncover it, but a financial position audit should give some pointers to how this might be done.

Squeeze working capital

Working capital is an area rich in possibilities to release cash for expansion. Debtors and stock control are perhaps the most fertile areas to start.

Debtors

According to research at Cranfield (*Business finance in today's challenging environment*, an Independent Business Finance study, 2003), collecting money from customers is still a major problem for most owner-managed businesses, despite copious legislation across Europe to outlaw late payment of bills. It is salutary to remember that the total cost of providing customers with the extra 48 days of credit, the difference between the best and worst collection periods in different countries in Europe, is equivalent to 5.7 per cent of the average business's turnover, and, assuming a net profit margin of 10 per cent, more than half its net profit. Instead of companies being able to borrow to grow the business, they often need to borrow just to fund their sales ledger.

Here are some things you can do to manage your debtors more closely and so make better use of your working capital:

1. Carefully consider your terms of trade. Can you ask for part payments up front, or for staged payment? Do you need to allow credit? If so, how much?
2. If you are going to give credit, always take trade references and look at the customers' own accounts to see how sound they are.
3. Make sure that your invoices are accurate. Don't give your customers an excuse to query them.
4. Send out invoices promptly, if possible on delivery.
5. If you sell on credit, set out your terms of trade very clearly on your invoices. Unless customers know when you expect to be paid, they will pay when it suits them.
6. Find out when your biggest customers have their monthly cheque run and make sure your bills reach them in time.
7. Send out statements promptly to chase up late payers, and always follow up with a phone call.
8. Bank cheques and cash promptly. It's not only safer, but the sooner you get money into the banking system, the sooner you are either saving interest cost or earning interest income.

Stock control

Stock of all types (raw materials, work-in-progress and finished goods) ties up capital. You only benefit from this investment once the finished goods are sold and you receive the payment in return. Stock also occupies space and needs people to manage it. Therefore, minimizing the amount of stock and maximizing the speed with which stock flows through the business, are key levers of releasing working capital.

On the other hand, you need enough stock to meet demand. So, it's important to have detailed and accurate forecasts of demand and then to match your stock requirements to these forecasts. In larger businesses, this is often done through sophisticated software known as material requirements planning (MRP) and enterprise resource planning (ERP). Growing businesses can achieve considerable improvements in stock management by relatively simple changes in the way they purchase and monitor their stocks including:

- Having accurate stock records for each individual stock item. Regularly review for any slow moving items.
- Regularly forecast your sales for each individual stock item. Review forecasts against actual sales so that you can improve the accuracy of your forecasts. Match stock and work-in-progress to these forecasts.
- Where possible, buy from suppliers with short delivery times.
- Buy more frequently but in smaller quantities (e.g. monthly instead of quarterly). You may need to consider the effect of price discounts for bulk orders but generally speaking the working capital advantages outweigh these discounts.
- Much of the cost of many products is incurred in the final stages of manufacture. So potentially big stock savings can be made by holding stocks of semi-finished items. Only put the finishing touches to an item when the customer wants it.
- Re-examine any automatic stock re-order points to see if lower levels can be set.

For businesses which have failed to monitor stock levels closely, the introduction of tight controls can prove daunting. A 'quick and dirty' way of making improvements can be achieved by grading stock as A, B or C according to the value of individual items or of the total number held. Attention is then focused on items in the A category which can provide the greatest savings. These items can then be subjected to regular stock-takes; patterns of demand can be studied to see how frequently orders are placed, if there are peaks or troughs, or whether demand is seasonal. Managers can then decide the quantities they require and when to place their next order, or start their next production run, if they are making the item in-house. B and C items can be brought into this programme once it is well established.

Other ways to squeeze working capital

You can also improve your working capital management by managing your own credit and cash better. For instance:

- Take the maximum credit from your suppliers. Once you have a good track record, try to negotiate extended terms with major suppliers. Many will say no, but some may not. A good time to start these negotiations is when a price rise comes along!
- Make any cash you have work harder. Overnight money markets, now more easily accessible through internet banks, could allow you to get interest on cash, rather than having it sitting in the banking system doing nothing.
- Work out if it makes sense to pay bills quickly to take advantage of early settlement discounts. Sometimes, usually by accident, suppliers offer what amounts to high rates of interest for settling promptly. If you are offered 2.5 per cent to pay now rather than in two months time, that is equivalent to an annual rate of interest of 15 per cent (12/2 x 2.5%). If your bank is charging you 8 per cent then you would make a good extra profit by taking up this offer.

Make more profit and plough it back

Another internal source of finance is to make your present business more profitable and plough that profit back to grow your business. Five steps you can take to unlock the extra profit potential in your business are:

Recognize the iceberg

Just as the small tip of the iceberg showing above water conceals an enormous mass below, the small(ish) percentage of profits the average business makes (typically under 10 per cent of sales), conceals a great volume of money being used to arrive at that profit. It requires only a few percentage points reduction in costs to dramatically improve profits, as Table 2.13.1 illustrates.

In the example given in Table 2.13.1, the last profit margin was 5 per cent. Costs, the 'below the water line' mass, are 95 per cent of sales. By reducing those costs by a mere 2 per cent, bottom line profits have been increased by a massive 40 per cent (this is a simplified example from a real life case).

This extra profitability can then be used to finance extra investments, saved as a reserve for bad times, or be used to compensate for lower sales. In Table 2.13.1, when costs are reduced by 2 per cent, turnover from sales can drop by over 25 per cent to £714000 before profits will dip below £50000. That should take care of even the worst recession seen since the 1920s and 1930s.

	Before		After 2% cost saving		Extra profit		But if sales drop ...	
	£000	%	£000	%	£000	%	£000	%
Sales	1 000	100	1 000	100	—	—	714	100
Costs	950	95	930	93	—	—	664	93
Profit	50	5	70	7	20	40	50	7

Table 2.13.1

Effects of cost savings on profits

Much of this will come as no surprise to you – after all most of this is your money, so naturally, you are well informed as to where it goes. But, the people who work for you have probably never considered, or been given the chance to consider, the phenomenal impact that relatively small savings in costs can have on the bottom line. So, why not tell them? You could start by giving your key employees a copy of Table 2.13.1 and inviting their comments.

Use the 80:20 rule

Obviously, you cannot leave the whole responsibility of reducing costs exclusively to the people who, after all, created the costs in the first place. Just as with any other business task, objectives have to be agreed and strategies adopted.

Fortunately, here you have the 80:20 rule working in your favour. This rule states that 80 per cent of effort goes into producing 20 per cent of the results. Look at Table 2.13.2, which was prepared for one company on a recent business growth programme. This more or less confirms the rule, as 18 per cent of customers account for 78 per cent of sales.

A quick glance at figures in your own business will, in all probability, confirm that 20 per cent of your customers account for 80 per cent of your sales, and yet your costs are probably spread evenly across all your customers.

As an example of the way in which this affects your business, consider the way that sales staff spend their time. Sales staff tend to make their calls in a cycle that suits their administrative convenience, rather than concentrating on customers with the most potential.

Interestingly enough, when the salesman in the company used in the above example was asked where he thought his sales in two years' time would be coming from (see column 3, Table 2.13.2), he felt that his top 18 per cent of customers would account for 88 per cent of sales (up from 78 per cent of actual sales this year). And yet, an analysis of his call reports showed that he spent over 60 per cent of his time calling on his bottom 68 accounts, and planned to continue doing so. This activity-based – rather than results-based – outlook was being used to make out a case for an additional salesperson. What was actually needed was a call grading system to lower the call rate on accounts with the least sales potential. So, for example, accounts with the least potential were called on twice a year and phoned twice, while top grade accounts were visited up to eight times a year.

Number of customers	%	Value of sales £000	%	Value of potential sales £000	%
4	3	710	69	1 200	71
21	18	800	78	1 500	88
47	41	918	90	1 600	94
116	100	1 025	100	1 700	100

Table 2.13.2

The 80:20 rule in action

This grading process saves costs, as phone calls are cheaper than visits; it eliminates the need for an additional salesperson, which at first glance the projected growth would have justified; and it even frees up time so the salesman can prospect for new, high potential accounts.

The 80:20 rule can be used across the business to uncover other areas where costs are being incurred that are unwarranted by the benefits. In some areas, you just need to open your eyes to see waste. Did you know that the average executive spends 36 minutes a day looking for things on or around the desk? This can waste up to £6000 a year for a fairly senior person – you, for example. The same survey, conducted for the British Institute of Management, revealed that a quarter of the 500 executives they questioned spent 11 hours a week in meetings – equivalent to 13 weeks a year. Few were satisfied with their investment.

The chances are, if you are anything like many other chief executives, you feel that you and your management team waste too much time on the wrong priorities. It is not that managers aren't working hard enough – on average they work 20 per cent more hours than a decade ago. It is just that organizing time and daily priorities in a world in which there has been a 600 per cent increase in business information, and the average manager is interrupted every eight minutes, is difficult to say the least. But, the 'cost' of wasting time is very real in two senses. Firstly, you end up buying more management than you need – and that cost has to be spread across your products. Secondly, people are too busy doing the wrong things to have time to do the right things.

Zero-based budgeting

The 80:20 rule is helpful in getting costs back into line – but what if the line was completely wrong in the first place?

When you sit down with your team and discuss budgets, the arguments always revolve around how much more each section will need next year. The starting point is usually this year's costs, which are taken as the only 'facts' upon which to build. So, for example, if you spent £25 000 on advertising last year and achieved sales of £1 million, the expense would have been 2.5 per cent of sales. If the sales budget for next year is £1.5 million, then it seems logical to spend £37 500 next year. That, however, presupposes last year's sum was wisely and effectively spent in the first place, which it almost certainly was not.

Popularized by Robert McNamara, US Secretary of Defense in 1962, zero-based budgeting turns the cost argument on its head. It assumes that each year every cost centre starts from zero spending and, based on the goals of the business and the resources available, arguments are presented for every penny spent, *not just for the increase proposed*.

Cut out mistakes through training

According to the former chief executive of a major bank, basic mistakes by employees account for between 25 per cent and 40 per cent of the total costs of any service business – and not just in banking. It is certainly true that people learn from experience, and the more often they do a job, the faster and better they get at it (up to the stage where indifference sets in of course)! What a pity, however, that so many growing businesses let their employees practise on their customers, losing money and goodwill in the process.

As we have already seen in an earlier chapter, training your people, on a regular basis, in all aspects of their jobs, is a sure-fire way to reduce mistakes, and get costs down and customer satisfaction up. Training can be one of the fastest payback routes to cost reduction.

Incentivize everyone around profit

Lots of companies have incentive schemes, but most end up rewarding the wrong achievement. Some firms actually reward people by how much they spend! So, for example, buyers with the biggest budget get the highest pay and perks. Production staff are paid for greater output and salespeople for more sales, whether or not either activity is particularly desirable at the time it is achieved. In one company (name withheld to protect the embarrassed) one of the largest creditor items on liquidation was sales people's commission.

There are always hundreds of reasons for giving people intermediate incentives, such as sales commission. But, unless you build profit targets into your goals and incentives, nine times out of ten you'll end up with the wrong result. You get nothing if the company doesn't make a satisfactory profit, so rewarding others if they don't make money is only encouraging an illusion. Building incentives for everyone around the profit you make focuses the whole business around customers and costs, and that has to be good. It will make everyone look for:

- cheaper ways to do things
- ways to eliminate waste
- more effective ways to spend their time (and your money)
- ways to get more money out of more satisfied customers.

In short, all the ways to unlock the profit potential in your business.

Increasing margins

Increasing margins has the double effect of increasing the flow of cash into a business by increasing profits, whilst at the same time reducing the amount of money tied up in producing low or even no profit items.

To achieve increased margins, you need first to review the mix of your sales. This requires accurate costs and gross margins for each of your products or services. Armed with that information, you can select particular product groups or market segments that are less price sensitive and potentially more profitable.

For example, Robert Segesser, MD of Dairyborn Foods, a cheese component business, spent his first five years in business building sales – £3 million a year's worth – without making much profit. Then he defined the company's principal objectives as being to move its profit margin from 16 per cent to 25 per cent. This moved the business into what he likes to refer to as 'margin-protected' business, in other words, things that only Dairyborn can do, that certain groups of customers want badly and will pay for. Segesser believed that, if his customers got to the future before he does, they would leave him behind. He had to create solutions for customer's problems before they even realized they had one.

Refocusing on solving problems rather than selling cheese, and aiming for profit margin growth rather than turnover growth alone, has transformed the business into a £15 million sales and £2 million a year profit business. From being worth little, within two years the company had turned away a potential suitor with £20 million on the table.

Pricing

Pricing is one of the biggest decisions your business has to make, and one that it needs to keep constantly under review. It is certainly the decision that has the biggest impact on company profitability. Try the consultant's favourite exercise of computing and comparing the impact on profits of:

- A 5 per cent cut in your overheads.
- A 5 per cent increase in volume sales.
- A 5 per cent cut in materials purchased.
- A 5 per cent price increase.

All these actions are usually considered to be within an owner-manager's normal reach. Almost invariably, the 5 per cent price increase scores the highest, as it passes straight to the net profit, bottom line. Even if volume falls, because of the effect price has on gross margin, it is usually more profitable to sell fewer items at a higher price. For example, at a constant gross margin of 30 per cent with a 5 per cent price increase, profits would be unchanged even if sales declined 14 per cent. Yet, if prices were cut 5 per cent, an extra 21 per cent increase in sales would be needed to stand still.

Frequently, resistance to increasing prices, even in the face of inflationary cost rises, can come from your own team members, eager to apportion blame for performance lapses. In these instances, it is important to make detailed price comparisons with competitors. Mark Sanders, for example, when designing and launching his innovative folding bicycle, the 'Strida', into the mature 100-year-old bicycle market, recognized that a) his manufacturer's capacity was strictly limited and b) his target market was 'well-to-do, city commuters' or 'lifestyle weekenders'. An initial price of nearly £300 per bike was well above established competitive models, but gave good margins to dealers in taking up the product and left room for manoeuvre later in the product life cycle when competition would react to the Strida's unusual features. By selecting a less price-sensitive market segment, Strida's margins were maintained at a much higher level than they might otherwise have been had they gone for a blanket approach to the market.

Working smarter

Making more of your own money rather than having to raise money outside doesn't always have to mean working longer hours. You could just work smarter, and who knows you may even end up working fewer hours than you do now and still make more money.

One way to get everyone's grey matter working overtime is to create smart circles (and smart rewards). You could formalize the process of encouraging employees to rethink the way they work, and reward them in such a way as to make their working environment better still, as the owner-manager has demonstrated in the case example below.

Case Study

Dairyborn Foods products are used in the chilled ready meal market, the frozen ready meal market and the convenience food market. The market consists of chilled ready meals, prepared salads, chilled pizzas, fresh pasta, sandwiches and chilled pot desserts, and is one of the most dynamic sectors of the total food market in Europe. The market is relatively new but is developing quickly in response to consumer expectations.

For the past decade the total market for all chilled food has grown at a compound rate of 7.7 per cent and is forecast to continue this rate of growth over the foreseeable future. The market for chilled ready meals has grown at a compound rate of 10 per cent and is expected to continue this growth rate.

Operating in such a dynamic market has forced Dairyborn to find innovative ways to get even more output from her small production facility. To motivate and involve employees, 'Smart Circles' have been introduced to develop a culture of working 'smarter not harder'. Any employee can arrange a meeting with other staff members, to discuss a new idea or operational change, which will be of benefit to the customer or company. This meeting has a set time of half an hour, to ensure they are productive, but if the idea is worth pursuing there is the opportunity to have as many meetings as required. However, after six weeks, the idea must be 'taken on', or dropped.

This gives the staff a sense of belonging and responsibility for the way the company develops, and a Smart Team award acknowledges any 'outstanding' ideas, for each quarter. Presentation of this award is given by the Managing Director and published in the company's newsletter each quarter.

The Smart Team Award consists of a sum of money, relative to the value of the innovation. The money has to be spent on things of value to the team. It could be an evening out, or any other social event. It could also be used to buy a business asset that's nice to have but could not really be justified on business grounds. One winning team decided to have their own photocopier to save them going up and downstairs to use the one in the general office.

One final thought on internal sources of finance: Does your business really need to do everything it currently does itself? If not, you could release all the working capital and fixed capital tied up in that process and use it for better things.

External sources of funds

There are two fundamentally different types of external money which a growing company can tap into: debt and equity. Debt is money borrowed, usually from a bank, and which one day you will have to repay. While you are making use of borrowed money you will also have to pay interest on the loan. Equity is the money put in by shareholders, including the proprietor, and money left in the business by way of retained profit. You don't have to give the shareholders their money back, but they do expect the directors to increase the value of their shares, and if you go public they will probably expect a stream of dividends too. If you don't meet the shareholders' expectations, they won't be there when you need more money – or if they are powerful enough they will take steps to change the board.

In the UK, out of the total population of 1.5 million limited companies, about 1000 take on equity finance each year.

Debt (or borrowing)

Borrowing someone else's money to help you grow your business has many attractions. 'High gearing' is the name given when a business has a high proportion of outside money to inside money. High gearing has considerable attractions to a business which wants to make high returns on shareholders' capital, as the example in Table 2.13.3 shows.

In this example, the business is assumed to need £60000 capital to generate £10000 operating profits. Four different capital structures are considered. They range from all share capital (no gearing) at one end, to nearly all loan capital at the other. The loan capital has to be 'serviced', that is interest of 12 per cent has to be paid. The loan itself can be relatively indefinite, simply being replaced by another one at market interest rates when the first loan expires.

Following the columns through, you can see that ROSC grows from 16.6 per cent to 30.7 per cent by virtue of the changed gearing. If the interest on the loan were lower, the ROSC would be even more improved by high gearing, and the

Table 2.13.3		No gearing — £	Average gearing 1:1 £	Average gearing 2:1 £	Average gearing 3:1 £
Capital structure					
Share capital		60000	30000	20000	15000
Loan capital (at 12%)		–	30000	40000	45000
Total capital		60000	60000	60000	60000
Profits					
Operating-profit		10000	10000	10000	10000
Less interest on loan		None	3600	4800	5400
Net profit		10000	6400	5200	4600
Return on share capital	=	60000	6400	5200	4600
		60000	30000	20000	15000
	=	16.6%	21.3%	26%	30.7%
	=	N/A	10000	10000	10000
			3600	4800	5400
Times interest earned	=	N/A	2.8X	2.1X	1.9X

Effect of gearing on ROSC

higher the interest the lower the relative improvement in ROSC. So, in times of low interest, businesses tend to go for increased borrowings rather than raising more equity, that is money from shareholders.

At first sight, this looks like a perpetual profit growth machine. Naturally, if they could increase the return on their investment, owners would rather have someone else lend them the money for their business than put it in themselves. The problem comes if the business does not produce £10 000 operating profits. Very often, in a growing business, a drop in sales of 20 per cent means profits are halved or even eliminated. If profits were halved in this example, it could not meet the interest payments on its loan. That would make the business insolvent, and so not in a 'sound financial position'. In other words, failing to meet one of the two primary business objectives.

Bankers tend to favour 1:1 gearing as the maximum for a small growing business, although they have been known to go much higher. Gearing can be more usefully expressed as the percentage of shareholders' funds (share capital plus reserves), to all the long-term capital in the business. So 1:1 is the same as saying 50 per cent gearing.

All loans from banks take time to set up, attract an arrangement fee and it is generally frowned upon if you go back a few weeks later and ask for more money. The days when you could expect to cultivate a lifetime relationship with either a bank or a bank manager are long gone. Banks are into market segmentation and profit generation, so you need to be prepared to a) shop around and b) manage your relationship with the bank carefully.

As a rough guide, if you are with the same bank for over five years, you haven't pushed them hard enough. The Cranfield study mentioned earlier in this chapter indicated that around half of all owner-managed businesses had either changed, or seriously considered changing, their bankers in the preceding two years. There are a myriad number of things to negotiate with your banker, and there is even a new breed of consultants who advise on banking relationships.

Once your business is up and running you will have a wider range of financing options including those described below.

Working capital finance

Customers often take time to pay up. In the meantime, you have to pay those who work for you and your less patient suppliers. So, the more you grow the more funds you need. It is often possible to 'factor' your credit worthy customers' bills to a financial institution, receiving some of the funds as your goods leave the door, hence speeding up cash flow.

Factoring is generally only available to a business that invoices other business customers either in their home market or internationally, for its services. Factoring can be made available to new businesses, although its services are usually of most value during the early stages of growth. It is an arrangement, which allows you to receive up to 80 per cent of the cash due from your customers more quickly than they would normally pay. The factoring company in effect buys your trade debts and can provide a debtor accounting and administration service. In other words, it takes over the day-to-day work of invoicing and sending out reminders and statements. This can be a particularly helpful service to an expanding business. It allows the management to concentrate on expanding the business, with the factoring company providing expert guidance on credit control, 100 per cent protection against bad debts, and improved cash flow.

You will, of course, have to pay for factoring services. Having the cash before your customers pay will cost you a little more than normal overdraft rates. The factoring service will cost between 0.5 and 3.5 per cent of the turnover, depending on volume of work, the number of debtors, average invoice amount, and other related factors. You can get up to 80 per cent of the value of your invoice in advance, with the remainder paid when your customer settles up, less the various charges just mentioned.

If you sell direct to the public, sell complex and expensive capital equipment, or expect progress payments on long-term projects, then factoring is not for you. If you are expanding more rapidly than other sources of finance will allow, this may be a useful service that is worth exploring. Invoice discounting is a variation on the same theme. Factors collect in money owed by a firm's customers, whereas invoice discounters leave it to the firms themselves. However, the majority of growing businesses continue to prefer factoring to invoice discounting because it enables them to outsource their financial management controls. Invoice discounting is, in any case, typically available only to businesses with a turnover in excess of £1 million.

Invoice factoring and invoice discounting now account for £8 billion of business financing, up from £2 billion in 1990.

Case Study

In the first few years, Cobra Beer sales turnover grew rapidly as more and more Indian restaurants chose to stock the beer that was designed specifically to eat with Indian food. As is customary in the industry, the restaurants were allowed credit. In the meantime, Cobra had to commit to increases in production, to meet the increasing demand, and to pay the brewing, bottling and importation *before* receiving payment from the restaurant owners. Founder, Karan Bilimoria, a qualified accountant, realized that the business would run out of cash if this situation continued.

He decided to bridge this gap by means of an invoice factoring arrangement whereby Cobra would receive 75 per cent of the value of the goods as they were delivered to the restaurants, with the factoring company then responsible for collecting the payments.

Asset-backed finance

Physical assets such as cars, vans, computers, office equipment and the like can usually be financed by leasing them, rather as a house or flat may be rented. Or they can be bought on hire purchase. This leaves other funds free to cover the less tangible elements in your cash flow.

Leasing is a way of getting the use of vehicles, plant and equipment without paying the full cost at once. Operating leases are taken out where you will use the equipment for less than its full economic life, for example a car, photocopier, vending machine or kitchen equipment. The lessor takes the risk of the equipment becoming obsolete and assumes responsibility for repairs, maintenance and insurance. As you, the lessee, are paying for this service, it is more expensive than a finance lease, where you lease the equipment for most of its economic life and maintain and insure it yourself. Leases can normally be extended, often for fairly nominal sums, in the latter years.

The obvious attraction of leasing is that no deposit is needed, leaving your working capital free for more profitable use elsewhere. Also, the cost is known from the start, making forward planning more simple. There may even be some tax advantages over other forms of finance. However, there are some possible pitfalls, which only a close examination of the small print will reveal. So, do take professional advice before taking out a lease.

Hire purchase differs from leasing in that you have the option to eventually become the owner of the asset, after a series of payments.

Government assistance

Unlike debt, which has to be repaid, or equity, which has to earn a return for the investors, grants and awards from governments or the European Union are often not refundable. So, although they are frequently hard to get, they can be particularly valuable.

Almost every country has incentives to encourage entrepreneurs to invest in particular locations or industries. The US, for example, has an allowance of Green Cards (work and residence permits) for up to several hundred immigrants each year prepared to put up sufficient funds to start a substantial business in the country.

In the UK, if you are involved in the development of a new technology, then you may be eligible for a Research and Development award (previously called a SMART award). This is open to individuals or businesses employing fewer than 50 people. The grant is in two stages and can be for amounts as high as £100 000 in total. You may also get help with the costs of training staff, gaining quality recognition, or carrying out market research to identify export opportunities.

Support for business comes in a very wide variety of forms. The most obvious is the direct (cash) grant, but other forms of assistance are also numerous. The main types of grant also include soft loans that are money lent on terms more advantageous than would usually be available from a bank, equity injections, free or subsidised consultancy or access to valuable resources such as research facilities.

Many grants are location specific. There are several schemes that operate across the whole of the European Union, and are available to all businesses that satisfy the outline criteria. In addition to these, there are a myriad of schemes that are administered locally. Thus, the location of your business will be absolutely crucial, and funding that might be available to you will be strongly dependent on the area into which you intend to grow or develop. Additionally, there may well be additional grants available to a business investing in or into an area of social deprivation, particularly if it involves sustainable job creation.

For further information, try Business Link (www.businesslink.org/), The Department of Trade and Industry (www.dti.gov.uk/), Funders online (www.fundersonline.org) and Grants On-line (www.co-financing.co.uk/).

Money for 'free'

If you enjoy publicity and like a challenge, then you could look out for a business competition to enter. Like government grants, business competitions are ubiquitous and like national lotteries they are something of a hit or miss affair. But one thing is certain: if you don't enter, you can't win.

There are more than 300 annual awards across Europe, aimed at new, small and growing businesses. For the most part, these are sponsored by banks, the major accountancy bodies, chambers of commerce, and local or national newspapers, business magazines and the trade press. Government departments may also have their own competitions as a means of promoting their initiatives, for exporting, innovation, job creation and so forth. The nature and the amount of the awards change from year to year, as do the sponsors. But, looking out in the national and local press, or contacting one of the organizations mentioned above, should put you in touch with a competition organizer quickly, as will an internet search.

Money awards constitute about 40 per cent of the main competition prizes. For the most part, these cash sums are less than £5000. However, a few do exceed £10 000, and one UK award is for £50 000. Other awards are for equally valuable goods and services, such as consultancy or accountancy advice, training, and computer hardware and software.

Equity (or venture capital)

Having already invested your own money in getting the business started, you may now be interested in getting outside investors to provide some of the funds for growth. And, at the same time, you are in a much better position to attract venture capital investment.

Venture capital is a medium- to long-term investment, of not just money, but of time and effort.

Venture capital is rarely a means of financing start-up ventures, but for development, expansion or for pursuing a strategy of acquisition this means of financing comes into its own.

The venture capitalist acquires an agreed proportion of the share capital (equity) of the company in return for providing the requisite funding. Venture capital firms often work in conjunction with other providers of finance in putting together a total funding package for a business.

Venture capital providers are investing other people's money, often from pension funds, and seek to achieve large returns by investing in businesses with the potential to grow and develop into major businesses of tomorrow. Worldwide there are several hundred venture capital firms.

Venture capitalists will go through a process known as 'due diligence' before investing. This process involves a thorough examination of both the business and its owners' past financial performance. Accountants and lawyers subject all the directors' track records, and the business plan, to detailed scrutiny. Directors are then required to 'warrant' that they have provided *all* relevant information, under pain of financial penalties. The cost of this process will have to be borne by the business raising the money, but will be paid out of the money raised, if that is any consolation.

In general, venture capitalists would expect their investment to have paid off within seven years. But they are hardened realists. Two in every ten investments they make are total write offs, and six perform averagely well at best. So, the two stars in every ten investments they make have to cover a lot of duds. Venture capitalists have a target rate of return of more than 30 per cent to cover this poor hit rate.

Raising venture capital is not a cheap option. The arrangement costs will almost always run to six figures. They are not quick to arrange either. Six months is not unusual and over a year has been known. Every venture capitalist has a deal that they did in six weeks in their portfolio, but that truly is the exception.

Venture capital providers will want to exit from their investment at some stage. Their preferred route is via flotation on a stock market, but a trade sale is more usual.

Whilst venture capital is big business, the value of funds invested in early stage companies has remained modest, at just a few per cent of all the funds invested. While this is mainly attributable to the risk–reward relationship, the due diligence and transaction costs involved in investing in smaller businesses are similar to those associated with investments in large companies, and so they are far higher per unit of funds invested. But, don't despair. New venture capital funds are coming on stream all the time and they too are looking for a gap in the market. Figure 2.13.1 shows the recent explosion in venture capital investment.

British Venture Capital Association (www.bvca.co.uk/) and The European Venture Capital Association (www.evca.com/) both have online directories giving details of hundreds of venture capital providers.

Mezzanine money

Mezzanine finance (also known as subordinated debt) is a type of debt that, from a security perspective, typically ranks behind senior debt finance such as invoice discounting and factoring, leasing, traditional bank loans and overdrafts, but ranks in front of equity investment. This means that the mezzanine finance provider has the second claim on a company's assets should the loan need to be recovered.

This increased risk, and the fact that there is often little security available, means that an increased charge is required to justify the risk. Charges vary but can be up to 8 per cent more than the cost of ordinary debt and can also include share options or warrants that can be converted into a company's equity. Options or warrants may be necessary if the available cash flow is insufficient to support a level of interest that will compensate for the risks associated with a given transaction.

The benefit of mezzanine finance is that it often bridges the gap between the funds that a clearing bank will provide and the funds provided by the company's management and a venture capital or private equity backer. Between 15 and 30 per cent of management buyout finance is provided by mezzanine finance, making it a crucial element in successfully structuring a transaction. Mezzanine finance can now also be considered a stand-alone funding solution, often as an alternative to more expensive equity finance. Mezzanine is now commonly used to provide acquisition finance, development capital, replacement capital as well as finance for the more traditional management buy-out, buy-in scenarios.

Figure 2.13.1

Venture capital explodes: annual investment in the US and Europe from 1990

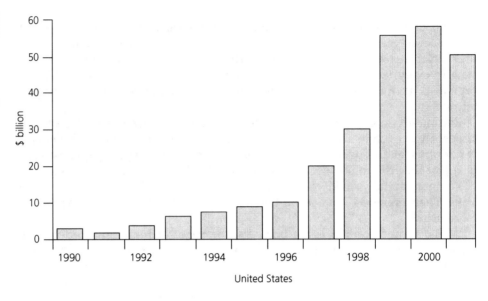

United States

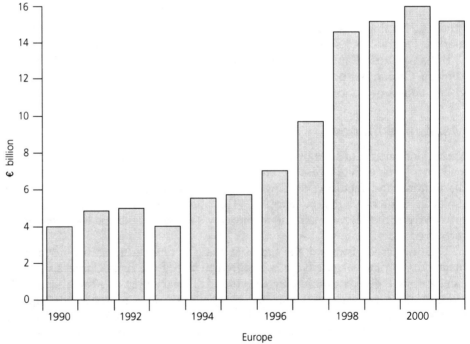

Europe

Sources of mezzanine finance include many of the clearing banks and insurance companies as well as specialist finance boutiques. With larger transactions, it is possible to access the capital markets using an investment bank to achieve public offerings of high yield or 'junk' bonds. These are typically sold to institutional investors such as insurance companies and pension funds.

The amount and cost of funds under a mezzanine arrangement will depend on many factors including industry sector, historic performance, credit ratings, seasonality and predictability of revenues, forecasts for future cash flow and profitability, as well as the strength of management, nature of a company's financial backers and structure of the overall financing package.

It is usual for mezzanine finance to be provided on an interest only basis until some or all of general bank debt has been repaid, typically after four to five years, with typical loan terms ranging up to ten years. Loans are usually secured with a second charge on a company's assets such as property, plant and equipment.

Other ways to fund growth

Franchising

Have you ever wondered why Tie Rack has survived and Sophie Mirman's Sock Shop has gone to the wall? Both are (or in Mirman's case were) niche retailers; both need small high street locations; both founders came from Marks and Spencer and knew all about their product; neither product is essential for survival – indeed, if anything socks seem more essential than ties!

One of the key differences lies in the way these businesses were funded and managed. All the Sock Shop outlets were funded by the company itself and, in the last year of its life, this was largely provided by the banks. In Tie Rack's case, the situation is rather different. Most of their outlets are effectively owned by the people who manage them. These franchisees, as Tie Rack's 'managers' are called, have stumped up at least £60 000 each for the privilege of following the Tie Rack formulae for business success. That was a fairly staggering £6 million of new money for every 100 franchisees, which is completely risk- and cost-free to Tie Rack. For Mirman, a similar sum would have cost her £1.25 million a year in interest charges alone – and it probably did as £2 of every £3 in Sock Shop was put up by the banks.

Case Study

Miles O'Donovan's franchise, Material World (named after the Madonna hit record, Material Girl), is a good example of how to turn a successful conventional business into a franchise. O'Donovan is an up-market version of a market stall trader, buying up manufacturers' ends-of-lines and seconds and selling them to an apparently appreciative public. 'It is a very simple business', he says. And he never doubted that it would succeed because, the way he looks at it, it is providing a service at both ends of the equation. Not only is he helping out those people who would love to make their home 'very Sanderson' but currently find themselves strapped for cash, but he is also helping out the manufacturers who have to rid themselves of their surplus stock somehow.

This mutually beneficial system is already well established in the clothing business, where disposing of chain store cast offs is the basis of several retail chains. O'Donovan, however, operates with goods from rather further up-market. Much of what he stocks would normally sell at £15 to £20 per metre but he

▶

has a blanket price of £7.95 per yard. The fact that he sticks to yards is not just hankering for days gone by; it gives him a 10 per cent price advantage.

O'Donovan woke up one morning and decided that, with nine of his own shops, he was about as exposed as he would like to be. Watching others in his sector sink without trace, he decided the time had come to share the risk with others. After a brief flirtation with the idea of venture capital, he plumped for franchising and has never looked back. His new franchisees have helped lift turnover from £1.8 million to £3 million in the present year and his business is now expanding fast, both in the UK and Europe. Best of all, he can sleep easy at night with the comfort of knowing his franchisees are as exposed as he is to the consequences of failure.

Corporate venturing

Corporate venturing is a term widely in use for an activity which has been around for at least 50 years. However, there is quite a lot of confusion about what exactly it is, since the same term is frequently used to describe different things.

Internal corporate venturing essentially describes large companies' attempts to generate new business activity from inside the organization but outside their existing core activity. Usually, in internal venturing, the new activity is set up as an entirely separate unit and sometimes as a stand-alone business, so as to maximize the sense of entrepreneurism in the new venture. IBM attempted this in the 1980s, with mixed results, when it created the PC division to compete head-on with Apple. Until that time IBM was focused solely on large, centralized computing systems. More recently, several big UK financial institutions, notably Halifax, Abbey and Prudential, have successfully incubated and launched internet-based banks which not only have very different business models compared to the parent business, but are also entirely separate businesses.

External corporate venturing, on the other hand, refers to investments made by big businesses in new or early-stage ventures that are outside their organizations. Sometimes, these investments are made directly, sometimes indirectly through an investment fund controlled by the company but typically managed by investment professionals. In both direct and indirect investing the usual model is that the investing company injects cash, and possibly other resources (e.g. industry know-how, customer introductions), in return for a minority shareholding. This is the dimension of corporate venturing which is of interest to us here, since it is a potential source of funding for growth-hungry, early-stage businesses. As a general rule, external corporate venturers will invest in early-stage businesses, but not start-ups.

What's in it for the larger partner?

In 1999, the UK's employer organization, the Confederation of British Industry (CBI), surveyed its members to find out the benefits of corporate venturing from their point of view (the report is called 'Connecting Companies'). CBI members are overwhelmingly medium and large-sized companies, and those who took part in the survey replied that the main advantages were:

- access to new ideas, people and skills
- developing a more entrepreneurial culture
- exploiting managerial talent and intellectual property to their full potential
- pre-empting competitors.

Those views have been echoed in other surveys (e.g. the 'Captains of industry' report compiled by MORI and featured in *Corporate Venturing*, issue 1, April 2003), although profit has also figured strongly as a motive.

What's in it for the growing business?

For the growing business partner, the principal reasons given for entering joint ventures with larger firms were:

- access to sales and distribution
- collaboration on research and development
- access to products and processes.

In every case, however, there is one common purpose shared by the partners: achieving growth.

Corporate venturing can be a great option where the parties bring complementary skills and assets to the table. However, the growing business needs to think carefully about this method of building the business. In particular, consider the following:

- The corporate venturer will behave in a very similar way to a venture capital firm. They will require the current owner of the business to surrender some shares in return for the investment and, as a corollary of this, they will usually be in the picture for the long term. Therefore, you will need to give careful thought – and take some (expensive) legal advice – on what to do if the relationship goes sour, and how to provide for that in a shareholders' agreement.
- Corporate venturing has something of a reputation as a management fashion, and tracks the economic cycle closely. Thus, Venture Economics, a leading consultancy in this area, estimated that European corporate venture investing peaked at $US 5.1 billion in the last quarter of 2000 and dropped to $2.8 billion in the first quarter of 2001. Since then it has been in steady decline as the technology bubble burst and the European economy has hovered uneasily between recession and low growth. The implications for the investee company are clear:
  - Be clear that the interests of both partners are aligned for the long term.
  - Make provision so that, if the corporate investor is not prepared to invest more money if needed at a later stage, there are no obstacles to other investors putting money into the business.

If this *does* seem like a suitable route forward for your business, where should you start? A good place to begin is with your existing network of business contacts. If this leads nowhere, then look to see who is making trade investments in your industry – usually not too difficult to discover via the trade press or the internet. Professional advisers often have good networks and, increasingly, government agencies are seeking to act as brokers between large businesses and growing businesses seeking finance (see, for example, www.corporateventuringuk. org). To see how one large multinational corporation presents its corporate venturing activities look at www.unileverventures.com.

Don't forget, however, that this is one aspect of business where it definitely pays to get expert advice.

Chapter summary

As you grow the business, it is almost certain that you will require extra money to fund that growth. This is not a cause for concern. Businesses, after all, exist in part at least to turn money into goods and services, which can be sold on for a profit. It usually takes a while for this process to take place and so you are likely to need money to fund the acquisition of raw materials and people before you can sell them on. So unless you are throwing off very large amounts of cash, the faster you are growing, the more money will be needed.

The key issue for managers of the growing business is where the money comes from. As we have seen in this chapter, there is a wide range of possible sources which can be broken down into the broad areas of internal and external sources. A detailed review of your existing operations can identify useful ways to squeeze out extra funding through measures such as reducing excessive stock holding, or collecting money owed to you more quickly. Nevertheless, in many cases, new outside money may be required at some time, and perhaps several times, during the life of the business. This chapter has reviewed the main sources of external finance and the criteria for deciding which forms of finance are appropriate at each stage of growth.

Assignments

1. How much money can you squeeze out of your business by:
   a) Greater working capital efficiencies, i.e. getting paid faster, reducing stock holding, etc.?
   b) Reducing the amount of fixed assets tied up?
2. How much extra capital is required to fund each £1000 of growth in sales?
3. So, how much new capital is required to meet your growth objectives?
4. Which sources of funds would be most appropriate for you?
5. Research potential industry backers or corporate venture firms in your sector.

Suggested further reading

Barrow, Colin, (2001) *Financial Management for the Small Business*, London: Kogan Page.
Barrow, Colin, (2003) *The Complete Small Business Guide*, Oxford: Capstone Reference.

The challenges of deciding whether to re-invest or exit

To exit or not to exit?

You have your growth strategy in place, the business is in a sound financial position, you've built a good management team to support you and the business is growing nicely. At some point, just like every entrepreneur, your mind will stray to thoughts of exit. This may be driven by an external investor wanting to obtain a return on their investment or by an unexpected approach from a potential acquirer. Or it may be that you decide that the business has outgrown you and it's time to harvest the value and do something else. Or it may simply be that age has inexorably caught up with you and it's time to stop.

Some entrepreneurs plan their exit right from the very start of the business. At the other extreme, there are entrepreneurs who have no particular exit plan, either at start-up or later as the business grows. Their rationale for not thinking about exit is usually one of the following

- 'I started the business so that I could be my own boss. So, why would I want to sell it to someone else?'
- 'I can't predict when, or even if, someone will want to buy the business. So, I can't possibly plan for it.'
- 'I don't want to sell the business. I intend to pass it on to my children.'
- 'The business is my life. What else would I do with myself?'

Succession or selling the business

Firstly, it's important to distinguish between the founding entrepreneur exiting the business, that is no longer being in the business themselves, and selling the business. For every entrepreneur there will come a time when he or she stops working in the business they founded – even if this is when they get carried out in a box. Less dramatically, the entrepreneur may decide that it's time to retire, or that it's time for a new generation of management to take over or that the business has outgrown them. In all of these circumstances, there are significant issues to be considered and planned. For instance, in businesses which are passed on through families, there is a whole raft of complex issues around succession planning, including identification and grooming of the successor, share ownership among successor generations, tax management, and so on.

Conversely, we are familiar with many instances where a sudden and/or unplanned departure of the founder has had dramatic effects on the value of the business and its future sustainability – and that is in no one's interest.

Case Study

The founder of a business that we know well died suddenly while on a rare, but deserved, holiday. He had founded the business 30 years earlier and had built it into a highly respected niche manufacturer with a presence in several countries. Although one of his sons had worked in the business for a number of years, and there was a general assumption that this son was the 'heir apparent', the founder had never made his intentions about the future of the business clear to anyone, including his wife and family.

When the founder died there was no plan in place as to who would take over the running of the business or how the ownership of the business would be passed on. After some difficulties with existing directors and senior managers, it was agreed that the son would take over as Managing Director, while the shares passed to the founder's wife. It took a further five years of friction, during which time some of the existing directors left the business, for the son to reach a point where he was fully accepted by the management. Much of this could have been avoided had a simple succession plan been put in place.

Fortunately, the son has been a resounding success as Managing Director and the business has grown even more rapidly under his stewardship. Although he is still only in his late thirties, he is already planning for what happens after he is gone!

Selling the business, on the other hand, is primarily a way of the current owner(s) realizing the value of their investment. For many entrepreneurs, the ultimate expression of their original driver to 'be their own boss' is to be completely financially independent. The most likely way to achieve this is to sell part or all of your business and capture the value.

Selling your business often includes the current owner-manager moving out of the business, but this is not necessarily the case, since many acquirers will want you to stay on at least for a transitional period.

Contents of this section

Since selling the business has at least one other party involved in addition to the entrepreneur, planning the precise timing and nature of an exit is, if anything, even more difficult than planning for start-up. Nevertheless, just like the challenges of starting out and the challenges of growing the business, there are distinct advantages in having an effective exit plan. Not least of these being that you can significantly increase the value of your business by preparing it for exit.

Case Study

One entrepreneur we know decided to sell up and so had his business professionally valued. The valuation given was £10 million. Eighteen months later, he sold the business for £15 million. The additional value had been achieved through a thorough and planned series of activities to build value in the business prior to the actual sale.

Essentially, the *Challenges of Deciding Whether to Re-invest or Exit* are highly personal and revolve around the following issues:

- Has the business reached 'maturity'? In other words, has it changed from a big small business to a small big business?
- Can you make the transition from owner to manager? This is not an easy metamorphosis and one that most entrepreneurs either cannot or will not make.
- What are you options for realizing the value?

The chapters in this section consider each of these three key topics in turn.

Assignments

As before, each chapter concludes with a series of assignments which suggest work to be done in applying the ideas introduced in that chapter. If you are an owner-manager who is considering whether to re-invest or exit, then by working through these assignments applied to your business, you will build up most of the information you need to help you make the decision and prepare for what to do next.

If you are using this book to learn about growing businesses, but do not have a business of your own, then we suggest that you work through the assignments using one of the recurring case studies. World Golf, Cobra Beer and ChocExpress (renamed Hotel Chocolat) would be appropriate choices for this section. Full teaching cases of all the recurring case studies are available on the companion website.

14

Are you a 'big small business' or a 'small big business'?

Introduction and objectives

From start-up, through the years of early growth, successful companies are those which demonstrate product or service differentiation and a clear customer focus. While these qualities endure, the *business model* can change significantly over time. The pursuit of new opportunities sometimes leads a business into new market sectors, and creates new revenue streams. The senior management is strengthened, often from outside the business, which can impact on the focus of the business. New divisions or profit centres are created. The business which emerges is, in important respects, no longer the same business as the one which started up several years before. At some point – and there is no clear dividing line – a big small business, if it continues to grow, becomes a small big business.

In this chapter, we will look at the *strategic* and *marketing* challenges of taking a growing business into this phase of mature management. By the end of this chapter, you should have a clear understanding of the following key topics:

- *Your product portfolio*: How you should structure it to exploit the inevitable changes in the marketplace.

- *Your structure*: Are you a multi-product/multi-service business or are you becoming multiple businesses?

- How professional advisers can help you address these challenges.

Case Study

In early 2003, Angus Thirlwell and Peter Harris took the decision to re-brand their consumer chocolates business from ChocExpress to Hotel Chocolat. The new name and design were more than a new look; they reflected the move to a new phase in the company's development.

▶

ChocExpress had been in existence for ten years and the name had been chosen to describe succinctly the company's mission: to provide high quality chocolates through mail order. However, in recent years, Angus and Peter had begun to feel that the brand was too constraining given the way they saw the business developing.

In 2000, they had established the Chocolate Tasting Club as part of the business. As well as buying gifts for other people, customers could also subscribe to a service which delivered a box of artisan-crafted chocolates every month to their own home. This activity continued to grow, but was sold and marketed under the ChocExpress brand. After three years, Angus felt that they needed a brand which exuded some of the qualities of the business at an emotional level, rather than merely being a description of the service. 'ChocExpress is an effective brand, but it's only part of what we do now. Hotel Chocolat provides us with an umbrella brand for ChocExpress and the Chocolate Tasting Club, and it also allows us to take the business into new areas, such as retail. We have ambitions to double, or even treble, our size, and our branding has to reflect that.'

Product portfolio analysis

Most businesses which have been in existence for five years or so will have multiple revenue streams, from a mix of products and services. The common term for this is the *product portfolio*, although the term applies to both products and services. Some products/services in the portfolio will produce cash; others will almost certainly consume cash. The most widely used tool for analysing the product portfolio is the Boston matrix (see Figure 3.14.1), a framework developed by the Boston Consulting Group (BCG) in the late 1970s and early 1980s.

The Boston matrix classifies products on two dimensions:

- the rate at which their market is growing
- and the share of that market relative to competitors.

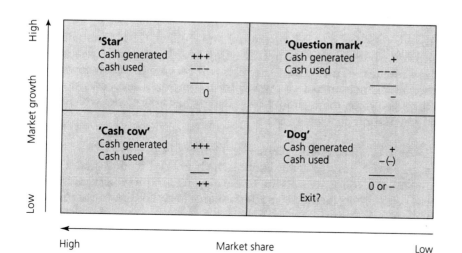

Figure 3.14.1

Boston matrix

The resulting analysis creates a two-by-two matrix, in which the business's products/services can be located. The *Star* box, on the top left, reflects a market which is growing strongly and where the business has a strong market position. Typically, in this situation, Star products/services are either cash-neutral or consume cash. The *Cash cow* box, in the bottom left, shows a market where the firm also has a strong market position, but the rate of growth has slowed, usually because the market is more mature. Products in this box generate the cash that powers the business. The *Dog* box, on the bottom right, is occupied by products which have a small share in a declining market. These products tend either to be cash-neutral or to produce smaller amounts of cash. Finally, the *Question mark* box, on the top right, is reserved for products which have a low share in a fast-growing market. These products invariably consume cash, because they require lots of financial support but are not yet producing a return. They are Question marks because it is unclear whether their market share will improve, and so move them into the Star box, or whether they will continue to under-perform and, eventually, as the market matures, become Dogs. (If you use this analysis when you are still a small growing business, where you may have very small shares of very large markets, it is important to define share in terms of *your market niche versus the direct competition.*)

The Boston matrix has enjoyed widespread popularity because it is seen to be a versatile, general-purpose business tool. The analysis can be conducted at the level of an industry, within a group of companies, or for the product/service portfolio of one business. The underlying idea is that businesses (above a certain size) have a portfolio of activities, developed in response to new market opportunities, and sufficiently diversified to spread their commercial risks (a little like the way investment portfolios are diversified to account for risk). That portfolio is *dynamic*, that is, it evolves over time, and should be *actively managed*. The key points of this active management are:

- Cash cows fund the investment needed to support Stars and a selected number of Question marks.
- The business must create action standards for Question Marks, to identify which should be encouraged.
- Dogs have no long-term future and should receive limited or no investment.
- In the longer term, as markets mature and decline, Cash cows will cease to generate cash and move towards the Dog box. The business needs to have other activities – ideally Stars – which will become the Cash cows of the future, as the market rate of growth for the current Cash cows slows down. At the same time, there should be suitable Question marks which are now ready to assume the role of Stars.

The direction of investment is shown in Figure 3.14.2

It is, of course, *cash flow*, not profit, which is used in this model as the real determinant of a company's ability to develop its products/services. The overall business aim is to achieve market share and continuing growth while maximizing cash flow.

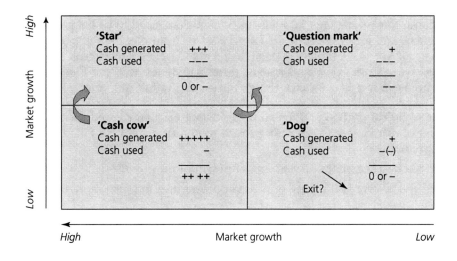

Figure 3.14.2

Boston matrix: direction of investment flows

Arguments for using the Boston matrix

The Boston matrix is used by countless businesses, small and large, across the world, as one of the primary tools for strategic planning. Every year, in our work with smaller growing companies, we meet business founders who rely on it heavily. It has certain undoubted advantages:

- The analysis imposes a valuable degree of rigour and clarity on your thinking about the business. Many businesses become emotionally attached to activities which can no longer be justified on commercial grounds, and thus dilute and divert their resources. A Dog is a Dog!
- We have already discussed the need for successful businesses to continue to respond quickly and effectively to changes in their markets. The Boston matrix forces you to think carefully about how your markets are changing, not just today but in the longer term.
- This analysis can act as an early warning system to alert senior management to the dangers of spreading resources too thinly or underinvesting in the wrong places. In the longer term, no business can support an unlimited number of Question marks, nor be reliant on too few Cash cows.
- As we have emphasized before, all businesses are viable only insofar as they generate cash. The Boston matrix focuses on *cash* as the ultimate business driver, not profit.

Proceed with caution

On the other hand, this approach will not work for every business. First, the analysis cannot be undertaken for young businesses or businesses which do not have a portfolio of products and services – although it may usefully prompt managers to examine whether they are too dependent on a narrow revenue stream from only one or two areas.

Second, like all managerial tools, the conclusions need to be balanced against judgement and experience. In the late 1980s, for example, the big players in the UK tea market were united in their belief that packet (loose) teas were Dogs, teabags were Cash cows and instant (granulated) tea was the Question mark ready to become a Star. In fact, things turned out rather differently:

- The technical challenge of creating an instant tea that catered for the British habit of drinking tea with milk proved too hard. Instant tea failed to take off as predicted.
- The tea bag segment still had lots of potential for growth.
- And there were still plenty of niche opportunities to make money in packet teas.

Those businesses that were very dependent on the Boston matrix for their strategic planning were paralysed in their thinking for a while, because the model had not successfully predicted the future.

The third point follows from this example. It is always dangerous to rely wholly on one way of looking at the world. We recommend using the Boston matrix, only if it is appropriate for your type of business at its stage of maturity. If so, you must then apply your judgement and experience to interpreting the analysis and the conclusions. Discuss this across the management team and with advisers whose opinions you respect.

Structure – are you a multi-product company or multiple companies?

So far, we have looked at the issue of growth on the assumption that your business is still essentially one business. There is, however, one final issue to be addressed in this chapter. As you cross that invisible line from a big small business to a small big business, you may question that assumption. Richard Branson, founder of Virgin, is notorious for splitting his businesses up once they reach a certain size. He justifies this on the basis that the entrepreneurial culture that distinguishes Virgin will be slowly strangled if a business unit gets too big. Others do so on the basis that different commercial entities are necessary to take advantage of different opportunities.

Case Study

By mid 2003, Steve Jolliffe had restructured his business interests into three separate entities.

One business would be the master franchisor, or licensor, of the TopGolf concept. This business was called World Golf Systems, and it was the owner of all the intellectual property which lay behind TopGolf. World Golf's role was to appoint franchisees, who would pay an up-front fee plus a percentage of revenues for the right to operate TopGolf centers. During 2003 and 2004, World Golf had held negotiations with potential franchisees in North America,

▶

◀

Russia, Japan, Spain, Dubai, Thailand and India.

A second company would be the master franchisee for the UK and would be funded largely by a venture capital company. Its role was to operate the TopGolf centre near Watford and to identify other sites in the UK. By mid 2004, a second site was opened in Chigwell, east of London.

The third company would operate the master franchise in North America.

The new structure reflected the very different roles in developing TopGolf. Steve believed that each needed dedicated management focus. He planned to withdraw completely from an active role in the Watford centre and the UK franchisor operation, and focus on rolling the business out globally through World Golf.

How does the management team know if and when some kind of restructuring is necessary? The answer is that there are usually some fairly clear indicators:

- The business is serving several different market sectors with fundamentally different requirements. Sometimes a business 'slides' into this situation and, at a certain point, must take action. Other businesses plan for this from the beginning.

Case Study

Hotel Chocolat supplies boxed chocolates to both individual and corporate buyers. But, the needs of the corporate sector are very different. Peter Harris runs that side of the business, through Geneiva Chocolates, as a distinct business unit. 'We have a separate profit and loss account. The sales and marketing activities are quite distinct from those of ChocExpress or the Chocolate Tasting Club. On the other hand, we share common supply chain functions. So, in some ways we resemble a small group of companies.'

- Servicing different markets imposes excessive strain on the business's internal systems and processes. There are, for example, two quite distinct classic types of supply chain (and some variants in between). Firstly, there are supply chains which are geared to dealing with a largely routine, predictable demand, for example, basic consumer goods, such as baked beans or soup, where consumption patterns are broadly similar year in, year out, and seasonal variations are well known. The second type of supply chains are those built to deal with volatile and unpredictable demand, for example in the fashion industry, where demand is notoriously hard to forecast accurately. It is not hard to see that a single business trying to satisfy both types of demand with a single set of processes would have a near impossible task.

- Internal conflicts cannot be resolved unless the businesses are made separate. In the Top Golf/World Golf example cited above, there are clear potential differences of interest between the different entities. The global franchisor, World Golf, is seeking to maximize its licensing income from franchisees. For the UK master franchisee, it makes commercial sense to *minimize* its licence payments to World Golf! Therefore, it makes sense *to separate clearly the operating structure from the shareholding structure.*

Using professional advisers

Even if the indicators are clear that restructuring is required, there are no hard and fast guidelines on how exactly you should undertake this. One piece of advice we would give, however, concerns the role of the professional advisers you need to help you.

By this stage of business growth, you will be using regularly the services of both lawyers and accountants. When they start, many firms engage both types of adviser on the basis of whom they know personally, or who comes recommended to them by friends and family. It is an unpalatable but established fact that the local firm of professional advisers who were appropriate to help the business in the early days, may not be the right people to work with the business in the future. If you have serious ambitions to grow, you need advisers who understand the business you want to become, not the business you were. Ever since the early days, Karan Bilimoria of Cobra Beer has always hired advisers who normally work for much bigger firms. The downside is that they are more expensive. The upside is that, he believes, you get what you pay for – and he is himself a qualified accountant and lawyer! If you are reviewing the future structure of your business, now is also the time to review the calibre of your professional advisers. Do their experience and skills qualify them to do the best possible job for you?

This raises the question of how you would find new legal or accountancy advisers. In our experience, professionals of integrity are usually the first to recognize that a client firm has outgrown their ability to service it, and will recommend you to a suitable alternative. But, you can easily do some market research yourself. Who do you know personally who has built the kind of business you aspire to? What advice can he or she give you? Alternatively, which firms do you admire, in your sector or others? Their published accounts will identify their advisers. Pick up the phone and make an appointment to meet the appropriate partner. The rest is up to you!

Chapter summary

At a certain point of its growth path, a business which was once small, begins to take on the characteristics of a larger business, and needs to review its strategy accordingly. In this chapter, we have looked at the following key topics

- *Product portfolio*: The Boston matrix is a useful starting point here and the resulting analysis focuses the management team on the choices available for future investment or divestment.
- *Structure*: Consider whether it would be useful to re-organize the business into several separate entities.
- How professional advisers can help you address these challenges.

Assignments

1. If appropriate, apply the Boston matrix analysis to your business. What are the directional implications for investment or divestment? Where should you be focusing your efforts?

2. Are there good arguments for restructuring the business significantly? If there are, what form should this take?

Suggested further reading

Dick, R. and M. Kretz de Vries (1995) *Richard Branson: The Coming of Age of a Counter Culture Entrepreneur*, Fontainebleu: INSEAD. (European Case Clearing House, Cranfield University, Cranfield.)

15 Can you change from owner to manager?

Introduction and objectives

The characteristics and management styles most appropriate for a founding entrepreneur are very different to those required by the CEO of a mature business. It is also unusual for a single individual to possess both sets of characteristics and to be able to change styles successfully. Many entrepreneurs cannot, or will not, make this transition. And, for many, this need to operate in a very different style is often a key factor in the decision on whether to continue to invest in the business or to exit.

By the end of this chapter, you should have a clear understanding of the key characteristics and management styles required in the mature business, and that you will need to develop if you are to move successfully from owner to CEO. These will be examined under the following key topics:

- How much management does your business need?

- What kind of leader are you?

- Growing into leadership, including delegation.

- Managing yourself, including managing your time, managing meetings and communication.

Case Study

Although it is unusual for an individual to be both a successful entrepreneur and a successful CEO, Karan Bilimoria of Cobra Beer has no intention of stepping aside from the top job of the company he founded. With his own diverse cultural roots and connections, who better to steer Cobra through the next stage of international growth?

What is interesting is that Karan does not believe in the idea of the lone entrepreneur, but places significant responsibility and trust in his management team. Whilst wanting to take the big decisions, he seems just as keen to develop the Cobra team today as he was to share the building of the business with his partner, Arjun, in the early years. This team spirit is no doubt a significant contributor to the creativity, energy and innovation the Cobra team continues to deliver. As Cobra pursues rapid international expansion, moving from offices in one country to four countries in 2002 alone, close teamwork and the cultivation of personal networks will be vital to the continuing success of the Cobra story.

How much management does your business need?

Most large organizations today have grown up according to basic management principles. If you started your business career working for a bigger organization, or if your present managers have worked in such enterprises, you will know the scenario. Managers in these organizations plan, organize and control in a way that produces consistent, if unexciting results. It is a formula that worked remarkably well for much of the twentieth century when all a successful company had to do to prosper was more of the same.

But management, which is all about maintaining order and predictability is ill-equipped to deal with change, which is the order of the day for the new millennium. To cope with change effectively, you need to be a leader as well as a competent manager. Leadership and management are not the same thing, although many business people fail to make the distinction. A professor at the University of Southern California summed up the difference between leaders and managers thus: 'A leader challenges the status quo; a manager accepts it.'

Peter Drucker says that the first task of a leader is to define a company's mission. In a world where product life cycles are shrinking, new technologies have an ever-shorter shelf-life and customers demand faster delivery and higher quality, this increasingly means defining and inspiring change within a company. By setting a company's direction, communicating this to its workforce, motivating employees and taking a long-range perspective, a leader adapts the firm to whatever volatile environment it does business in. In short, the leader becomes the change master in his own business.

There are certain attributes you need to lead a growing business.

- *High energy levels and drive*: This is vital to overcome the inevitable setbacks and be able to work long hours.
- *High intelligence*: This is required to cut through complex information and get to the root of problems.
- *Good mental and emotional health*: This allows leaders to sustain good interpersonal skills.
- *Honesty*: To manage people requires long-term trust which can only be built up through honesty and integrity.

These personal characteristics sound very ordinary. But, remarkably few people apparently possess all four, maybe one in 50. Still, that means that there are plenty of people around with the potential to lead a larger business than the one they currently run.

Your business will need different amounts of leadership and management at different stages in its life and when the environment around you becomes more (or less) turbulent. Use the matrix in Figure 3.15.1 as a guide to deciding how much leadership and management you need now. The vertical axis shows how much change your company 'needs' at present. This change can be either caused by external factors such as your competitors, customers or the economic climate; or it can be self-imposed because you want to change from running a low-growth to a high-growth business. The horizontal axis is the complexity of your business. It can be complex because of its size, for example, the number of products or services offered or the number of locations in which business is carried out.

The top left-hand box is the typical profile for a start-up business. Here, the business is relatively simple, but the change required to create something from nothing is enormous. Leadership is the key skill needed and by definition there is little to manage at this stage. If the business grows very slowly and stays very simple, doing much the same as when it started, only more so, then it will never need very much leadership or management. The firm will evolve and tick over until it is overcome by a calamity or its profits decline to the point where it would be more profitable to do something else.

More complex businesses, which operate in relatively stable environments, can usually prosper with lots of management and very little leadership. The problem here is that it is becoming increasingly difficult to locate friendly backwaters that will support a sizeable business. These businesses need to be sure-footed enough to inject sizeable quantities of leadership when the environment becomes unstable, or they too will be swept away.

If you want to achieve rapid growth and, not unnaturally, expect to have to do different things to achieve that growth, your business will need management and leadership in depth. The myth of the solitary hero leader attached to popular entrepreneurs of the last decade has largely been exploded. An army in peacetime needs good leadership at the top and good management below. In wartime, it needs competent leadership at all levels. The business world today is undoubtedly 'at war' and clever companies must learn how to find and recruit

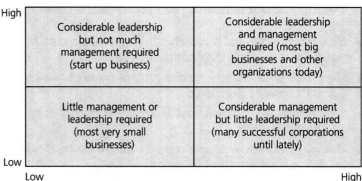

Figure 3.15.1

The leadership/
management matrix

people with both leadership and management potential – growing businesses cannot afford separate leaders and managers so the skills must often be combined in one person.

Decide from the leadership attributes given above which of your managers have leadership potential, and give those that have it challenging assignments as quickly as you can. This will stretch them and allow them to grow. Keep them in each job for a reasonable amount of time so they can learn from both success and failure. Don't make the mistake of promoting too rapidly – this means people are not around long enough to see the impact of their actions and encourages that scourge of strategic thinking, short-termism. Move your potential leader/managers sideways as well as upwards. Assignments which broaden their base allow people to build relationships across the whole business and encourage them to develop the full range of interpersonal skills and empathy needed to motivate the whole business, not just the part they are currently responsible for.

What kind of leader are you?

Are you a 'hero' or a 'meddler'? The dividing line might be thinner than you think, according to our research carried out at the Cranfield School of Management. And, your answer may reveal whether you company will grow or stagnate. We've been studying the behaviour of owner-managers and their relationship with key staff in some 600 growing UK companies. We've concluded that owner-managers can be clustered into four dominant types of relationship with their staff:

- heroes
- meddlers
- artisans
- strategists.

This research project follows on from an earlier study which uncovered the alarming fact that 60 per cent of senior staff in small businesses leave within two years of their appointment. Poor recruitment is one of the reasons for these premature departures – half of all key staff in small businesses are recruited via personal contacts, a notoriously variable method at the best of times. But, unsatisfactory relationships between key staff and the owner-managers of the business is another important reason.

The research studied two key elements of this relationship. First, how much time the owner-manager spent at marketing, selling, analysing figures, reviewing budgets or arbitrating between senior staff. On average, with the exception of the group of entrepreneurs who were still preoccupied with basic non-management functions such as delivering their service or making their product (e.g. architects, small builders, retailers, etc.), over 85 per cent of the entrepreneur's working day was spent on these routine management tasks.

The owner's behaviour can be more easily understood by showing this graphically, as set out in Figure 3.15.2. A low score on the y axis indicates either that most time is spent on basic non-management functions, or that most time is

Relationship
between owner-
manager and key
staff in a growing
firm

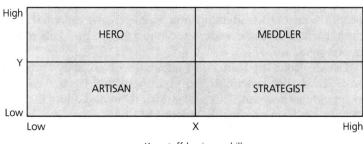

spent on strategic issues such as new product or market development, improving market share, acquisitions and divestments or diversification. A high score indicates that the owner-manager is still largely preoccupied with routine management tasks. The second element examines what level of business skills has been attained by key staff and this is plotted on the x axis of the graph. Here, a low score would be where most of the management team were relatively new to their tasks or largely untrained for their current job. An example (true, believe it or not) of this would be an unqualified book-keeper trying to produce the management accounts for a £5 million business. A high score would be where people were mostly either specifically qualified or trained for their current job. If, for instance, we had replaced the unqualified book-keeper with a fully qualified accountant.

Types

The artisan

The artisan is typified by low occupation with routine management tasks, because most time is spent producing a product or delivering a service. Every hour that can be sold, is sold and little time is left over to improve the quality or profitability of today's business or to consider strategy for tomorrow.

The level of business skills in the company are also low as most of the artisan's staff are employed helping on 'production' or carrying out primary tasks such as book-keeping or selling. The owner-manager is very much 'one of the boys' still. Artisans can encompass professional firms such as architects and surveyors, manufacturers, sub-contractors or small building firms; owners of small retail chains such as chemists, video stores and proprietors of hotels and restaurants.

The artisan has low growth prospects, relative to his or her market. Training and development is needed to raise awareness of the importance of management as a business task of equal importance with daily revenue earning.

The hero

The hero by contrast probably heads up one management function such as sales or production. But, if, for example, the hero heads up sales he or she will do little selling except for handling some key accounts. Time is now spent on managing the business. As the level of business skill among employees is still relatively low, such a hero will take the lead initiating routine management procedures. Typically he or she will read up or attend one-off courses on topics such as Value

Added Tax, accounting business ratios, market segmentation, sales management and staff appraisal systems. He or she will introduce them to the firm, and be the only person who really understands them. To a managerially illiterate team, he or she will consequently be seen as a hero.

Unfortunately, the hero has a Herculean task on his or her hands. Shedding the day-to-day tasks is relatively simple as working skills in most businesses are either readily available in the local community or people can be trained up. But passing out routine management tasks will almost invariably require the owner-manager to train up their own management team. And, individuals to make up this team are difficult to come by (as we have already noted in an earlier chapter).

The hero has a high capacity for improving the performance of the firm but still has low growth prospects relative to the market. There is no time for strategic thinking and no depth of management to handle growth effectively.

There is a need for training and development to help raise the general level of management skills in the business, while at the same time increasing his or her own grasp of motivation, leadership, organization development and strategic management issues in general. If the hero fails to do this, as many do, the hero becomes a meddler.

The meddler

The meddler raises the firm's level of management skill either by training or recruitment, but then fails to let go of routine management tasks. At this stage, the owner-manager probably has no functional responsibilities and has assumed the role of managing director. Typically, much time is spent second-guessing subordinates, introducing more refined (but often unnecessary) management systems. The meddler also goes on courses or reads books that make him/her even more knowledgeable and, sometimes, better at routine management tasks than subordinates, who anyway are doing a perfectly satisfactory job of managing today's business. He or she typically gets in early, and leaves late and practises 'management by walking about'.

The meddler's problem is he or she has been used to a 70–90 hour week, with only 10 days holiday each year and is scared that his day will feel empty if he or she relinquishes responsibility. Once the management team is in place and trained, he or she is out of a job. Until involvement with routine management tasks is reduced, the meddler will limit the growth capacity of the firm for two reasons. First, the management team won't take on more responsibility if the reward for taking on the last lot was being nagged and criticized. Second, he or she is too busy checking on people to develop sound strategies for growth.

The strategist

The strategist is the best type of entrepreneur to develop a growing business. The management skills of the team are developed to the highest appropriate level and depth. He or she may introduce staff to help line managers in such areas as personnel and market research. This will free up key managers to think strategically too.

The strategist will devote roughly a third of working time to management tasks such as monitoring performance, co-ordinating activities, resolving conflict, and helping manage today's business. Another third of time will be spent developing strategic thinking to form the shape of the future business. The strategist's training needs are to update constantly the core leadership and motivation skills to increase depth of knowledge on strategic issues, acquisition/divestment activity, financing sources and the City.

The natural path of development for the relationship between owner-manager and the team is to progress from artisan to hero and, if possible, to strategist (hopefully by-passing meddler), so that energies can be directed to making 'a new business for a new tomorrow', to borrow Peter Drucker's phrase.

Growing into leadership

To grow into the leadership role requires a fundamental shift in attitudes for many owner-managers. One of the most profound of these shifts lies in appreciating why people work at all. Most owner-managers – indeed most managers for that matter – believe that people work largely for money. However, as we saw in an earlier chapter, most of the research shows money ranking third or even fourth in order of importance as to why people work.

Theory 'x' and theory 'y'

These two alternative theories were developed by Douglas McGregor, an American social psychologist, to try to explain the assumptions about human behaviour which underlie managerial action.

Theory 'x'

Theory 'x' is characterized by the following assumptions:

- The average human being has an inherent dislike of work and will avoid it if possible. So, management needs to stress productivity, incentive schemes and a 'fair day's work'; and to denounce 'restriction of output'.
- Because of this human characteristic of dislike of work, most people must be coerced, controlled, directed, threatened with punishment to get them to put forth adequate effort toward the achievement of organization objectives.
- The average human being prefers to be directed, wishes to avoid responsibility, has relatively little ambition, wants security above all.

Theory 'x' has persisted for a long time, because it has undoubtedly provided an explanation for some human behaviour in organizations. There are, however, many readily observable facts and a growing body of research findings which cannot be explained on these assumptions. McGregor proposes an alternative.

Theory 'y'

The foundation of theory 'y' consists of the following precepts:

- The expenditure of physical and mental effort in work is 'as natural as play or rest'. The ordinary person does not inherently dislike work; according to the conditions it may be a source of satisfaction or punishment.

- External control is not the only means for obtaining effort. Humans will exercise self-direction and self-control in the service of objectives to which they are committed.
- The most significant reward that can be offered in order to obtain commitment is the satisfaction of the individual's personal business needs. This can be a direct product of effort directed towards organizational objectives.
- The average human being learns, under proper conditions, not only to accept but to seek responsibility.
- Many more people are able to contribute creatively to the solution of organizational problems than do so.
- At present, the potential of the average person is not being fully used.

Delegation – a remedy for overwork

Overwork is a common complaint of the growing business owner. Too much hard work and never enough hours in the day to do it. However, it is a problem that could easily be remedied by some effective delegation.

Delegation is simply the art of getting things done through other people. And, if you show any of the following symptoms you should consider working harder on delegating in your business. Do you:

- Have problems with deadlines for jobs that you do?
- Have to work late regularly?
- Take work home regularly?
- Avoid accepting help with jobs?
- Devote a lot of your time to details rather than planning and managing?
- Feel insufficiently confident about your employees' ability to take on greater responsibility?

Delegation will help to keep the work flowing smoothly and so prevent a pile-up on your desk which is both stress-inducing and counter-productive.

Fear of delegation

Most owner-managers are proud of the fact that they have built up their own businesses from nothing. In the beginning, reasonably enough, entrepreneurs often perform all the tasks of running the business. But, as the business grows they may hang on to too many jobs. They may believe that nobody else can do the job, and conversely it is just possible they may fear being shown up. It is also possible that, through pressure of work, or else the gradual nature of the expansion, they simply have not reviewed the day-to-day management of their time.

Another reason for small business owners not delegating is that sometimes the routine is preferable to the difficult. Writing invoices is easier than preparing the new cash flow for the bank. What has to be recognized is that when you delegate, both you and your employees grow. The work gets done and your employees get a chance to broaden their skills. Through delegation you can ease your job of managing and thereby increase the effectiveness of both yourself and your workers – and thus your organization.

Benefits of delegation

Delegation is a 'win, win, win' proposition – there are benefits for you, for the employees and for the business

- Benefits for the owner-manager:
  - *Allows time to achieve more.* An owner-manager who can delegate effectively is likely to achieve greater output. Through the proper selection, assignment and co-ordination of tasks, a manager can mobilize resources to achieve more results than would have been possible without skilful delegation.
  - *Allows time for managerial activities.* Delegation allows the owner-manager an opportunity to handle aspects of the job that no one else can do – project planning, plans for developing the business, monitoring how the business is doing, monitoring staff performance and dealing with any problems arising.
  - *Provides you with back-up.* By delegating responsibility in different areas, you will create a back-up workforce who can take over in times of emergency.
- Benefits for the employees:
  - *Develops employees' skills.* Owner-managers who fail to delegate effectively deprive employees of opportunities to improve their skills and assume greater responsibility. Since employees are likely to realize that they are not learning and gaining experience, they may well leave your firm in order to find a more challenging and supportive environment. This happens most frequently with those employees who are most talented – precisely the people that you least want to lose. What is a routine job for you is often a growth opportunity for an employee.
  - *Increases employee involvement.* Proper delegation encourages employees to participate more in understanding and influencing their work. By increasing their involvement in the workplace, you will also increase their enthusiasm and initiative for their work.
- Benefits for the business:
  - *Maximizes efficient output.* Delegation enables the best use of available human resources so as to achieve the highest possible rate of productivity. It also provides the right environment for employees to offer new ideas that can improve the flow and operation of the workplace.
  - *Produces faster and more effective decisions.* Since an organization is most responsive to changes in the environment when individuals closest to the problems are making the decisions about resolving those problems.
  - *Increases flexibility of operations.* Effective delegation trains several people to perform the same tasks. As a result, when someone is absent or when a crisis requires others to assist with functions not regularly a part of their job, several individuals will already be familiar with the assignment.

– *Improves contingency and succession planning.* Delegation prepares more people for promotion or rotation of responsibilities. It also eases your job of finding someone to supervise when you are absent.

Your five-point delegation plan

1. Decide what and what not to delegate.

   The general guidelines for deciding what should be delegated are:

   - the work can be handled adequately by your workers
   - all necessary information for decision-making is available to the worker being delegated the task
   - the task involves operational detail rather than planning or organization
   - the task does not require skills unique to the owner's position
   - an individual other than you has, or can have, direct control over the task

   Therefore any routine jobs, or information collection or assignment involving extensive details such as making calculations, etc., are things that can be delegated. Tasks that should not be delegated include the delegation process itself, employee evaluation and discipline, planning and forecasting, confidential tasks, complex situations and sensitive situations.

2. Decide to whom to delegate.

   Obviously your ability to delegate will be governed by the size and quality of your workforce at any given time. However, three factors are of primary importance when selecting the right person for an assignment: (a) an employee's skills (b) an employee's interest and (c) an employee's workload.

3. Communicate your decision.

   Describe what it is you are delegating and give the other person enough information to carry out the task. Presenting the directive in writing, as well as verbally, will prevent the 'I didn't know' syndrome. If a gap exists between the assignment and an employee's skills, you must be very clear and concise in describing the steps of the task. Bear in mind that a new assignment, particularly one involving several stages, is unlikely to be completely understood on the first explanation. Make yourself available for further clarification as the employee works through the assignment. Closely monitoring the employee will save time in the long run.

4. Manage and evaluate.

   From the beginning, clearly establish set times when you will meet with the person to review their performance. The secret of delegation is to follow up.

5. Reward.

   Results that are recognized get repeated. You must monitor and respond to the person's performance. Otherwise it's like playing a game without score, which in the end is not motivating.

Part of the essence of delegation is thoughtfully judging when a new employee is ready to handle a more stimulating assignment. If necessary delegate in stages, starting with small tasks and working up to more challenging projects.

Delegation is a form of risk-taking. If you can't deal with a few mistakes, you will never be able to delegate. Nevertheless, effective delegation which is carefully planned and well executed will result in a freeing up of your time and a more efficient and more profitable business.

Of course, the one thing you can never delegate is accountability. No matter which employee handles the task, as the business owner, it is your reputation that is on the line.

Managing yourself

It is hard to see how anyone can seriously expect to become an effective business manager until they can first manage themselves. There are three aspects to managing yourself that need to be kept under regular review and these have a major impact on the ability of the rest of your staff to be able to perform.

The first is managing your own time – vital if you are to win back the opportunity to think and plan; the second is managing meetings – or other people's time – vital if your team is going to have a chance to do their job effectively; the third is communication.

Managing your time

Most owner-managers have a false impression of how they use their time and how it affects their performance. There is a strong body of research that suggests that a typical MD could improve his or her output by at least 10 per cent and save time by as much as 20–30 per cent in a typical working day. A prize such as having an eight or nine-day week at your disposal, is surely worth a modest investment of time and energy.

There are many time management systems in the market, but you can realize many of the benefits yourself immediately without any expertise.

- *Step 1: Have a daily and weekly 'to-do' list.* Most senior people in business have diary scheduling meetings and the like, but do not have a list of key tasks to be completed each day and each week. It follows that without a set of daily objectives key priorities cannot be established, nor can you commit to driving hard to achieve those objectives.
- *Step 2: Establish the key priorities.* A manager's day is made up of different types of priorities:
  - 'A' priorities are highly essential activities which must be completed or progressed substantially.
  - 'B' priorities are less essential activities which can be deferred because the time element is less critical and the impact on job performance is lower.
  - 'C' priorities are non-essential activities which can be scrapped, screened out, handled by other people or handled at low priority times.

– 'X' priorities are activities which require immediate attention. There may be queries, requests for information, crises and emergencies, boss demands or interruption. You can have 'AX', 'BX' or 'CX' priorities.

One of the golden rules of time management is based on the Pareto or 80:20 rule. This suggests that 80 per cent of your performance will come from 20 per cent of your activities and 20 per cent of your performance will come from 80 per cent of your activities.

- *Step 3: Review how you spend your time.* This is a simple technique whereby you sum the total amount of time (in percentages) you spend in certain categories of activities. Typical categories are: meetings, telephone, secretary, correspondence, project work, report writing, reading, etc. Each manager will have different categories and different times; however, managers usually find they spend at least 40–50 per cent of a typical day in some sort of meeting.

  If you made an assessment of the amount of time you saved by 'crisper' management of these activities you would find that your time saving could be between 20 per cent and 30 per cent. The four priority areas for time saving and better self-management are: delegation, meetings, planning and personal organization.

  You can make a start on improving your time management by keeping a daily time log for three or four days, reviewing how you spent your time and then look for ways to save time, improve performance or delegate tasks (see Figure 3.15.3).

  You will almost certainly find that you are not spending enough time on your top priority work, and that the majority of your time (which could be as high as 60 per cent or 70 per cent) has been spent on lower priority work of which you could have saved at least 20 per cent by better control and discipline.

Managing meetings

Meetings consume between one and three days of a typical business week. It follows that anything that can be done to make them more effective must be good news. Meetings are vital. They are a forum for exchanging business ideas and gaining fresh thinking – a way to communicate complex information – a way to gain consensus and commitment to key decisions. Unfortunately, most people see most meetings as a complete waste of time – including often the person who called the meeting.

Here are some points to help make your meetings more effective:

- *Define the purpose*: Before you go in to a meeting, you should know exactly what you expect to achieve. Meetings without set objectives demotivate people. The purpose might be to inform staff of new initiatives/procedures (in many instances, a memo would be a quicker, cheaper and just as efficient a way of doing this); it might be to identify and resolve a particular problem, to review progress and give people an opportunity to express their views.

  Asking yourself what would happen if the meeting was not held is a great help in defining its objectives.

Figure 3.15.3

Daytime log

Time	Start and finish time	Activity	Time taken (minutes)	% of the total day	ABCX priority (%)	Was this a main goal activity?	Estimate of time saving on this activity. How?	Could this activity be delegated? Why not?
					A			
					B			
					C			
Totals					X		%	%	%

- *Decide who should attend*: The fewer attendees the better if the meeting is going to achieve its objectives in a reasonable length of time. However, research has shown that larger groups often come up with sounder decisions than individuals or a small number of people – but take much longer to do so.

- *Ensure everyone prepares properly*: A meeting is going to be much more successful if all the participants have prepared in advance, yourself included. If possible, circulate beforehand a note giving notice of the meeting with the agenda items. The note should state the purpose of the meeting and its probable duration (to give people a chance to organize the rest of their day).

An agenda is vital for any meeting – it acts as the control device, establishing order and sequence, assigning tasks and providing guidelines for the timing of each item. If a meeting is called on the spur of the moment, it should still have an agenda, even if it is just jotted down on the back of an envelope. An agenda sent in advance, though, gives people a chance to do their homework.

If participants need to have absorbed specific information before they can discuss it, e.g., budgets, plans, proposals, it is much better to send these out well in advance since nothing wastes time more than people sitting reading during a meeting.

- *Be a good listener*: People who chair meetings need to listen more carefully than anyone else in the group since it is their job to make sure the real point of someone's contribution is not being missed. They need to pick the right moment to move on; clarify points when people are getting in a muddle and summarize all the views when it is time to push for a decision.

- *Involve all the participants*: People are likely to feel far more committed to the meeting and the decisions reached if they have had a chance to say their piece. And, indeed, people should not be at the meeting unless they have something to contribute. It is your task to ensure that everyone has a chance to participate. Use open-ended questions to get people to talk (questions that start with words such as 'how', 'what', 'why', 'when' – these are impossible to answer with a yes or a no). Making positive noises throughout the session – 'Can anybody add to that?' 'Any more?' – also encourage the shy, and check round the group – 'Let's see where we all stand on that, Tim you first' – not only forces people to speak but generally mobilizes and motivates the meeting.

  Closed questions (those that begin with 'do', 'can', 'are', which are usually only answerable with a yes or a no) can be used to bring the talkative to a halt – 'So, do you think we should proceed on that basis?'

- *Keep the meeting on course*: Red herrings and ramblings are the chief dangers when you are trying to stay on course and keep to time limits. There are polite ways to stem the speaker's flow – cough, lean forward, raise your eyebrows – or the more positive: 'We're getting off the point, aren't we?', 'That's your two minutes up, we have to move on.' Don't be too tolerant with people who regularly take the meeting off at a tangent or you'll lose the respect of the others who want to see your hand firmly on the wheel.

- *Control aggression*: Conflict can be healthy in that it encourages new ideas and new ways of solving problems, and it is the chairperson's job to ensure that everyone has a fair say and a fair hearing even if they are disagreeing. However, some control may need to be exercised if things are getting particularly ugly, or someone with strong views is being very vocal. You must avoid taking sides or apportioning blame. This almost always provokes an argument and the chairperson who loses his or her temper loses credibility in the process.

- *Check that everyone understands*: You need to know both that the rest of the group is not at cross-purposes with the speaker, and that they understand what he or she is trying to convey, so check assumptions by asking follow-up questions: 'So you mean that if we improve x we'll get better results from y?' Make a habit of providing a summary of what has been said.

- *Decide on action*: The purpose of meetings is not impose decisions but to achieve decisions by consensus. Once decisions have been made, define clearly how they are to be acted upon, by whom and by when. Memories being short, it is essential to produce minutes (or at least some notes) of every meeting, if for no other reason than to prevent subsequent arguments over who was responsible for what. Another of the chairperson's tasks is to ensure that this is done, although he/she may well prefer to delegate minute-taking to someone else in the group or a secretary. The minutes should be brief and strictly factual, describing what happened without distortion or comment, sticking to suggestions and proposals with the names of the people who made them, actions agreed and the name of the person responsible for each action.

- *Make sure decisions are implemented*: If the meeting was worth having, the decisions are worth implementing. So, your job doesn't stop when the meeting finishes. You need to monitor progress which may involve holding a follow-up meeting, asking for interim reports or carrying out day-to-day checks.

Case Study

John Harris is MD of Carpaints, a ten-year-old company supplying car refinishing paints which employs 20 people and has an annual turnover of around £2 million. John knew where he wanted to go, and how he wanted to get there, but he realized, when considering the company's future while on holiday, that he needed to acquire the skills to ensure success. He applied to go on the Business Growth and Development Programme (BGP) at Cranfield and, in his own words:

I enjoyed the course right across the board, it covered so many things which were all thought-provoking. Ours is a business which has undergone constant expansion, but with the recession really starting to bite we realized we had to control our development with the help of a good business plan. Carpaints needed a kick-start to budge it from a position of

complacency and to do that I needed to stand back, take a good look and get ready to really develop.

Basically the effect of BGP has meant changes in practically everything, including the way we answer the telephone! Even the sales team, in what I thought was the 'organized' side of the business have made changes. They now all have clearly defined roles, so there aren't black holes in responsibilities – and we're on the scent of a new £500k account at the moment. With six-weekly sales meetings, and working towards formal bi-weekly joint meetings for sales and technical staff as well as office meetings on a weekly basis, I'm looking forward to everyone setting their own targets, being sales driven, so that should I disappear tomorrow the company could pretty much run itself.

Communication

The principal ways to communicate are by the spoken word and in writing.

The objective of verbal communication is to give a message in such a way that it can to be readily understood by the listeners – and to be sure that they understand it. Good verbal communication is a two-way process. The speaker gives the listeners the opportunity to ask questions and make comments about what has been said in order to clarify.

There are, however, a number of barriers that get in the way, distorting or even shutting out, the messages we try to send. Such barriers include physical distractions, such as noise, temperature, lighting; and emotional distractions such as personal prejudice, experience, assumptions or values and beliefs. Finally, certain words can cause us to stop listening altogether. This can happen when people are moralizing, threatening, criticizing or just using jargon. So, a good starting point in improving communication is to think about these barriers and prepare your communications with them in mind. Talk to people in an atmosphere free of interruptions and use words that don't rub people up the wrong way. While you can't do much about other people's emotions, you can do something about your own. Stay calm and neutral. If you sense emotional barriers in others, either keep your conversation brief and to the point, or postpone it.

Speaking effectively

Research has shown that each of the following elements has a specific value in transmitting the 'true' message:

- the actual words 7 per cent
- the tone of voice 35 per cent
- non-verbal or body language 58 per cent.

You may disagree with these percentages, but think about it for a moment. You have complete control over the words that you use. You have less control over the tone as your emotion begins to take over. Try saying the phrase 'Where did you go last night?' without emphasizing any of the words. Repeat it, putting an emphasis on the first word, then again, this time emphasizing the word 'you'. Three different 'true' messages will be conveyed to the listener and they will respond accordingly.

You have virtually no control over the non-verbal, your body language. Subconsciously, your body will reveal what you really mean and think. If you sit with your arms and legs crossed, this is a defensive posture and indicates a hostile attitude towards the other person and/or the message. Sitting with your arms folded with your thumbs up, shows a superior attitude. Leaning forward indicates either interest or intimidation. People who rest their chin on one hand and have a finger in or near their mouth, need reassurance. Those who rub their chins are thinking or making a decision and will not be listening to you, so stop talking.

You may be able to control your body language at the beginning of a conversation, but the more you become involved, the more your subconscious will take over. To back up the importance of body language at the beginning of a conversation, it should be noted that of information relayed:

- 87 per cent is via the eyes
- 9 per cent is via the ears
- and 4 per cent is via the other senses (taste, touch, etc.).

Gestures are intentional movements and should not be confused with body language.

A vital part of speaking effectively is being sure people understand what you mean. This is best done by asking questions. Never say 'Do you understand?', as this puts the onus on the listener and, rather than appear stupid, they will probably say 'yes'. If you say 'Have I explained that satisfactorily?' then the responsibility rests with you. The listener does not feel threatened and can answer honestly.

Written communication

Much of our written communication is made unnecessarily hard to follow. Research into the subject has shown that two things make life hard for readers: long sentences and long words. Back in 1952, Robert Gunning, a business language expert, devised a formula to measure just how tough a letter, report or article is to read. Called the Fog Index, these are the four steps:

- *Find the average number of words per sentence.* Use a sample at least 100 words long. Divide the total number of words by the number of sentences to give you the average sentence length.
- *Count the number of words of three syllables or more per 100 words.* Don't count (a) words that are capitalized, (b) combinations of short easy words like 'book-keeper', (c) Verbs that are made up of three syllables by adding 'ed' or 'es' – like 'created' or 'trespasses'.
- *Add the two factors above and multiply by 0.4.* This will give you the Fog Index. It corresponds roughly with the number of years of schooling a person would require to read a passage with ease and understanding.
- Check the results against this scale:
  - 4 and below very easy, perhaps childish
  - 5 fairly easy: tabloid press, hard-selling letters
  - 7 or 8 standard: *Daily Mail*, most business letters
  - 9–11 fairly difficult: *The Times*, good product literature
  - 12–15 difficult: *The Economist*, technical literature
  - 17 or above very difficult: *New Scientist*, no business use, except to bamboozle!

Chapter summary

As you will have seen, the characteristics and management style required by the CEO of a mature business are often very different to those most appropriate for a founding entrepreneur. Most individuals do not possess both sets of characteristics and the transition from one style to another is often not one which entrepreneurs are able or willing to make. As a result, this need to operate in a very different style is often a key factor in the decision on whether to continue to invest in the business or to exit.

Assignments

1. How much management does your business need? Locate your business on the matrix at Figure 3.15.1. Do you have the right amount (not too little and not too much) of leadership and management for the position you are in? If not, what are the implications of this on the business and your plans for it?

2. What kind of a leader are you (i.e. hero, meddler, artisan or strategist)? What consequences do you think this has for your firm's growth prospects?

3. Prepare a five-point plan for delegation along the lines shown in this chapter.

4. Keep a log of how you spend your time over the next week and analyse it as suggested in this chapter. Do you need to improve the way you manage your own time? If so, how?

5. Review the last three meetings that you have run and identify ways in which you could improve the way you manage meetings in future.

6. Get some feedback on the way you communicate verbally. What can you do to improve your verbal communication?

7. Calculate the Fog Index for the next six important letters or reports that you write. Are you happy with the result and, if not, what can you do about it?

Suggested further reading

Armstrong, Michael (2003) *A Handbook of Human Resource Management Practice*, London: Kogan Page.

Greiner, L. E. (1972) 'Evolution and Revolution as Organizations Grow,' *Harvard Business Review*, July–Aug, 37–46.

Huselid, Mark, Brian Becker and Dave Ulrich (2001) *HR Scorecard: Linking People, Strategy and Performance*, Boston: Harvard Business School Press.

McGregor, D. (1960) *The Human Side of Enterprise*, New York: McGraw-Hill.

Maddux, Robert B. (1998) *Effective Performance Appraisals*, London: Kogan Page.

Taffinder, Paul (1995) *The New Leaders: Styles and Strategies for Success*, London: Kogan Page.

Tichy, Noel M. and Nancy Cardwell (2002) *The Cycle of Leadership: How Great Leaders Teach their Companies to Win*, Basingstoke: HarperCollins.

16 What are your options for realizing value?

Introduction and objectives

Having considered whether you are now a 'small big business' rather than a 'big small business', and having reviewed whether you can (or indeed want to!) change from entrepreneurial owner to strategic manager, you may well conclude that you do indeed want to exit the business and realize the value that you have built up over the years.

By the end of this chapter, you should have a clear understanding of the following key topics:

- Why entrepreneurial business owners sell up and realize value.

- The options for value realization. We briefly look at a range of options including trade sales, selling to other managers, floating on a stock market, winding up and passing the business on through the family.

- Preparing the business for sale so as to maximize its attractiveness to potential purchasers.

- How privately owned businesses are typically valued.

- Using professional advisers.

- Life after the sale.

Why realize the value?

Every year, tens of thousands of entrepreneurs seek to realize all or part of the value in their business. The reasons for doing so are legion. Some want to retire, others are bored with the business and want to move on to something else, and others feel that their business has reached a point where association with a larger business is desirable or even essential. And, if you have taken venture capital funding, you may find that your investors become restless after a few years and look for a return on their investment.

A study at Cranfield on why entrepreneurs exit identified that the most common reason was retirement (51 per cent), followed by reasons to do with the strategy and development of the business (34 per cent), the entrepreneur wanting to explore other interests (8 per cent) and ill-health (7 per cent).

What are your options?

The routes to selling are also numerous and the one chosen will probably be governed by a number of factors, some personal and some economic. We've described below some of the most common options for selling the business open to the entrepreneur.

Winding down

One option is simply to allow the business to wind down of its own accord, then close the business and sell off the assets. However, even if your business is not in the greatest of shape, or even if it is financially troubled, selling an operating business, almost always brings more money than closing it down and selling off the assets. Before you give up and conclude that no one would ever buy your business, consider that people buy businesses, even businesses with financial problems, for all sorts of reasons.

Private sale

A very large number of companies, particularly smaller ones, are sold privately to other individual entrepreneurs.

So called 'sweetheart deals', where you sell out to someone you know or already do business with, are a popular strategy for retiring entrepreneurs. On the surface, this seems appealing since it can be done in a friendly way and should be straightforward once the price has been agreed. However, the reality is that they are almost always bad deals for the seller. In setting the original price, without an auction or controlled auction, you could be short-changed by as much as 50 per cent. Even having got your price, how can you be sure you will get your money? Warranties, missed earn-outs, and bad tax advice could take 70 per cent of that headline price out of your pocket.

An alternative, which at least creates an auction-like scenario, is to advertise the business through the press or a specialist business broker.

Trade sale

A trade sale is where you sell some or all of your company to another company – usually a larger one and often one that is publicly traded. This is a very popular route, particularly for those entrepreneurs who are selling for strategic reasons since the larger acquiring business can often provide key resources to enable further growth (such as finance, access to markets, research and development, and so on) which the acquired business would not otherwise be able to afford.

As far as the acquiring company is concerned, the attractions of the acquisition are usually to do with some form of 'strategic fit' with their existing portfolio of products/services, or possibly taking out a competitor. There may be other reasons, such as access to particular people or skills, access to a more entrepreneurial culture, which are attractive to the acquirer also.

In the particular case of a publicly quoted company, there is an extra incentive to acquire privately owned companies. Because the shares of unquoted companies are 'illiquid', that is they cannot be bought and sold easily, they are viewed as being less valuable than shares of a similar type of quoted company. So, whilst a quoted company's shares might trade on a P/E (price/earnings) ratio of 12, a similar unquoted company would be more likely to be valued on a P/E of 8. Thus, if your profits were £250 000 and your company was unquoted, it might be valued at £2 million (8 × 250 000), whilst a public company undertaking identical activities could be valued at £3 million (12 × 250 000). Were a public company to buy your company for £2 million and absorb its profits into its own, the value of the acquiring company could rise by £3 million, without any change in the level of business undertaken. That is £1 million more than they paid in the first place.

Clearly, the more desirable your company is to the acquirer, the better the price that you will achieve. Therefore it is worthwhile thinking carefully about what types of company might be a good fit with yours and actively approaching them, usually through an adviser, with a proposition.

For these reasons, a trade sale usually results in a better price than a private sale. On the other hand, the acquirer very often demands that the existing owner-manager stays with the business for a minimum period, sometimes up to two to three years, so that a successful transition can be made. Part of the price that the acquirer is paying is usually linked to performance during this period in what is known as an 'earn-out'.

Selling to your existing management team

Just as larger companies often sell off parts of their operations to the existing management team of that particular unit, so can you sell your business to your management team. This is known as a management buy-out or MBO.

MBOs are very popular with venture capital providers. The reasons are not hard to see. The business is usually well established and profitable, and the people in the best position to run the business are probably there already. The existing team can then be incentivized with shares and options to take the business to even greater heights. The result is much happiness and wealth all round! This is one of the reasons why developing a truly effective management team around you is so crucial to growth and building value.

On the other hand, smaller firms can often find it difficult to attract much venture capital interest in funding a buy-out. The reason is usually that the venture capitalist believes the owner-manager makes all the key decisions, leaving the management to 'obey orders'. As the venture capitalist has no intention or desire to manage the business, it will be necessary to convince them that the existing management team can really run the business without you.

Selling to an incoming management team

A close relative of the MBO is the MBI, or management buy-in, where you sell the business to an incoming manager or management team. This may be an appropriate route if you believe that your current management team lack expertise and/or experience. By injecting new management resources, the business is better placed to continue to grow and the new managers can share in the future profits and value.

As with MBOs, MBIs are popular with venture capital firms. Usually, the venture capital firm will have had a successful relationship with the buy-in team in a previous venture. Alternatively, a business angel with experience in your industry or market may fund the buy-in and take an active role in the future management of the business themselves.

There are also combinations of MBIs and MBOs where some of the company's existing management team join with a new incoming manager to buy the business. This arrangement goes under the strange sounding title of a BIMBO.

Passing the business on through the family

If your inspiration is to build up an enduring family business, then you may plan to pass the business on to the next generation. However, beware the old adage 'clogs to clogs in three generations'. Only 33 per cent of family businesses reach the second generation, less than two-thirds of these survive through the second generation while only 13 per cent survive through the third generation! On the other hand, the average life cycle of a family business is 24 years, which is about the same as any other type of business.

Although these statistics illustrate the fragility of the continuing family business you should not despair: more than 50 per cent of US corporations, including some of the largest multinationals (Heinz and Campbell's soup, for example), are family owned.

If you have children, or other family members, involved in the business, they may well be the right people to take it over. Even if there is no obvious family succession candidate, it might be worth casting your net beyond the immediate family. One business founder wrote to all his family and relations, asking if anyone would like to join him. A stepdaughter accepted the challenge and quickly became a key member of the management team.

But, you will need to plan very carefully how you will extract any value you want or need from such an arrangement. It may be that you can allow the succeeding family members to pay for the company over a number of years. Alternatively, you might be content to retain a shareholding and take your reward by way of a dividend. On balance, a clean break is usually best, but in any event clear arrangements for payments agreed in writing is a prudent arrangement to ensure family peace.

Selling to the employees

Selling the business to the employees is not exactly the most popular notion in entrepreneurial circles. And yet, recent research by the Centre for Tomorrow's Company has found that employee-owned companies outperform companies with other forms of ownership. The case study below certainly makes interesting reading.

Case Study

Tullis Russell has 1200 employees making every sort of specialist paper, from that required to insulate high-voltage cable to that used for postage stamps. David Erdal, the sixth generation of the Erdal family to run the company, spent a year on the factory floor before going to Harvard Business School where he was the resident 'left-wing weirdo' in an annual intake of 800. He was the only one of 14 of his generation of the family working in the business and was appointed chairman of the company at the age of 37.

One of his jobs was to reconcile the interests of the family (25 interested parties), who had not been able to sell their shares since 1874 and who wanted to get their money out, with the future interests of the employees. There was nothing the matter with capitalism, he had decided, the problem was that it created very few capitalists:

A lot of rubbish is talked about capital taking the risk, therefore it must get the rewards. All managers know that a large part of their role is to shift the risk away from capital to the employees. If the share price is in danger of going down, you cut their wages or sack them.

Erdal decided that the best way to satisfy both sets of interests was for the family to sell their shares to the employees with the deal being financed from the company profits.

Two far-sighted provisions in UK company law made the deal work for both sides. The family could sell their shares to a qualifying employee share trust (Quest), financed by the company, and reinvest the £19.3 million they received without paying capital gains tax. Had they sold for cash to an outside bidder this tax would have come to about £7 million. By forming a Quest, the employees could finance the buy-out from pre-tax profits, all money (capital as well as interest) being allowable against tax. If there had been a management buy-out, the company would have had to repay the debt from after-tax money, which would have cost another £6 million. As it was, the employees put up no money themselves. The family also agreed to give the buy-out a fair wind by allowing the payments to be spread over nine years.

As a result, the employees and the employee benefit trusts now control Tullis Russell, owning 60 per cent of the shares. The rest are owned by a charitable trust set up by the family after the Second World War. This charitable trust, Erdal claims, gives stability to the company because it is a genuine long-term holder of shares. It has the power of veto over the future sale of the company, and it can veto the choice of directors put forward by the board. Nevertheless, the company is still very clearly management-led, which is the single most important factor in any business.

At Tullis Russell, things are going from triumph to triumph. 'It patently works without me,' Erdal is on record as saying. Profits have quadrupled over the last few years to more than £7 million, after £2 million of profit sharing. The management hopes to increase production to 200 000 tons a year in five years without buying any new paper machines, up from 117 000 tons this year, and 64 500 four years ago. This is among the fastest growth rates in the industry.

Going public

Perhaps the 'ultimate accolade' for any business is to float on a public stock exchange. In so doing, the shares of the company are publicly listed and can be traded by anyone. This provides a reward for both the owners and investors and also allows access to further fundraising possibilities by issue of new equity shares.

There are two possible types of stock market on which to gain a public listing. In normal economic circumstances, a full listing on the London Stock Exchange, the New York Stock Exchange or any other major country's exchange calls for a track record of making substantial profits with decent seven figure sums being made in the year you plan to float. A full listing also calls for a large proportion of the company's shares being put up for sale at the outset. In a frothy market, such as at the height of the internet bubble, these rules can be set aside.

In more recent times, many major countries have formed so-called junior markets such as New York's Nasdaq, London's Alternative Investment Market (AIM) and the Nouveau Marché in Paris. These markets were formed specifically to provide risk capital for newer ventures and have an altogether more relaxed atmosphere. They are, therefore, usually a much more attractive proposition for entrepreneurs seeking equity capital.

Public flotations tend to generate more value for the current share owners. A perfectly respectable private business that might have been sold privately on a multiple of six times annual profits, could float for anything between two and three times that sum. Why? Well, the logic is fairly simple. Placing shares on a stock market makes the companies shares liquid. In other words, shareholders can buy and sell at will, or nearly so. For the same reason, if you have raised any of your finance through either a venture capital firm or a business angel, then sooner or later the subject of a stock market float will come up.

On the other hand, since the shares are to be traded publicly, the markets have many safeguards. These safeguards place great demands on the company that is attempting to float. For example, to float on one of the major exchanges, you will need to appoint a sponsor (usually a merchant bank), a stockbroker, a reporting accountant and a solicitor. All of these will need to be well-respected firms, active in flotation work and familiar with your company's type of business. Such advice does not come cheap. As a result, floating is a very expensive and lengthy process which also places huge demands on the senior management team.

In fact, both the sales values achieved and the costs of floating vary significantly even between different stock markets as Table 3.16.1 shows.

Table 3.16.1   Where to float … and why it matters

Market	Number of stocks	Flotation cost	Entry requirements	Minimum market capitalization	Comparable price earnings ratios (P/E's)
Alternative Investment Market (AIM)	350	£0.5m	Low	None	1
London Stock Exchange	2 500	£1m+	High	£1m+	1
techMARK	200	£0.75m+	High	£50m+	X3
New York Stock Exchange	2 600	£7m	Very high	£12m+	X2
NASDAQ	5 500	£6m	Very high	£10m+	X5

Source: Exchange details

A final word of caution. If you have to pull the flotation for any reason, it can be like slipping down a long snake back to the bottom of the snakes and ladders board. Only about 10 per cent of companies who withdraw a flotation ever manage to go public at a later date.

Case Study

From the start of his new business, Nigel Apperley was keen to develop an internet brand for photographic equipment. Early in 2000, *The Sunday Times*, the UK's leading Sunday newspaper, reported that the best place to buy a Fuji MX1700 was InternetCamerasDirect. The brand was taking off. As a result of press coverage such as this, allied with keen pricing and effective sourcing, sales had been doubling every month.

With all the hype surrounding the internet at the time, all of a sudden the prospect of a flotation appeared realistic, and Nigel saw the opportunity to raise a large sum of money on AIM. He wanted to raise £10 million in return for 49 per cent of the business and to use this capital injection to build the business internationally. It was important to present a credible team to the market and with this in mind he went about recruiting a board.

He called an old friend, Paul, who was previously company secretary at Hickson Group plc. Paul was three-quarters of the way through his MBA at Bradford, not so far from InternetCamerasDirect's head office. Paul agreed to come on board as a director and company secretary. Next, Nigel decided he needed a chairman. Through his connections at Cranfield School of Management, Nigel approached John Constable, professor of strategy and non-executive director of Sage plc, to join the board in return for 2.5 per cent of the equity in the company. Nigel then approached the finance director of a publicly listed chain of wine bars. He also agreed to join

in principle, at flotation. With the top team agreed, Nigel set about writing the business plan.

In January 2000, at which point the internet stock market bubble was still at its peak, Nigel started approaching brokers to explore the appetite for a flotation. Unsurprisingly, given the market conditions at the time, their initial reactions were of keen interest. Based on these responses, the management team were extremely bullish. 'We think it'll be worth more than Lastminute.com,' said Apperley, referring to another internet business due to float the next month.

But it was not to be. In the spring of 2000, Lastminute.com became one of the last pure internet businesses to float in the UK and the way it was priced and its shares were allocated caused some resentment among private investors. Suddenly, market sentiment towards internet business-to-consumer (B2C) propositions changed. By the turn of the year, floating InternetCamerasDirect was a non-starter and even Lastminute.com was finding life on the public markets uncomfortable.

As it turned out, both InternetCameras-Direct and Lastminute.com have flourished in the years since the internet bubble burst. As at late 2003, Lastminute.com was profitable and was held up as a prime example of an internet business that 'survived'. Meanwhile, Internet-CamerasDirect obtained finance for growth from other sources and continued to increase it sales to a point where it had reached a turnover of £20 million.

Preparing the business for sale (dressing to kill)

Whichever route you choose, if you are thinking about selling, it certainly pays to plan ahead and prepare your business to look its best. Your buyer will look at your last three years' performance, at the least, and it is important that your figures for these periods are as good and clean as possible.

Taking the latter point first, private businesses do tend to run expenses through the business that might be frowned upon under different ownership. One firm, for example, had its sale delayed for three years while the chairman's yacht was worked out of 'work in progress'. There can also be problems when personal assets are tucked away in the company or where staff have been paid rather informally, free of tax. The liability rests with the company, and if the practice has continued for many years the financial picture can look quite messy.

The years before you sell up can be used to good effect by improving the performance of your business relative to others in your industry. Going down the profit and loss account and balance sheet will point out areas for improvement.

Once the business is firmly planted on an upward trend, your future projections will look that much more plausible to a potential buyer. You should certainly have a business plan and strategic projections for at least five years. This will underpin the strength of your negotiations by demonstrating your management skills in putting together the plan, and show that you believe the company has a healthy future.

Some entrepreneurs may wonder if such an effort is worthwhile. Perhaps the following example will show how financial planning can lead to capital appreciation for the founder.

Case Study

A 34-year-old owner-manager built up a regional service business in the United States that had a 40 per cent compounded annual growth rate for the five most recent years. He employed an experienced chartered accountant as his chief financial officer. This person developed budgets for one- and three-year periods and a detailed business plan charting the company's growth over the next five years. The owner's objective was to be ready to sell his business when the right offer came along.

A UK company interested in acquiring a leading service company in the region, and finding a manager with the potential for national leadership, carefully analysed the company and came away impressed with management's dedication to running its business in a highly professional manner. Because the previous year's after-tax profits had been $500 000 on sales of $10 million, the UK company offered $4.5 million on purchase, and $4.5 million on attainment of certain profit objectives (which were well within the growth trend). The transaction closed on these terms.

The $9 million offering price, representing 18 times net earnings, was 50 per cent higher than the industry norm and clearly justified the owner's careful job of packaging his business for sale.

Valuing the business

Whatever route you decide to take to selling the business, it will involve placing a value on it. One way to measure value is to work out what the various assets of the business would be worth on the open market. So vehicles, premises, equipment and any other assets could be professionally valued. From that sum, you would take any outstanding liabilities to creditors, bank borrowings, tax authorities and redundancy payments due. This might make sense if the business is actually going to stop trading, but it is unlikely to produce the best value.

Part, perhaps even all, that a business has to sell, in the final resort, is its capacity to make profit. At any rate, that is where the debate about value will start.

The ratio most commonly used here is the price to earnings (or P/E) ratio. This means the number of times annual profits a business is valued at.

If you look up a company's performance in the financial press, you will see a P/E ratio calculated in the following way

$$\text{Price to earnings} = \frac{\text{share price}}{\text{earnings (or profit) per share}}$$

The P/E ratio expresses the market value placed on the expectations of future earnings, i.e. the number of years required to earn the price paid for the shares out of profits at the current rate.

So, if the share price of the business in question was £10, and the earning per share was 80p, then the P/E ratio is 12.5. Which is another way of saying the company is worth 12.5 times this year's profits.

If you look up another company in a different industry sector, you might find a quite different multiple in force. At the height of the internet boom, the record P/E ratio was 135. More usually, P/E ratios are less than 20.

Differences in P/E ratios between industries indicate the different perceived growth prospects of the industries concerned. Differences in P/E ratios between businesses in the same industry indicate that the markets believe that one business has better growth prospects than the other.

The public stock markets are where the framework for values are set. So, if your business is in the food sector, and P/E ratios there are about 12, then that is where outsiders will start when they think about valuing your business.

After this, a few things can get added – and a few things can get taken away. The first seriously negative event is the discount that will be applied because your business is *not* on the stock market. Privately owned businesses are generally viewed as being worth at least a third less than a publicly quoted firm listed on a stock exchange. That is because shares in a publicly quoted company are much more liquid, i.e. there are more shares and more buyers and sellers.

If the privately owned company is a 'one man band' or is seen as being overly dependent on one person (e.g. the current owner-manager), then the ratio might be halved again. The reasoning here is that the customers are probably loyal to the current owner-manager and may not come over to any new owner. There is no certainty that the business will have a profitable life without the current owner. As a result, a potential buyer will adjust the industry standard P/E ratio and then multiply this adjusted figure by the operating profit to give an indication of the value of the business.

On the positive side, any expense seen as being unnecessary to running the business can be added back into operating profit before the sum is done. So, if you have three family members on the payroll who are performing no useful purpose, or if you are taking out more than a new owner would have to pay to have the business managed for them, then that sum would go back to swell the operating profit and, hence, the value of the business.

One last factor that affects private business valuations is the economic cycle. At the bottom of the cycle (a downturn), smaller privately owned businesses sell on average multiples of between 6 and 8. At the top of the cycle (a boom), the same business may sell on multiples between 10 and 12.

All these figures are illustrative only. Every business sale, and every circumstance, has unique elements to it that can greatly affect the final outcome. As you can see, perceptions are at least as important as figures, when it comes to valuations!

Professional advice

Nothing said in this chapter should be construed as a substitute for taking professional advice. Most people only sell a business once in their lives. The best professional advisers in the field sell a dozen or so each year. Getting the best value for your business may involve getting expensive corporate finance advice to maximize the price, in the minimum amount of time. In addition, a good tax and pension strategy can double the end value you receive and legal advice on warranties can make sure you get to keep the money.

Afterwards

What happens after you exit rather depends on your goals in selling up. If you are retiring, then your plans should be well laid beforehand. If you are staying on as a member of a larger group, then you need to be prepared for corporate rather than entrepreneurial life. This can be hard, and few people make the transition successfully.

Many entrepreneurs who have sold up seek to find another venture to start and/or grow. Sometimes, it can take years to find the right opportunity to get back into business. What many have found helpful is to set themselves up as a sort of one-man venture capital and management consultancy business. By putting the word out that they are interested in buying or backing ventures in the field they understand best, they receive a steady stream of proposals and presentations, from which they hope to fund their next venture.

Irrespective of your future plans, and even if you are walking away with a large cheque, your experiences may bear a close resemblance to a bereavement. You have probably invested a great deal of your time and a huge amount of emotional energy into your business. And now it's not yours anymore. Don't underestimate the significance of this change!

Chapter summary

In this chapter, we've looked at:

- why owner-managers sell up and realize value
- the range of options available for realizing value
- how to prepare the business for sale so as to maximize its attractiveness
- how to value a business
- the need for professional advisers
- life after the sale.

Like all good things, all businesses must come to an end. Hopefully, for you that 'end' is, in essence, a new beginning, for the business as it is sold or floated on a stock market, and for you as you develop new interests after the sale.

But, the most important thing to say, if you've got this far, having started, grown and then sold your business, is

CONGRATULATIONS!

Assignments

1. Prepare two lists, in balance sheet style, setting out the pros and cons of selling up now and in say five years time.
2. If you had to get out of your business for any reason, which exit route would you favour?
3. What value would you put on your business now and in say five years time?
4. What will you do when you exit?

Suggested further reading

Gladstone, David and Laura Gladstone (2002) *Venture Capital Handbook: An Entrepreneur's Guide to Raising Venture Capital*, New York: Prentice Hall.
Yegge, Wilbur M. (2002) *A Basic Guide to Valuing a Company*, London: John Wiley & Son.

References

Adair, John and Neil Thomas (2004) *The John Adair Handbook of Management and Leadership*, London: Hawksmere.

Adcock D., R. Bradfield, A. Halborg and C. Ross (1995) *Marketing: Principles and Practice*, London: Pitman.

Ansoff, Igor (1965) *Corporate Strategy*, London: Penguin.

Armstrong, Michael (2003) *A Handbook of Human Resource Management Practice*, London: Kogan Page.

Barrow, Colin (2001) *Financial Management for the Small Business*, 5th Edition, London: Kogan Page.

Barrow, Colin (2003) *The Complete Small Business Guide*, Oxford: Capstone Reference.

Barrow, Colin (2003), *E-Training and Development*, Oxford: Capstone.

Belbin, Meredith (1984) *Management Teams: Why They Succeed and Fail*, Oxford: Butterworth-Heinemann.

Bhidé, Amar V. (2000) *The Origin and Evolution of New Businesses*, New York: Oxford University Press.

Birch, David (1979) *The Job Generation Process*, Boston, Mass.: MIT Press.

Bowman, Cliff with D. Faulkner (1994) Measuring product advantage using competitive benchmarking and customer perception, *Long Range Planning*, **27**, (1), 119–32.

CBI (2000) 'Connecting Companies', London: CBI.

Crimp, Margaret and Len Tiu Wright (2000) *The Marketing Research Process*, Harlow: Pearson Higher Education.

De Bono, Edward (1990) *Lateral Thinking: a Textbook of Creativity*, Harmondsworth: Penguin.

Dick, R. and M. Kretz de Vries (1995) *Richard Branson: The Coming of Age of a Counter Culture Entrepreneur*, Fontainebleu: INSEAD. (European Case Clearing House, Cranfield University, Cranfield.)

Drucker, P. (1964) *Managing for Results*, London: Heinemann. Reprinted in The Essential Drucker: The Best of Sixty Years of Peter Drucker's Essential Writings on Management, New York: Harper Collins.

Drucker, P. (1999) *Innovation and Entrepreneurship*, London: Butterworth Heinemann.

Foster, Jack (1996) *How to Get Great Ideas*, San Francisco: Berrett-Koehler.

Galbraith, J. K. (1985) *The Anatomy of Power*, London: Hamish Hamilton.

Gladstone, David and Laura Gladstone (2002) *Venture Capital Handbook: An Entrepreneur's Guide to Raising Venture Capital*, New York: Prentice Hall.

Golzen, Godfrey (2003) *Working for Yourself*, London: Kogan Page.

Greiner, L. E. (1972) *Evolution and Revolution as Organizations Grow*, Harvard Business Review, July–Aug, 37–46.

Hall, G. (1995) *Surviving and Prospering in the Small Firms Sector*, London: Routledge.

Hertzberg, F. (1959) *The Motivation to Work*, New York: John Wiley & Son.

Huselid, Mark, Brian Becker and Dave Ulrich (2001) *HR Scorecard: Linking People, Strategy and Performance*, Boston: Harvard Business School Press.

McDonald, Malcolm (2002) *Marketing Plans: How to Prepare Them, How to Use Them*, 5th edition, Oxford: Butterworth-Heinemann.

McGregor, D. (1960) *The Human Side of Enterprise*, New York: McGraw-Hill.

Maddux, Robert B. (1998) *Effective Performance Appraisals*, London: Kogan Page.

Melkman, Alan (2001) *Strategic Customer Planning*, London: Thorogood.

Ogilvy, David (1995) *Ogilvy on Advertising*, London: Prion Books

Peters, Thomas and Robert Waterman (1988) *In Search of Excellence*, New York: Warner Books.

Porter, Michael E. (1998) *Competitive Strategy*, New York: Free Press.

Porter, Michael E (1998) *On Competition*, Boston: Harvard Business School Press.

Taffinder, Paul (1995) *The New Leaders. Styles and Strategies for Success*, London: Kogan Page.

Tichy, Noel M. and Nancy Cardwell (2002) *The Cycle of Leadership: How Great Leaders Teach their Companies to Win*, Basingstoke: HarperCollins.

Warnes, Brian (1984) *The Ghengis Khan Guide to Business*, London: Osmosis Publications.

Webb, Phillip and Sandra Webb (2002) *The Small Business Handbook*, Hemel Hempstead: Prentice Hall.

West, Michael and Lynn Marciewicz (2003), *Building Team Based Working*, Oxford: Blackwell.

Yegge, Wilbur M. (2002) *A Basic Guide to Valuing a Company*, London: John Wiley & Son.

Index

Lightning Source UK Ltd.
Milton Keynes UK
UKOW01f0729210514

232006UK00001B/45/P